ITEMS TO CONSIDER

*

It's unkind to point out the Obvious
To those who don't want to see it.

But it's worse to point out the Invisible
To those convinced it doesn't exist.

*

What, When, and Who are important, of course, but
Meaning is only achieved by understanding
the WHY

and which is one reason why the WHY
it hidden from easy access.

*

Enthusiasm collects Vital Energies

* * *

Ingo Swann (1933-2013) was an American artist and exceptionally successful subject in parapsychology experiments. As a child he spontaneously had numerous paranormal experiences, mostly of the OBE type, the future study of which became a major passion as he matured. In 1970, he began acting as a parapsychology test subject in tightly controlled laboratory settings with numerous scientific researchers. Because of the success of most of these thousands of test trials, major media worldwide often referred to him as "the scientific psychic." His subsequent research on behalf of American intelligence interests, including that of the CIA, won him top PSI-spy status.

His involvement in government research projects required the discovery of innovative approaches toward the actual realizing of subtle human energies. He viewed PSI powers as only parts of the larger spectrum of human sensing systems and was internationally known as an advocate and researcher of the exceptional powers of the human mind.

To learn more about Ingo, his work, art, and other books, please visit: **www.ingoswann.com**.

PSYCHIC SEXUALITY

THE BIO-PSYCHIC "ANATOMY" OF SEXUAL ENERGIES

A BIOMIND SUPERPOWERS BOOK
PUBLISHED BY

Swann-Ryder Productions, LLC
www.ingoswann.com

Copyright © 1999 by Ingo Swann; Copyright © 2015 by Murleen S. Ryder; Copyright © 2017 by Swann-Ryder Productions, LLC.

All rights reserved. No part of this book may be used or reproduced in any manner whatsoever without written permission.

For more information address: www.ingoswann.com.
Previously published in trade paperback by Ingo Swann Books and Crossroad Press and digitally by Crossroad Press.

First edition BioMind Superpowers Books.

Cover art: *Radiant* (1965) by Ingo Swann © Swann-Ryder Productions, LLC.

ISBN-13: 978-1-949214-21-5

PSYCHIC SEXUALITY

The Bio-Psychic "Anatomy" of Sexual Energies

INGO SWANN

With a Forward by Paula Gunn Allen, Ph.D.

This book is dedicated to
the Late and Very Great Zelda Suplee
Free Spirit, Sexologist, Social Critic,
Universal Earth Mother,
a Soul of Great Wonderment and Beauty

CONTENTS

FOREWORD X
INTRODUCTION XVII

PART I: TREMULOUS PULSATIONS 1

CHAPTER 1: THE UNIVERSALITY OF SEXUAL ENERGIES 2
CHAPTER 2: INANIMATE ENERGY—ANIMATE ENERGY 8
CHAPTER 3: BODY-MIND VERSUS BODY-ENERGY-MIND 18
CHAPTER 4: ANIMA AND THE LIFE PRINCIPLE 26
CHAPTER 5: MAGNETISTS OF THE RENAISSANCE PERIOD 37
CHAPTER 6: MAGNETIC FORCE—ANIMAL MAGNETISM 42
CHAPTER 7: ODIC FORCE 50
CHAPTER 8: ENERGIES PHOTOGRAPHIC 56
CHAPTER 9: PSYCHIC FORCE 64
CHAPTER 10: ORGONE ENERGY—BIONIC ENERGY 76

PART II: THE TREMULOUS PULSATIONS SEEN BY CLAIRVOYANCE 87

CHAPTER 11: PREVENTING KNOWLEDGE OF SEXUAL ENERGIES 88
CHAPTER 12: THE PSYCHIC FORCE AS AFFLUENT SUBSTANCE 100
CHAPTER 13: CLAIRVOYANCE—TELESTHESIA 108
CHAPTER 14: BEYOND CLAIRVOYANCE—LUCIDITY 115
CHAPTER 15: AURA 125
CHAPTER 16: "THE ENTANGLED MANIFESTATION" 133

PART III: THE COPPER MIRROR TRAINING DEVICE OF THE MAHATMAS & EXPERIENCING THE ENTANGLED MANIFESTATION 143

CHAPTER 17: PERSONAL EXPERIENCING OF AURA ENERGY FIELDS 144
CHAPTER 18: THE COPPER MIRROR TRAINING DEVICE OF THE MAHATMAS 154
CHAPTER 19: UNANTICIPATED LUCIDITY BEGINS 165
CHAPTER 20: CHAKRA 174
CHAPTER 21: NETWORKS WITHIN THE ENTANGLED MANIFESTATION 179
CHAPTER 22: TURNING OFF WHAT THE COPPER MIRROR TURNED ON ... 185

PART IV: "ANATOMY" OF SEXUALIZING ENERGIES...190

CHAPTER 23: PARAPHERNALIA AND REGALIA OF HUMAN SEXUALIZING ENERGIES 191

CHAPTER 24: SOME ANATOMY OF SEXUALIZING ENERGY PARAPHERNALIA 196

CHAPTER 25: SOME ANATOMY OF SEXUALIZING ENERGY REGALIA......... 212

CHAPTER 26: SOME SEXUALIZING ENERGIES OF BIO-PSYCHIC CHANGELINGS... 226

CHAPTER 27: THE ENERGETIC MELDING FUNCTION............................... 237

CHAPTER 28: HUMAN ENERGETICS—A SCIENCE DENIED........................ 247

SUGGESTED READING 256

FOREWORD

When Sir Arthur Conan Doyle via Sherlock Holmes commented that "The world is full of obvious things which nobody by any chance ever observed," he had not been counting on people like Ingo Swann. For while Doyle's observation is depressingly true in this misbegotten time warp, there are those who, like, Swann, not only notice but experiment, experience, research, and record their findings.

Sadly, unlike Swann in his painstakingly researched *Psychic Sexuality*, most who write about these obvious but by most unobserved matters fall victim to several stylistic vicissitudes Ingo avoids.

Their writing is dense, troublesome, obscure, becoming part of the problem it attempts to solve. Or their approach is so oversimplistic, pointing to obvious truths while omitting much of the data that fleshes them out, that they are readily dismissed as childish.

Swann, by contrast, employs an engaging style while at the same time drawing on a vast store of data, personal experience, and deep reflection. He does not ignore the rules of reasoned argument, but instead imbues his text with the kind of fluid magnetic power he is elucidating, making his points simultaneously comprehensible and recognizable. As in, "Yeah, I remember that!" Or, "Wow, I wondered what that was when it happened!"

Swann doesn't make the common mistake of confusing the menu with the meal. Instead, he rightly makes the menu function as it should: a guide to gustatory experience—or, in this particular case—a guide to psychic experience.

Eluding the common trap of pursuing a point merely because it is trendy, or echoing what everyone in one's circle already believes, Swann chooses to observe, record, and think the problem through. He writes from material that in general supports, explains, expands, deepens, and clarifies matters he has experienced firsthand and reflected deeply upon. In short, he follows the Path of Wisdom, and through his carefully constructed reflections, makes it accessible to modern understanding.

In Chapter 12, "Psychic Force as Affluent Substance," Swann comments, "The only real problem with the whole of this [discussion] is that modern sciences do NOT admit that this kind of magnetism or force exists." He goes on to list a number of characteristics of the force taken from *Spiritualism Answered by Science* (1871) by Edward William Cox. According to Swann, Cox was the person who coined the now generally accepted term "psychic," to refer to psychological abilities that transcend mechanistic limits.

The list includes three characteristics I particularly want to draw attention to:

1. There is a Force proceeding from, or directly associated with, the human organization. (Read organism, or body structure.)
2. The strength, or power, of the Force is conditional upon the mental and emotional status of the individual and the individuals involved. The Force "is sometimes, but rarely, exhibited when the Psychic is alone. As a rule, the presence of other persons promotes the operations of the Force."
3. The Force "is materially influenced by the electric and magnetic conditions of the atmosphere and of surrounding bodies, by heat and cold, by moisture and dryness, and still more by the nervous conditions of the persons present."

Here, the most significant aspect not of the psychic alone, but the spiritual as well is highlighted. He focuses our attention on the basic Laws of Magic, of ritual and of transcendent consciousness. Upon reflection, one begins to realize why a social system that promotes and comprehends the true nature of human potential is so essential to our well-being as spiritual, PSYCHIC, entities who indeed do not live by bread alone.

True human consciousness—for that is what is being explored in Swann's work—is a by-product of community. No rugged individualism here! For true consciousness depends on the interplay of a variety of human organisms coordinated into a harmonious whole.

The psychic envelope (as I term the structure that arises out of community) created by the linkage of human organic magnetic or psychic force is dependent on its environment. Items such as weather, climate, season, placement on the planet, and within the constellations have direct impact on the clarity of any human operation.

The location includes the group and its purpose as they relate to sun, moon phase, and tide—that is, to the general tone of the magnetic flow this vast interlocking, energistic complex takes on in that precise moment.

It also includes "what time it is"—as Native Americans put it.

That is, the time/space continuum—which to the Native American philosophy is a time-space never ending enfoldment-unfoldment-multidimensional helical interaction —and which is critical to all transactions among and within all communities in the universe. (Again, everything depends on everything else, and nothing can act in isolation or independence outside of the infinite/eternal confluence of energies-forces-intelligences.)

If any of these aspects of the grid is off balance or out of tune, either nothing, something unexpected, or things unlovely and downright evil will be generated by this link.

In other words, garbage in, garbage out; love and beauty in, love and beauty out; plenty in, plenty out; peaceful in, peaceful out—and so forth. As one of the basic occult texts of the tradition instructs: "For as ye sow, so shall ye reap;" "Sow the wind, inherit the whirlwind;" and "By their fruits [results] shall ye know them."

So various American Indian Peoples hold that "All life is a circle, and everything within it is connected." That is what they mean by the evocation "All my relatives."

In traditional American Indian languages, the sacred (that is, the higher, integral energy field) which practitioners manipulate in ritual manner, is known variously as "orenda," "iyanyi," "hobomak," "manitou," and so forth.

In their study of magnetic fields in New England, James Mavor and Byron Dix compare "manitou" to the ancient Chinese geomantic practice called "feng shui."

They write that Manitou appears to be "inseparable from geomancy, the concept of the world as a place where all activities and objects, both in the natural and supernatural domains, are connected in some subtle manner. Geomancers believe that the natural order can be sensed, and tuned into by traditional practices." [See: Mavor, James W. & Dix, Byron E.: *Manitou: The Sacred Landscape of New England's Native Civilization.* Rochester, Vermont: Inner Traditions International, 1998, pp. 330-331.]

Native peoples' philosophical systems have long assumed that the use of this power, this "orenda," "hozho," "hobomak," or "iyanyi," this "manitou," is subject to certain laws: for example, that it doesn't work for loners, except as negative sorcery—the sort that blights, distorts, and destroys.

In his book *The Manitous: The Spiritual World of the Ojibway*, [New York: Harper Collins, 1995, p. 242], Basil Johnston, the noted Anishinaabeg (Ojibway) scholar, defines manitou. He gives characteristics of "Mystery, essence, substance, matter, supernatural spirit, anima, quiddity, attribute, property, God, deity, godlike, mystical, incorporeal, transcendental, invisible reality."

The community use of manitou, orenda, iyanyi, hozho, etc., that is, of geopsychic energy, however, results in an almost infinite variety of positive results, many chronicled in reports on spiritual events in Indian Country by travelers, antiquarians, anthropologists and missionaries. Just about all of these both misunderstood what they saw and, either horrified or disbelieving, mischaracterized it.

But there are those who have got it right. One such source is provided by Peggy V. Beck (anthropologist) and Anna Lee Walters (Otoe-Pawnee writer) in their book *The Sacred: Ways of Knowledge, Sources of Life* [Tsaile, Navajo Nation: Navajo Community College Press, 1971; pp. 41-42].

One of the many intriguing and points they make (in their study of American Indian systems of the sacred) highlights the means by which these geopsychic, spiritual energies are used to benefit all life.

"The expression we are using to describe this power of prayer [dance and song-chant] and the concentration brought to an idea or thought by a lot of people at the same timethinking and praying for the same thing—is 'collective mindfulness'" they write. "One is mindful when one is aware, respectful, careful." Beck and Walters provide examples of this "collective mindfulness," and include prayers given by native speakers, such as this, from a Winnebago officiant:

"... Ancestors, we greet you, we greet you!

You who sit around me here, we relatives, we greet you again.

Soon the dance song will start up and we will try to dance and sing as did the Indians of old in the beginning. This was always an Indian ceremony and, in the old days, everything was done with the greatest of care and circumspection. ... all who were present had been blessed by the spirits. ... When it was time to begin the dance song, all arose and danced." (Beck and Walters, pp. 41-42).

As so much of this has crucial matter has been known for so long, in so many civilizations, why don't contemporary authorities encourage all of us together to do whatever we do "with greatest care and circumspection?"

Why not join in patterned, focused attention on psychic energies that surround us, and manipulate them harmoniously for the planet and humanity's greater good? Maybe in that way we could transform the hostile, violent, fragmented, alienated, sick energies we have been generating.

The question must arise: Who benefits from the world-wide transformation of essentially Life-making force-energy into that which is so powerfully negative that even the air can't survive its assault?

In PSYCHIC SEXUALITY, Swann explores many of the reasons why knowledge of basic life-enhancing processes is denied, even prohibited. He suggests that should "we, the people" ever learn how to consciously amplify and utilize the psychic force that flows through us and through all that is, then all bets are off.

Talk about power! Imagine paradigm shift!

I venture to say that the deepest cause behind most of the war, poverty, disease, and phenomena both too vast and too subtle to quite comprehend, is lust for power.

Distortion of human-cum-planetary psychic force by oppression, repression, and suppression of our creative energy is the means by which we are locked out of our creative power.

By distortion of creative urges, and chief among them being our own sexuality, we are prevented from making full use of the "inalienable rights" given us by "God" and "Nature's God" in order to secure the blessings of liberty with and for all the people of the world.

For one thing, without the vital Life-making force that nourishes sexual and all creative energies, no one could get "turned on," no community could be formed, no learning could take place, and nothing would live.

More than carbon, oxygen, nitrogen, and hydrogen, that which brings them into harmonious relation is the essential ingredient of all that is—organic or inorganic, animal, vegetable, or mineral connecting all that is into "All my relatives" as a fact, not a pious wish.

How is it the poet Dylan Thomas named that energy: "That force that drives the greeny flower?"

Ingo probes into many of the causes of officialdom's mindfuck: it boils down to who's to have power. Since about 1769 the industrial civilizations of the Western world have, by regulating human creative energies, attempted to change, bypass, kill, or obliterate the obvious in the name of Progress; in the name of Empire; in the name of vested interests both religious and secular; in the name of science as only materialism; in the name of formalism and uniformitarianism.

Now comes Ingo Swann, just in time to make best use of the energetic potential of *what time it is*. In the 1970s, he published *To Kiss Earth Good-bye*, then went on to train a group at the heart of the beast—rubbing its nose, as it were, in the Obvious. Eventually his efforts resulted in their liberation—which each presently explores in their own bemused way.

He offers *Psychic Sexuality*, a work that will help widen a path of reclaiming information about the Obvious; at least the publication of this work gives us a fighting chance to survive the smoggy pollution that obscures the radiant vitality of all this is.

Given half a chance, the human spirit—that is, the human organization or organism—harmonized with the time and the spirit of the time, with the vast magnetic interlocking quaternary of Great Wheels, will break free from its chains.

Together knowing more of the magnetic interlocking, we might exit the deep cave we've been mucked about in for far too long, and abandon our fascination with the chimerical shadows that masquerade as truth.

Read *Psychic Sexuality*. Ponder it. Make its observations part of your experience, always remembering we are all part of one another. Observe the Obvious—the fruits, the effects of our efforts on ourselves and all our relatives, the change in you that entails the change in me and them and all of it everywhere. Find out what time it is, how the energies flow, and set sail. Begin now—and may the Force be with you.

Paula Gunn Allen
May 1998
Los Angeles

[PAULA GUNN ALLEN, Ph.D. is Professor of English, American Indian Studies, and Creative Writing at UCLA. She is spiritual visionary and Matron of Oak Clan (Laguna Pueblo, New Mexico); an award-winning scholar and writer; author of *The Sacred Hoop: Recovering the Feminine in American Indian Traditions*, a novel entitled *The Woman Who Owned the Shadows*. Recent publications include: *Song of the Turtle: American Indian Literature 1974-1995, Life is a Fatal Disease: Collected Poems 1968-1995*, and *Off the Reservation: Reflections from a Border-Crossing, Boundary-Busting Loose Cannons*, 1998.]

INTRODUCTION

As most people are aware, the topic of SEX is composed of a vast panorama populated by multitudes of subsidiary topics bound together by an enormous array of associated activities. The whole of the panorama is then crowned by that mysterious life-essential factor we refer to as ECSTASY, but whose nature and place in the scheme of all things is not understood very well.

In its bigger picture aspect, the topic of sex is so complex that it can't really be sorted out by relying on simplicities of smaller picture ideas about it. But some few seemingly permanent aspects can be established within any reasonable perspective.

The foremost of these is that the mysterious ecstasy is the virtual hallmark of all sexualizing activities, for without it interest in pursuing any sexual matter would decline dramatically.

Another permanent aspect is that the topic of sex perpetually outlives almost all other topics that the fertile minds of humans can invent and set going. Thus, while powerful intellectual ideas arise and ultimately deflate into faulty historical remembrance, the topic of sex persists in all cultures and in all generations.

Yet another permanent factor is quite impressive. A very large proportion of human life depends on nurturing the inflow of knowledge with respect to whatever is involved. In this sense, much of life is stratified depending on how much or how little is acquired via intellectual understanding.

But essential experiencing of sex and sexuality automatically arises from within each human individual.

Thus, if all intellectual understanding about the topic of sex was somehow to be erased by societal efforts, the topic itself is refreshed anew each time a human in born, and which individual will, for sure, commence sexuality experiencing.

This is much to suggest something both confounding but wondrous: that sex and sexuality have a life, and even a will, of their own.

My own interest in sexual matters grew out of the fascination of watching people undergo sexuality-oriented activities and contortions in the environments of my childhood.

By the time I was eight or nine, I understood that here was a topic subjected to impressive intellectual social control oversight.

But just beneath its platitudinal surface, the oversight had a high degree of inefficiency and failure—mainly because it sought to contain sexual behavior rather than perceptively address the issues of innate sexual forces involved.

Simply put, and all things considered, the intellectual oversight was frequently no match for the sexual forces.

By the time I was thirty-five, I had accumulated a rather large library having to do with all kinds of sexual activities and various studies of them.

Meanwhile, the age of sexual liberation had opened up, and so a plethora of new studies and books was suddenly available. But in the end, these more or less emulated the contours of what had gone on before, in that sexual behavior continued to be the principal focus.

But to me, then as now, the behavior resulted because of sexual forces or energies, which stimulated the behavior into identifiable existence. Although the phrase "sexual energies" was broadly used, actual studies of sexual energies as real energies remained few and far between.

Indeed, the modern West is highly deficient with respect to knowledge of sexual energies as really existing substantively. One obvious reason for this is that the topic of human energetics as a whole is either avoided or suppressed, and for reasons that are only partially explainable.

Ancient Eastern texts, however, do not avoid the issue of human energetics, and many of them are in fact based on the real, virtual existence of such energies.

My first exposure to such Asian information came from attempts to comprehend the nature of the Tantric arts and crafts, and which consist of many different categories besides the sexual ones more commonly treated in the West.

TANTRAS comes from Sanskrit, and literally refers to "a loom" upon which all things can be woven—and among which are enhancements of balanced sexuality, creativity, power, the achievement of desired objectives, and the attainment of six super-human faculties.

Most Asian texts stipulate the real existence of intangible, invisible energies that download into material representation and affects. The Chinese have long referred to these energies as Ch'i, while the Ch'i disciplines advocate understanding and working with, not against, those superlative energies.

Basic knowledge of such energies downloads from pre-antiquity sources usually referred to as shamanistic, and in this sense some kind of operational knowledge regarding invisible energetics is found in most pre-modern cultures world-wide.

With regard to the modern West, most will not really be aware (1) that the study of invisible human energetics really needs to flower into existence, and (2) that it does not enjoy accepted existence because societal forces have suppressed it.

As mentioned, the precise reasons for the suppression are vague and mysterious. But vivid, and awesome, elements of the societal suppression can be recovered from historical aspects usually deleted from conventional histories, and it is a full part of this book to recover a sampling of those elements.

But additionally, if the invisible energies do exist, as the ancient Eastern texts hold, then they are universal to our species and as such will constantly be encountered even by those not knowledgeable about their existence.

Such energies, including sexualizing energies, were encountered in modern psychical research. But they were concealed from popular knowledge because organized psychical research evolved smack in the middle of Victorian attitudes about sex, including even deleting the term from proper discourse.

Then there is the matter of clairvoyance via which invisible, intangible energies can be sensed or seen. It is with this matter of psychic clairvoyance that a large proportion of this book proceeds.

There are many misunderstandings regarding clairvoyance, a rather recent term, but the phenomena of which are entirely consistent with the long history from the earliest forms of shamanism to the present: sensing or seeing invisible energies and their relationship to all other more concrete factors.

It is quite clear that human power and creativity carry considerable energetic components, to the degree that neither can fully be explained without studying and incorporating them. But in some sense at least, creativity and power often are sensed only as potentials, largely because their energetic activation needs deliberate cultivation.

The sensing of sexual energies (sex vibes), however, seldom needs deliberate cultivation. They are very broadly sensed in the "raw," so to speak, among all humans, and sensed as distinct from physical, behavioral, and moral circumstances.

Thus, while the sensing and appreciation of power and creative energies may require special cultivation, the sensing of sexualizing energies is flagrantly omnipresent and easily accessible to almost everyone.

One of the benefits of this is that an examination of sexual energies can open a quite large intuitive door to studies of many other kinds of energies.

During the early months of 1989, I was invited by Dr. Elmer Green to travel to the Menninger Foundation in Topeka, Kansas, to take part in a particularly interesting series of experiments.

Elmer Green, together with his wife and co-worker, Dr. Alyce Green, had become widely known and respected during the 1970s in the realm of researching brainwave biofeedback and "the image-making faculty."

Their work inspired and energized the birthing field of bio-feed-back training both to cure many ailments and to enhance states of consciousness. The use of biofeedback techniques resulted in an individual gaining voluntary control over many physical and perceptual processes.

The Greens were a wonderful and dynamic duo, fully committed to discovering all they could about consciousness and its many phenomena and states.

Elmer Green had taken his doctorate in bio-psychology at the University of Chicago in 1962. Alyce Green had done graduate studies in counseling and creativity. She later focused on exploring brain-wave training in psychotherapy and had been the first president of the Association of Transpersonal Psychology.

The Greens had established at Menninger a research facility referred to as the "Voluntary Controls Program." The work of the Program focused on the alpha-theta brainwave biofeedback process and was at first funded primarily by the National Institutes of Mental Health (NIMH), constituting very high societal approval and support.

Research progress led to encounters and wonderment regarding physical energies and fluctuating states of consciousness. So within the Voluntary Controls Program, in 1983 the Greens incorporated a "Physical Fields and States of Consciousness" research project.

The concept of "physical fields" refers to field-like magnetic and electromagnetic functions that interpenetrate the physical body and also extend outward from it.

Within the physical fields project, the Greens and their coworkers conceptualized a very curious and extraordinary research direction referred to as "The Copper Wall Project." It was in this project that I agreed to act as an experimental subject.

Because they are quite complicated and require copious background information, details of the Copper Wall experiment will be completely described in chapter 18.

But generally speaking, the Copper Wall experiment incorporated large sheets of copper constructed into an environmental surround within which an individual sits.

There were two expectations. The first was that the energies radiating from the human body would impact with the copper walls which were hooked into sensitive equipment to detect the impacts. The second consisted of the expectation that the copper surround would act in ways that might stimulate and increase extraordinary states of awareness and consciousness.

The idea of INCREASING awareness and expanding consciousness is not new or unusual, of course. On its surface, the idea is attractive and widely discussed, for the prospect has to do with unlocking human potentials. Thus, the idea seems logical, and is one that might be pursued with enthusiasm.

But just beneath the glowing surface aspects of the idea exists a rather curious history of mainstream societal repression that is quite difficult to explain, and which has hardly ever been opened up for inspection.

In part explanation, though, let us identify what might be a strategic reason. What might be perceived, via conditions of increased awareness and expanded states of consciousness, certainly will differ from what might be perceived via average, or conventional, conditions of awareness.

So although the general idea of increasing awareness and

consciousness seems logical and attractive, there is the matter of what realities will be perceived if indeed such enhancement does happen.

Here is something apparently quite problematical to all major societal concerns, especially if they are founded upon states of awareness and consciousness developed only in accord with the conventional average.

Since most social structures are quite rooted in conventional parameters of awareness and perception, if one begins to think about what might be involved, any increases of them automatically have societal implications.

Most will recognize this kind of situation, of course. But it needs particularly to be pointed up that all forms of psychic perceptions encounter difficulties in this regard. Most forms of psychic awareness and perceptions can easily be said to constitute perceptual increases beyond the conventional average.

As it was back in 1989, I sat in the copper wall environment twice a day for five working days, each session consisting of forty-five minutes. Exceptional dynamic forms of consciousness, and awarenesses appropriate to them, gradually began manifesting.

This was very confusing at first. But over time it could gradually be concluded that the whole consisted of perceptions of various kinds of energies normally invisible to conventional perceptions.

With continuous exposure to this kind of thing, the energies could be isolated into many overlapping, but reasonably separate categories, with three of them seeming to be major: sexualizing energies; creative energies; and energies having to do with various kinds of human power.

This book, of course, constitutes an extended consideration of the sexualizing energies, the importance of which has been quite strangely treated by societal concerns, especially those of the modernist period.

At this point, it must clearly be stated that in no way was the Voluntary Controls Project at Menninger, or the copper wall experiments, set up to enhance perception of sexual energetics. Nor did the design or goals of the experiment have any foreseen or expected sexual concomitants in the minds of anyone involved—including myself.

In explanation here, if we abide by the conventional concept that sexuality has a lower-order status and spiritual matters have a higher-order one, then the Greens and their co-workers were entirely representative of the latter, and in very wonderful ways.

But when, on my part alone, the exceptional types of awareness commenced, they gradually went from (1) what might be expected (such as enhanced seeing of auras around physical bodies) to (2) what was totally unexpected, especially the perception of DYNAMIC energetics associated with creative and sexual activity.

Part IV of PSYCHIC SEXUALITY comprises my tale of encountering various aspects of the dynamic sexual energies, and which are of such a nature as to test even the most vivid powers of fantasy.

Indeed, so fantastic might the dynamic sexual energies seem that I would not make an attempt to present them herein unless corroborative and substantiating historical background could be located.

Thus, under the rubric of "tremulous pulsations," I review this background as Part I of this book in order to partially reconstruct a larger panorama what is apparently involved regarding energetics not generally visible within the limited scope of conventional perceiving.

This background history can be traced to many cultures in antiquity. But I enter into it during the Renaissance period, which some historians indicate as the early beginning of what later came to be known as the modern scientific age.

There is an advantage to entering into the history at the Renaissance point. Not only does the research topic of human energetics become identifiable, but societal repressions of that research are quite well recorded.

One of the detriments of the history is that in the modernist West the topics of sex and sexuality became increasingly taboo during the eighteenth century, and the taboo slopped over into the nineteenth.

Most of the general history we depend on in any official mainstream sense was compiled by eighteenth-century historians, who, because of the taboo attitudes, bleeped open and frank references to sex from their volumes. Thus, except as they pertain to the procreation of family lines, the conventional historical overviews from antiquity onward are sex-less.

This has made it very difficult to recover information about how sex and sexuality were treated in earlier times, and in different cultures.

But outside of the pall of conventional modern histories, enough has been recovered by intrepid researchers to indicate that sexualizing energies (as contrasted to physical sexual behavior) were acknowledged as existing in antiquity.

It is also quite well established that what we today would call psychic sexuality was often treated as having ceremonial, cathexis, and psychic implications.

CATHEXIS refers to a ceremonial investment of libidinal energy in a person, object or idea.

Perception of energetics, invisible to conventional awareness, requires that human organisms possess faculties to sense or to "see" them, faculties that can become functional or awakened under various circumstances. This kind of "seeing" has been scooped into the general category called CLAIRVOYANCE.

That term is a rather recent one, having many nuances not immediately apparent. I utilize Part II to sort through several of the nuances, thereby hoping to establish a wider comprehension of what is involved regarding the wonders of clairvoyance.

I utilize Part III to present a picture of what happened to me in general as a result of sitting in the copper wall environment during which lucidity, a super form of clairvoyance, turned on —and why extraordinary measures were soon required to turn it off.

As already mentioned, Part IV consists of my tale of perceiving sexualizing energetics, the whole of which was a rather mind-blowing, but completely fascinating experience.

PART I

TREMULOUS PULSATIONS

Chapter 1
THE UNIVERSALITY OF SEXUAL ENERGIES

Human sexuality has very many facets, faces, and nuances. The whole of these constitute a collective phenomenon that is monumentally complex in its contexts and dimensions. Thus, the exceedingly complex nature of human sexuality does not easily lend itself to simplified understanding—except in rather gross terms which themselves often increase confusions instead of sorting things out or making it possible to grasp the whole of what is involved.

The topic of human sexuality is also very dynamic and charismatic, and this places it among the few topics that have enduring high interest and fascination in almost all levels of life.

Indeed, during the modern period many thousands of books have been produced exposing to print various data, statistics, theories, and a wide assortment of factors which, in some respect, can be associated with sexuality-based dynamics.

FOUR CONVENTIONAL APPROACHES TO THE EXAMINATION OF SEXUALITY

The general topics of sex and sexuality have suffered extensive confusions by having been taboo for a number of centuries preceding the modernist period. Indeed, it became possible only about a hundred years ago to open somewhat organized examinations of sexuality.

For the most part during this period, human sexuality overall has tended to be officially considered within only four general categories.

What might be called the clinical way is derived from the structural anatomy of the two sexes.

The psychological way which tends to discuss sexuality as behavior.

Social approaches to sexuality are very likely to discuss it via modes of moral and ethical precepts—and which differ from culture to culture, and even among smaller social groupings.

Sexuality can also be studied via its "erotic splendors" expressed in some kind of representational form in the arts, music, and literature.

While elements of the four categories briefly enumerated above can be inter-mixed, societal forces tend to keep them separate, and so each of them tends to be limited by static mindset boundaries that often preclude any inter-mixing. The four categories, however, have a factor in common, in that they establish generalizing contexts that tend to obviate or ignore what individuals dynamically experience. Indeed, what individuals dynamically experience is often at odds with the general, non-dynamic parameters of each of the conventional categories.

Thus, while the contexts of the four categories are interesting enough as far as they go, the individual doesn't benefit very much from them in terms of their own dynamic experiencing.

THE AVOIDED ISSUE OF SEXUAL ENERGIES

While it might not be the case among all individuals, it is possible to suggest that they do not, in the FIRST instance, experience sexuality as anatomical, behavioral, or morally, but rather as dynamic energies that have sexuality concomitants.

Indeed, of all the many human activities DRIVEN by "energies," sexual energies seem not only to be the most powerful, but the most universally shared by all individuals of our species.

How the energies are interpreted AFTER experiencing them is a matter that does not particularly pertain to the essential existence of the energies themselves.

If the foregoing is considered, it would appear that there can be a fifth existing category via which human sexuality can be considered. This would be a category of sexual energies, or sexual energetics, but which category is seldom examined.

That a category identified as "sexual energies" does indeed exist can be made clear by the following consideration.

If humans possessed sexual equipment, or sexual response

systems, and if the sexual equipment was not or never ENERGIZED, then sexual matters would never come to anyone's attention.

Indeed, even if the existence of the sexual whatever was known, no one would know what it was for in the absence of energization.

In this sense, then, it can be considered that sexualizing energetics pre-exist any subsequent manifestation of sexuality, whether the ultimate manifestation be anatomical, behavioral, or is subjected to moralistic considerations.

So, for the purposes of this book, we can more or less leave behind the conventional categories and focus principally on the energy category. There are plenty of sources in the modern world that discuss sexuality in the light of the conventional categories, but extremely few that discuss it in the light of the basic energetics of the sexualizing processes.

PRE-MODERN CONCEPTS OF SEXUAL ENERGIES

An historical overview establishes that most pre-modern societies did incorporate what might be called energetic aspects or precepts regarding sexualizing processes.

Indeed, in antiquity most societies elevated the sexualizing energies to the status of demigods and goddesses—and seem to have done so fully aware that they represented not beings per se, but different kinds of archetypal energies.

One of the ironies of the modern world is that although the demigods and goddesses have been relegated to the realm of unfounded myth or superstition, the energizing archetypes are still recognized and utilized.

For example, the Venus and Mars sexual archetypes—which just about everyone today still recognizes as the principal embodiments of feminine and masculine energies.

Beyond that simplicity, people SENSE and/or FEEL sexualizing energies, and in fact identify and describe them as such. Indeed, in both pre-modern history and today, sexualizing energies are described as fields, beams, coils, intrusions, radiances, engulfing auras, impacts, energies, touches, electricity, magnetism, tinglings, heat, and etc., all of which have more or less TANGIBLE substance.

SEXUAL ENERGIES AS TANGIBLE "SUBSTANCES"

While it is exceedingly difficult to define what these tangible substances consist of, they none the less stimulate some kind of sexualizing responses in those who experience them, even if the response tends to be confusing.

Now, it must be pointed up that there is nothing strange about any of this.

Most take it on board and deal with the whole of it the best way they can. It is even safe to say that most people, to some degree anyway, would not live without it.

In fact, without experiencing some kind of sexualizing energetics, most would not consider themselves completely alive.

And that somewhat represents the unofficial status quo regarding sexualizing energies. Although the status quo has no official platform, it will none the less be found unofficially endorsed at the individual experiential level—and this universally so among the millions and millions, no matter their socio-cultural parameters.

THE STRANGE SOCIETAL AVOIDANCE OF SEXUAL ENERGIES

However, an element of strangeness begins to enter in when it is realized that the real existence of sexual energies is seldom included in the conventional line-up of sexual phenomena.

This is to say that the phenomena of the conventional line-up are officially accepted, while the very real existence of omnipresent sexual energies perpetually experienced by each individual human is not officially accepted.

And, as will be discussed ahead, the strangeness takes on heightened intensity because of a peculiar factor—a factor that, itself, is strongly avoided by most societal mainstreams.

This factor comes to light where it can be shown that any attempts, in modern terms, to research sexualizing energetics, and thus to make their existence official, are socially and actively condemned.

Exactly WHY research into sexualizing energetics is put down is something of a mystery.

Yet another form of strangeness definitely enters in when it transpires that clairvoyants, sensitives, psychics, and healers can, among other kinds of energies, perceive at least some formats of the sexualizing energies.

When perceived, such energies are then given description by the clairvoyants that more or less correspond to what ordinary people only sense-feel in distinctly tactile ways, although the psychic descriptions are usually and wonderfully elaborated with colors, textures, shapes, lights, and various other nuances.

Like sexualizing energetics, however, the realm of psychic energetics and perceptions does not enjoy any official socio-cultural acceptance, or in some cases not even slightly amenable toleration. Indeed, the arising of organized psychical research in 1882 (and later parapsychology) was aggressively treated and stigmatized by official modernist enterprises.

The sociological hoopla surrounding mainstream condemnation of Psi was sometimes tremendous and led to the official disenfranchisement of any kind of Psi research.

The overall result of all this socio-cultural denial has established the findings of any kind of Psi researchers in a negative light—no matter how careful, real and relevant those findings might be—and thus the topic of Psi is still considered taboo within our contemporary mainstream sciences and philosophies.

The cumulative findings of the Psi researchers thus remain as capsules of rejected knowledge within the contemporary societal mainstreams.

EARLY RESEARCH CONTEXTS REGARDING SEXUALIZING ENERGIES

Research into sexualizing energetics, however, inadvertently began about three centuries before the inauguration of organized psychical research in 1882. Although the two kinds of research occasionally coincided thereafter, the former more or less has acquired its separate history as capsules of rejected knowledge.

A review of that background history at least makes for interesting tragic-comic, and often quite hilarious reading. But its different epochs also serve as revealing background not only as regards social resistance to sexualizing energetics, but to the field of human energetics as a whole.

The history of the rejected knowledge involving human energetics began during the Renaissance.

This was a period when there were still important functional distinctions between inanimate and animate energy, and between the body-mind concept and the body-energy-mind concept.

Modern concepts along these lines differ from the earlier ones, and so we would be in error in applying contemporary understandings to them.

So, as a full part of the rejected history, and in order to achieve a more near authentic background, it is necessary to reestablish certain definitions and meanings as would have been in use back then.

The reader might at first think that doing so is far afield from the present context of psychic sexuality. But it will illuminate a lot of factors and bring us very much closer to the entire contexts of sexualizing energies.

Chapter 2
INANIMATE ENERGY— ANIMATE ENERGY

With the title of this chapter, we encounter a mix of topics so massively complicated that even partially conceptualizing them will require reserves of patience. But these topics are entirely relevant to sexualizing energies, and so untangling them is necessary to achieve a larger framework for understanding much that is to follow.

For openers, it is not only important but necessary to state that although the modern sciences do distinguish the inanimate (the nonliving) from the animate (the living), no such distinction is made regarding inanimate ENERGY and animate ENERGY.

But if such distinction was made, we would once more, as we so often do, encounter the modernist distinctions of the acceptable scientific and the unacceptable unscientific.

Inanimate energy would fall into the scientific category, and roughly speaking, animate energies would fall into the unscientific category.

This difficulty, peculiar to the modern scientific age, was not always the case.

THE PRIMITIVE IDEA OF THE "LIFE FLUID"

Most pre-modern societies held vivid concepts regarding animating energies. But as the modern scientific period advanced, such concepts were devalued as primitive and naive, and hence as unscientific in principle.

As but one example of the primitive "naivete," as revealed in early anthropology studies, is that "the Life" was flatly identified with an energetic animating "fluid" akin to breath or blood, but invisible or ethereal and rather more fiery.

As it was later and often put by early modern critics of the "fluid," the "etherealization of Life" naively culminated in the view that Life IS an energy-like fluid, but one that is assigned no properties other than its power of animating an organism.

This "primitive" idea more or less required the existence of another format of energy, a Life principle, in addition to the energies that could be derived from inanimate matter. This primitive concept ran counter to the modern sciences after they became infused with the philosophy of materialism.

Thus, without much in the way of deeper examination, the primitive concept of an energetic Life principle independent of matter was hastily relegated to the unscientific category, a little too hastily, perhaps, if certain scientific advances in the late twentieth century are any indication.

A slight confusion in all this has to do with the idea that the fluid had no properties other than its power of animating AN ORGANISM. But IF the fluid had the power of animating an organism, it FIRST also needed to have the power of seizing upon and organizing inanimate matter INTO the format of the organism.

However, when science became trenchantly based in materialism, it was assumed that if the Life principle existed it would be found to have a material origin, not an ethereal one.

In any event, by the turn of the century the modern sciences had jettisoned into the unscientific category the whole of this independent Life principle thing, especially the concept of the ethereal.

But if the sciences were successful in achieving this, an entire new set of problems and confusions emerged. It shortly became quite difficult to explain invisible energies whose existence could not be confirmed by direct material observation but could be confirmed by deduction.

One example involved the historically accepted phenomenon of "thought transference" (later renamed as "telepathy") across space and through intervening material barriers.

Indeed, the thought-transference phenomenon was an insult to the integrity of "scientific" materialism. But this was neatly handled by relegating it to the unscientific category, a category quickly to become much enlarged as time went on.

One of the results of dumping the fluid Life principle and accompanying ethereality, was that the entire scenario involving all animating energies was first marginalized, and then also dumped.

The only factor left was the general idea that life forms are animate life forms. But this was a residual descriptive contrivance only, having no scientific substance otherwise.

THE MODEL OF MECHANISTIC "WORK" ENERGIES

The concept of "mechanistic energies" generally filled in the vacuum left by the jettisoned animating energies, even in the so-called Life sciences.

The materialistic sciences indeed proved their worthiness by developing, via physics and chemistry, those energies into the stellar and vivid heights of technological wonders of the Modern Age.

Energies, as mechanistic, became the model for how energy of any kind was to be considered and conceptualized. A brief review of the history involved here is not only interesting in itself, but somewhat necessary with regard to many animating energetic aspects to be presented ahead.

The very great English mathematician and natural philosopher, Sir Isaac Newton (1642-1727), summarized his discoveries in terrestrial and celestial mechanics in a lengthy tract published in 1687.

The tract was a compilation of mathematical principles of "natural philosophy"—later being dubbed as "physics."

In Newtonian mechanics, energy was conceptualized as "a property of moving masses."

But at some point in the later 1700s, the definition of energy underwent various changes—and, by the late 1800s, ended up being defined simply as "the ability or capacity to do work."

Although this definition of energy is brief, it immediately calls for an explanation of WORK itself, and of another important factor, that of power.

As noted in many encyclopedias, "in the strict physical sense, work is performed only when a force is exerted on a body while the body moves at the same time in such a way that the force has a component in the direction of motion." In turn, POWER is defined as "the rate at which work is performed."

MAJOR SOURCES OF MECHANISTIC ENERGY

It is scientifically observed that energy can exist in a variety of forms, some more recognizable as being capable of performing work than others. The major known forms of energy are:

- Gravitation
- Energy of rotation
- Energy of orbital motion
- Nuclear reactions
- Electromagnetic energy
- Internal heat of stars
- Sunlight
- Sound
- Chemical reactions
- Terrestrial waste heat
- Cosmic microwave radiation

Scientists note that energy usually flows from higher levels to lower levels. Thus, "cosmic microwave background radiation is defined as the ultimate heat sink." In other words, the SINK representing "the ultimate in energy degradation with no lower form in which to be converted."

Forms of energy in which the energy is not dependent upon mechanical motion are generally referred to as forms of POTENTIAL ENERGY. KINETIC ENERGY is defined as energy associated with mechanical motion of bodies.

The availability of energy is found in many SOURCES of energy—for example, oxen, horses, coal, peat, geothermal, nuclear, electric, petroleum, gas, hydrogen, tidal, horses, wind, water, wage earners, etc.

The energy indwelling in these sources is potential energy, and which, via human genius, can be converted or transformed into kinetic energy that permits work energy to manifest and be utilized.

Some dictionaries ALSO define ENERGY as "power forcefully exerted," and thus power is the single synonym for ENERGY.

ANIMATING ENERGETICS

Moving now to the term ENERGETIC, it is easy to see why most will understand it to mean "marked by energy, operating with vigor or effect"—with VIGOROUS being a good synonym.

ENERGIZE is defined as "to impart energy to, so as to make energetic or vigorous."

It is to be noted that the term ENERGETICS is not found in a number of respectable sources. If it appears at all, its meaning is usually given as "a branch of mechanics that deals primarily with energy and its transformations."

Now, to point up a necessary observation. As defined and described above, in the scientific sense ENERGY is fundamentally associated only with inanimate phenomena (although as sources of kinetic energy some animate resources can be transformed into work).

Direct observation can easily establish that animate life forms are marked by potential work energy, often operating with vigor or effect, and sometimes can forcefully exert power.

Referring to the list given above regarding scientifically recognized forms of energy, it can be assumed that animate life forms can be affected by any one or all of the forms of energy given. But effected only AFTER they have become an animate life form.

It is true that the listed forms of energy-cum-sources can, so to speak, animate WORK. But what about the nature of the energies that animate the life-forms that utilize the work?

The essential difficulty here is that in the sense of the scientific, the modern West has only one major definition for energy: the capacity for doing work.

Additionally, that definition can be extended a little in that the capacity for doing work is seen as power forcefully exerted.

However, in the scientific sense these definitions for the most part apply to objective mechanistic factors external to the human.

Even though the terms ENERGY and POWER are applied to the human in a popular sense, the human is filled, so to speak, not so much with mechanistic energies, but with animating energies.

These animating energies are not served very well by the mechanistic definitions of energy/power. So, difficulties arise that are ambiguous and not a little confusing.

SEXUALITY AS BEHAVIOR?

As but one example of such a confusion, the nature of sexual energies cannot convincingly be described in mechanistic terms as the capacity for doing work, because even the most intellectually challenged would giggle at this.

Between 1890 and 1925, give or take a little, this particularly ludicrous factor was neatly disposed of in modern scientific terms by shifting the emphasis away from the "hard" idea of sexual energies to the "soft" idea of sexual behavior.

In the context of sexual behavior, then, the ambiguous difficulties landed in the lap of the various modernist psychologies (i.e., the "soft" sciences) which were in process of evolving in order to examine the many remarkable phenomena and paradoxes of human behavior.

This resulted in the concept, still prevalent, that human sexuality was solely a matter of behavior, not energetics.

As it then transpired in psychological (and psychiatric) terms, it proved exceedingly difficult to arrive at specific definitions that could be relevant to all kinds of BEHAVIOR.

Of the literally hundreds of definitions, the one most relevant to most visible kinds of behavior was established as "The manner in which anything acts or operates. With regard to the human being, the term usually refers to the action of the individual as a unit."

As will be reviewed in the next chapter, this definition suggested that the human being was composed of parts, which parts taken together composed the individual human unit. The dominant modern concept held that this unit was majorly composed of two basic parts: body and mind.

The concept was entirely convenient, in that the human could be segregated into two different major parts: the body, which could be studied in the hard-biological sciences; and the mind, which could be studied in the soft psychological sciences.

More specifically put, the body could be considered, philosophically and scientifically, within the theories of reductive materialism, while the mind could be studied within the theories of reductive behaviorism.

Modern discussion of reductive behaviorism, however,

began with the work of John Broadus Watson (1878-1958), the American psychologist generally credited with originating the modern school of psychology called behaviorism.

Watson aimed to establish psychology as a science. He held that because states of consciousness are private and thus directly inscrutable, there could not be a scientific psychology of consciousness. Only observation of behavior would provide the necessary data for a scientific psychology.

Because it is rare for any two behaviorists to generally agree on anything of importance, arriving at exact definitions for BEHAVIOR have proven to be somewhat elusive.

ORGANISM—ORGANISMIC

In any event, in its original context, BEHAVIOR is defined as "any movement of an organism."

This definition received refinement via the most general definition of BEHAVIORISM, which consists of "the observable evidence of organismic activity to the exclusion of introspective data or references to consciousness of mind."

One can cogitate on these and eventually come up with any number of interpretations. But the two definitions respectively refer to "an organism" and to "organismic activity" as the subject, while the behavior refers to what the subjects do when they can be seen as being in motion.

This is to attempt to point up that there are important distinctions between what an organism IS, and what an organism DOES when in movement.

Further, if "introspective data" refers to certain subjective and/ or psychological factors that might serve as motivations for the activity, then the activity takes place in the absence of such motivations. Here is something of a complexity, since when we observe an organism exhibiting such and such a motion (behavior), we usually try to comprehend why it is doing so and to what ends.

To transliterate this mess into something that can more easily be understood, sexual behavior is either caused by or originates in "organismic activity," while the processes of the behavior do not involve either subjective or consciousness of mind processes.

However confusing this may be, the central message is quite clear: The behavior, so-called, is the result of the organismic activity or the organismic activity causes the resulting behavior.

One has to wonder why Western societies have focused almost entirely on sexual behavior rather than "organismic activity, and whether this focus is simply voyeuristic thrill or on behalf of clinical aspects as alleged.

ORGANIC VITALITY—A FORM OF ANIMATING ENERGETICS

The word ORGANISMIC is a terminological extension of the term ORGANIC, and which in turn is extended from the Greek term ORGAN, which meant "instrument" that functions because of vibrations.

Thus, ORGAN came very early to refer to any number of musical instruments which, in the sonic sense, vibrated in that part of the electromagnetic spectrum for which human ear systems possessed sonic receptors.

In English, the term ORGAN, as referring to a vibrating thing, was not attached to plant or animal physiology until about 1420.

At that time, it was more or less seized upon to indicate an instrumental (vibrational) part or member of a plant or animal body that performs some particular vital function, such as digestion, respiration, excretion, reproduction, locomotion, and perception, etc.

But it needs to be pointed up with regard to this physiological meaning that the earlier comprehension of the term VITAL differed considerably from later modern concepts of it.

In the modern concept, it became associated with VITALITY, referring to physical or mental vigor, especially if highly developed.

The pre-modern meaning of VITAL referred specifically to "existing as a manifestation of Life."

The pre-modern concept yielded the concept of VITALISM, defined as "a doctrine that the functions of a living organism are due to a vital animating principle distinct from inanimate physico-chemical forces."

The distinction between animate and inanimate forces will

play a considerable role in the chapters ahead.

But here it should be pointed up that since ancient times ANIMATE specifically referred to a universally existing "something" that was likened to breath.

Breath is clearly a universal indicator that life is present, and so it could be considered a principle, whether completely understood or not.

The term VITAL referred to this principle, which itself was life.

Taking all of the above into consideration, an organism was an instrument of the life animating principle, an instrument of the life energetic principle. By associating the term ORGAN to life, organisms unquestionably also associated energetic vibrations to the life principle whether or not embodied in otherwise inorganic matter merely made up of physico-chemical forces.

And it is then possible to see that the concept of "orgasmic activity" refers only indirectly to behavior, but more directly to some kind of animating activity as contrasted, for example, with "inorgasmic activity."

In this sense, the term ORGASMIC is entirely redolent with vital, vitalizing, and animating functions.

Thus, what the definition of BEHAVIORISM is actually doing, is allocating behavioristic activity to primary vibrating, vitalizing, and animating functions, and which, on their own, manifest secondary results identifiable as behavior.

SELF-VIBRATING ENERGIES

Whether the whole of this small discussion makes sense to various readers, it is quite visible via sexual behavior.

This behavior, as most people realize, clearly manifests animating functions, and these functions are often in complete defiance of whatever serves as introspective data, consciousness, and mind.

Indeed, it is frequently observed that sexual activity "has a mind of its own."

More simply put, perhaps, sexual behavior is the result of some definitely self-animating, self-vibrating energies, and whatever vibrates certainly will resonate upon other organisms possessing the necessary receptor systems.

On definitional grounds alone, it is possible to theorize that sexual activity consists of resonating vibrations that can be sensed by other organisms, and that those organisms will demonstrate some kind of energetic reacting.

None of this can be allocated to, or explained by, body or mind alone, or by any mix of body-mind.

Any explanation of "organismic activity" requires the inclusion of an energetic principle between body and mind, a concept that links the two into an animate organism.

Chapter 3
BODY-MIND versus BODY-ENERGY-MIND

That the human being consists of only two parts—body and mind—is a concept so much taken for granted in the Western societal mainstream that its authenticity is hardly ever questioned.

Indeed, the body-mind concept in its modern status has been science-sacrosanct—so much so that mainstream workings can feel justified in relegating contrasting phenomena and data into the nebulosity of the unscientific.

Thus, the modern "image of man" is as body-mind. The culture-shaping influences of this image have been exceedingly strong. The image is so powerfully and redundantly prevailing in the overall societal sense that hardly anyone even knows how to begin challenging it—not even scientists themselves.

The image conceptually divides the basic perception of the human into two parts. This, of course, is a dualistic dividing, and is in keeping with the somewhat demented love affair the cultural West has conducted with the reductionism philosophy of dualism.

One importance of this dividing is that it omits, or does not permit, a logical tripartite dividing that includes human energies, human energetics, and phenomena accompanying them.

So it is perpetually difficult, for example, to account for and give authentic place to sexual energies, creative energies, mental energies—and, as well, to morphological energies that shape inanimate matter into animate formats.

In order to discuss the concept of the human as body-energy-mind, it is first somewhat profitable to review when and why the decidedly faulty dualistic concept became established.

IMAGES OF MAN

During the early decades of the twentieth century, anthropologists dug deeply into the cultural aspects of past societies.

Those studies reinforced the concept that human societies need what is referred to as an "Image of Man," in order to have some idea of what men thought MAN (including women) to be. In the past, therefore, human societies erected different kinds of images of man, based on whatever was seen as consensus reality by those societies.

This need is an exceedingly interesting revelation overall about the "nature" of societal humans. But it has always led into problems—especially among those societies which felt that only one Image of Man was needed, and this was the one THEY had constructed. Many Images have come and gone, of course.

In this light, the modernist body-mind Image is, in the nearing future, likely to be replaced as not quite authentic and all-inclusive, largely because advancing scientific discoveries are leading toward new knowledge packages.

Many early anthropologists noted that different Images of Man were established and adopted by each given society. Each society, then, saw all other Images as useless, and sometimes as a threat to the integrity and sanctity of its own Image.

Some wonderful books were produced regarding images of man. But when investigated species-wide, the fact that there were so many images, each differing, clearly established that all Images of Man were only artifacts of societal thinking.

Further, it could be surmised that the realities upon which the Images were based might only consist of supposed realities that somehow gained mainstream support.

So in actual fact, the Images were considered authentic only by virtue of the mainstream support. And since most societal mainstreams demonstrate authoritarian tendencies, perhaps many Images were in fact empty of everything but authoritarian insistence and conditioning.

The anthropological studies further revealed that the realities upon which the Images were incorporated could consist as much of the illusory as of reality. By direct implication, then, the anthropological revelations touched upon an issue quite sensitive to the modernist mindsets.

This sensitivity specifically involved the authenticity and durability of the Image of Man that the modern sciences and philosophies were working so diligently to construct.

The most important issue along these lines was that the modern sciences were working to ELIMINATE illusory, religious, and superstitious contexts that the moderns felt had been incorporated into all earlier Images. But anthropologists more or less suggested that all earlier societies also had thought they were eliminating the same things.

Even a hint that the modern sciences, however unsuspectingly, might be replacing earlier illusions with new illusions of their own was untenable. So various brouhaha's erupted in scientific and academic circles, all eagerly fueled by philosophical Intellectuals.

These arguments increased in pitch when anthropologists began reporting on certain conditions that were notable in earlier societies:

1. awareness of invisible energies;
2. different sexual formats, often ritualized;
3. connections of apparent sexualizing energies with "higher powers of mind"; and
4. the use of erotic methods to enhance creative and psychic capacities.

THE MODERN EMERGENCE OF PHILOSOPHICAL DUALISM

The body-energy-mind concept was entirely visible and relevant during the many decades of the European Renaissance, one of the most significant reculturalizing events in human history.

Indeed, it could be said, with historical justification, that the sciences of the Renaissance were focused on cosmic, natural and biological "energetics."

However, at some point during the post-Renaissance decades, this important trinity passed from mainstream consideration, with the result that the human was increasingly explained as body-mind only.

After the disappearance of Renaissance energetics, and until the 1930s Soviet introduction of bio-energetics, no comparable official concept really existed in the modern scientific and philosophical West. Although human energies could be talked about in popular, layman terms, there existed no official scientific or philosophical substance for them.

The concept of dualism is quite ancient, some of its formats dating back to Manichaeism arising in Persia about A.D. 226. Earlier formats are found in ancient Greece and among the even earlier Sanskrit-speaking people of India.

Most dictionaries usually offer three principle definitions of DUALISM:

1. a theory that considers reality to consist of two irreducible elements or modes;
2. a view of man as constituted of two irreducible elements; and
3. a doctrine that the universe is under the dominion of two opposing principles, one of which is good and the other evil.

Even though dualism does have a lengthy history, the particular concept of dualism that came to overwhelm modern thought is acknowledged as originating from the famous French philosopher and scientist, Rene Descartes (1596-1650).

Descartes is unquestionably accepted as major among the founders of modern thought, but also among the most original philosophers and mathematicians of any age.

It is interesting to learn of an unusual element in Descartes' early background. On the night of November 10, 1619, while in Germany, he had certain dreams which he interpreted as a divine sign that his destiny was to found a unified science of nature.

At the time of the dream it seemed that this new unity would be based on mathematics. He did not, however, immediately set about to write works of philosophy or science but continued to travel widely.

His first substantial work was "Rules for the Direction of the Mind" written in 1628-29. Although "Rules" was never completed, what did exist was published in 1701, but probably only because Descartes had become a philosophical superstar by the time of his death in 1650.

In November 1628, Descartes was in Paris, where he distinguished himself in a famous confrontation with one

Chandoux, who held that science could be founded only on probabilities (probability theory later becoming a significant issue in physics at about 1928).

Descartes eloquently attacked Chandoux, vigorously claiming: (1) that only absolute certainty (not probability) could serve as a basis of human knowledge, and (2) that he himself had a method of establishing this basis.

Here is made visible one essential ingredient regarding the nearly absolute charisma Descartes' thinking was to have, a charisma that is by no means dispelled even today.

Simply put, most humans prefer to deal in absolute certainties rather than in amorphous probabilities. Thus, Descartes was not only to become an exponent of certainty, but a comforting icon of it as well.

As regards Cartesian Dualism, Descartes held, in absolute certainty of course, that there are only TWO causally unrelated substances, the physical and the mental.

Accordingly, for Descartes, a human being must be some kind of union of two distinct things: a soul, or mind, and a body. The body is part of mechanical nature, the mind, a "pure thinking substance."

Since the body is merely a physical mechanical system, the pure thinking substance must be the principle of life that energizes the mechanical system.

For Descartes, live bodies differ from dead ones as stopped watches differ from working ones. Moreover, there are many actions that the bodily machine performs on its own, without any intervention of the thinking substance (a.k.a., the soul).

This Cartesian division of the human being into two distinct categories of body and mind apparently disposed of the "soul" which was a religious concept by renaming it "mind." And in this sense, Cartesian dualism was seized upon by later scientific materialists as the battle between religion and science heated up in the eighteenth and nineteenth centuries.

Descartes later changed his mind and became prepared to identify a close union between soul and body as a "substantial union" of MOTION. He does suggest that this union is in fact a "primitive" and thus unanalyzable union.

Nonetheless, he went to some lengths to analyze it. In fact, his increasing analysis led him to have a good deal to say about it, and he did so in his PASSIONS OF THE SOUL which he published in 1649.

As discussed in PASSIONS, the nature of the soul is quite complicated. But Descartes essentially offered a picture of the soul directly moving the pineal gland and thus affecting the "animal spirits," which he considered to be the hydraulic transmission system of mechanical change.

One might have to struggle a little regarding this concept, but a possible clarification is that "hydraulic transmission system" is a kind of energizing principle.

Descartes' picture also referred to what the soul was and was not conscious of, hut there are certain difficulties in understanding exactly how he envisioned this consciousness.

In any event, the pineal gland theory offered in PASSIONS was not a part of the Cartesian system that garnered wide favor in the developing patterns of the material, modern sciences.

The pineal gland idea, however, found wide favor in the occult sciences, so called to distinguish those sciences as areas of knowledge rejected by the modern science.

It is somewhat ironical, even humorous, that Descartes' ideas were seminal within both the modern materialistic sciences AND the modern occult sciences.

THE HUMAN AS BODY-ENERGY-MIND

One of the most common overviews of human energies, including those sexual, is that they constitute functions, "drives," or powers of some human aspect that is not actually physical by definition, but understood as being quite close to an "instinctual" something or other.

Most dictionaries give at least two definitions for INSTINCT. The second one (most usually emphasized in science and academia), defines INSTINCT as "consisting of specific responses to environmental factors, the responses being hereditary, unalterable, and not involving reason."

However, the term is drawn from the Latin INSTINCTUS, meaning "impulse." Thus, the first definition in English is given as "a natural impulse, capacity, or aptitude." So there is a "conflict" between the first and second definitions.

It is true that a "specific response" can be seen as an impulse. On the other hand, the word "specific" can bring up a number of questions if one takes time to reflect. A little further thinking can reveal that a response is not exactly the same as an impulse.

The principle reason is two-fold: while a response IS a reaction to a stimulus, an impulse, strictly speaking, is not a response or a reaction.

The center of this little difficulty is that IMPULSE is taken from the Latin IMPULSUS meaning "impel." In English, therefore, IMPULSE is defined in ways that cannot really be equated with the definitions of RESPONSE.

IMPULSE usually has at least three definitions: (1) the act of driving onward with sudden force; (2) a wave of excitation transmitted through tissues and especially nerve fibers and muscles that results in physiological activity or inhibition; (3) a force so communicated as to produce motion suddenly.

The distinction here is that RESPONSE to stimuli obviously is the effect of some cause, while IMPULSE as to impel is clearly describing a cause that will result in effects or responses.

Additionally, "a wave of excitation transmitted" obviously refers to some kind of energy, or to some kind of energetic or energizing process.

Furthermore, whether instinct, response, or impulse, none of them can be random or just flopping about. Otherwise, life forms that have them would quickly be reduced to a pulsating mess. Thus, some kind of "organizing intelligence" is implicit, and which, by all available clues, is energetic.

Various problems arise if it is accepted that the physical body is the fundamental reality regarding what the human is, because this relegates the human as energy to a less important conceptual place, or perhaps to no real place at all. Even if "mind" is added to "body," this dualism still omits "energy."

In actuality, the human is some kind of a "marriage" of active energies and physical body. Indeed, people refer to "body energy" and to "mental energy." It is thus somewhat difficult to see why the energetic components of the human are NOT included in science, or why human energetic phenomena generally fall into the unscientific category.

And if the energy aspect of the human is SUBTRACTED from the body aspect, and from the mental aspect, then the fate of the body will fall apart and back into the inorganic materials of which it is composed. The fate of the mind is much worse.

It is true that the rather recent concept of biophysical energies does exist. But it is also the case that the term "biology" came into German and French usage only in 1802, and into English usage in 1813.

Since then, the definition of BIOLOGY (or BIO) has referred to the science of physical life, the division of science that deals with "organized beings," their morphology, physiology, origin and distribution, but does not deal with their energies.

In the narrower, and most broadly accepted sense, biology refers to physiology—"the branch of biology dealing with the processes, activities, and phenomena incidental to and characteristic of life and living matter."

In the bio-physiological sense, then, the human is thought fundamentally to be living matter organized into a body. This concept is something of a derangement of the actual facts.

In actuality, the matter itself is NOT living since the atoms of organic and inorganic matter are exactly the same. Indeed, all atoms incorporated into any and all physical structures, including the skeletal and electronic nervous system, are gradually but completely exchanged every seven years by new atoms.

While the concept of biophysical energies has been making a slow comeback since the 1930s, the concept of bio-energetic physicals has not. In other words, we think PROM matter TO energies, not from ENERGIES to MATTER.

But even so, a vital question pertinent to both concepts remains: which of energy or body is the cart and which is the horse that pulls the cart? This is to ask, do the impulses of energy drive the automobile, or do the impulses of the automobile drive the energy.

Perceptive individuals can recognize that whatever the human IS, it is a complex and complicated affair, one that incorporates much more than body-mind alone.

The question can then emerge as to WHY, during modern scientific times, the most generally shared consensus REDUCES this complex affair to the simple parameters of the physical body, or to the body-mind duality.

This is a reductionistic concept via which the human as energy isn't only set aside but obviated into obscurity. To discover the WHY of this can be helpful and can lead to greater insights regarding human as energy.

Chapter 4
ANIMA AND THE LIFE PRINCIPLE

In most simple terms, throughout human history there have always been various kinds of distinctions between such things as (1) rocks that don't breathe, and (2) life forms that breathe, palpitate, sometimes demonstrate some kind of locomotion, and commence or enter into various kinds of activities.

Admittedly, the above is so simplified as to be almost inane. But even so, it adequately describes a double set of distinctions that were tremendously important in pre-modern societies, the distinctions between the INORGANIC and the ORGANIC, also known as the distinctions between the INANIMATE and the ANIMATE.

In order to emphasize the implication here, the pre-moderns had neither an overload of opportunities to deaden the real-life observational faculties, nor was there any particular kind of information glut to stress their memory storage capacities.

In explanation of this, there is a good deal of anthropological evidence indicating that such primitives devoted a great deal of observational time to what characterized the living from the not living, and in doing so became more sensitive to the existence of energetics.

Of course, such primitives did not possess the term ENERGETICS. And so they utilized terms more familiar to them. Those terms, when examined, clearly refer to something along the lines of energizing principles.

As described earlier, modern societies distinguished themselves from pre-modern societies by various methods, such as condemning the pre-moderns as superstitious, naive and primitive, and engulfed in myths having no credible basis within the modern philosophies and sciences. As it happened, though, since language is a fluid-like thing that flows from generation to generation, the modern societies could not altogether rid themselves of the pre-modern terms.

But meanings could be altered, and in this way the old meanings could be retired back into the primitive and unenlightened past, and new meanings could be assigned to old terms.

One not unusual fallout of this is that people utilize THEIR contemporary meanings to assess the past and are somewhat oblivious to the fact that in the past the meanings were different, and sometimes radically so. An example of different meanings can be realized by examining the word INFLUENCES, influences, of course, being one of the major constituents of sexual energies.

INFLUENCES

Of particular interest is that many terms used in modern times to identify THINGS were utilized in antiquity and up through the Renaissance period to specify various kinds of "influences."

The important distinctions in this regard are difficult to clarify, for at least three significant reasons.

First, although the concept of influencing has never been lost, the modern two-part formula of cause-effect is quite different from the three-part formula of pre-modern times.

Second, there are primary distinctions between the verb TO INFLUENCE and the noun AN INFLUENCE. The noun implies that an influence is an actual thing in itself, having its own identity. The verb implies an activity of some kind, usually a transient activity.

Third, although a cause or source can be seen to have influenced something else as an effect or result, the influencing process BETWEEN the cause and the effect tends to remain invisible.

In the light of the above considerations, it is thus possible, if only roughly so, to discern the essential differences between the modern and the pre-modern ideas of the cause effect formula:

The Three-part Pre-Modern Formula
CAUSE < > INFLUENCE < > EFFECT
The Two-part Modern Formula

CAUSE > EFFECT

In considering these two general formulas, it is interesting to remember that the study of the nature of influences was of extraordinary interest to the thinkers of the Renaissance.

But as the Renaissance vision came to a somewhat unexplainable end at about 1670, scientific and philosophic interest in the nature of influences had vanished almost entirely by the beginning of the twentieth century.

Thus, no science of influences evolved during the modernist period. The avoidance in this regard is important, in that many phenomena exist (sexualizing activity, for example) that cannot be adequately explained in the absence of knowledge about influences.

One clearly recognizable reason for this omission was that up until the advent of quantum physics, the modern sciences principally considered only physical and tangible phenomena where causes and effects could easily be observed and verified.

There remained, however, many "effects" for which no physical causes could be determined, such as how inanimate matter becomes organized into animate organisms.

Another reason, not so recognizable, but which can be identified by research, was that the topic of INFLUENCES had socio-political ramifications regarding power and empowerment. And indeed, influence and power have always been almost synonymous.

In the light of the above considerations, we can now examine the established definitions of INFLUENCE.

The verb, TO INFLUENCE, is defined as "to affect or alter by indirect or intangible means; to have an effect on the condition or development of something; also, to sway."

The noun form, (an) INFLUENCE, is taken from the ancient Latin INFLUERE (to flow in), and as such has some surprising definitions that have been carried into English, although shoved to the background:

1. An ethereal fluid thought to flow from the cosmos and stars and to affect the actions of men.
2. An emanation of hidden, intangible power held to derive from non-tangible sources.
3. The act or power of producing an effect without apparent

exertion of force or direct exercise of command.
4. The power or capacity of causing an effect in indirect or intangible ways.

These definitions share an obvious constituent, but which is not given verbal form, but is clearly indicative of an energetic principle.

To flow from so as to affect, emanation, act, or power of producing, power of causing, all these are more than suggestive of hidden, intangible, ethereal active principles, but which none the less have tangible effects.

In other words, to flow, to emanate, to produce, to cause, etc., are active, energetic principles. If they were not, it is quite difficult to see how they could influence anything at all.

One additional definition for INFLUENCE as both a noun and a verb is usually tucked somewhere into the lineup of its definitions: "Corrupting interference with authority for personal gain." In that influences might be "corrupting," authority in general doesn't like the idea of their existing.

And herein indeed exists a particular, if subtle, story quite relevant to why the modern West never developed a philosophy, a science, or a psychology, of invisible, intangible, energetic influences and functions.

As we will see, this subtle story has much to do with how and WHY the decidedly energetic phenomena examined ahead were treated in modernist societal contexts.

THE LIFE PRINCIPLE

It can be said of the modern period that no absolute philosophical or scientific explanation was considered necessary regarding the nature, essence and energies of what the ancients had generally dubbed the LIFE principle.

However, in terms of recorded history the need to do so was felt from at least 3,000 B.C., and continued up through the Late Renaissance, after which the modern sciences and philosophies departed from anything remotely involving supernal considerations.

Prior to the modern epoch, then, the need for a conceptual life principle had always been necessary, and this called for appropriate nomenclature.

In a number of cultural languages, the basic terms selected almost always had to do with "breath," since that is what living things basically did.

They also stopped breathing upon death, at which time it was conceived that the "breath of life" had departed from the physical body now empty of the life principle.

After the Life Principle departed, the body was no longer animated and turned back into its material "dust."

ANIMA

Although certainly deriving from earlier languages, the Latin term for this life-breath principle was ANIMA, in the first instance probably taken as meaning "breath."

However, as already stated, since it could easily be determined that the physical body ended up as non-living dust, it was considered that the life principle consisted of something other than, and independent from, the dust.

In LATE Latin (i.e., not in EARLY Latin), ANIMA also was taken to refer to "soul," in that soul represented the breath-factor of the life principle. But there are certain subsequent confusions.

The Latin ANIMA basically referred a life principle typified by breath; but in ancient times, there were concepts that referred to entity-like factors designated by the term SOUL or its many linguistic equivalents.

At some early point, ANIMA and SOUL became collapsed into each other, the earlier distinctions becoming ambiguous.

SOUL

In English, the soul concept is derived not from Latin but from early Old Nordic and Old Germanic sources. However, the terms "animate" and "animated" were incorporated into the principle definitions of "soul."

The earliest meanings of SOUL in Old English first referred to "animate existence," but this was later incorporated into "the principle of life in man or animals."

Somewhat later in English, but still very early, SOUL was

also established as referring to "the principle of thought and action in man, commonly regarded as an entity distinct from the body; the spiritual part of man in contrast to the purely physical."

SOUL also occasionally referred to "the corresponding or analogous principle in animals."

By about 1400, the concept of SOUL had taken on a number of meanings referred to as metaphysical—"the vital, sensitive, or rational principle in plants, animals or human beings."

Today, having in general lost touch with metaphysics, we would find it difficult to see why those vital, sensitive, or rational qualities should be considered as metaphysical.

In any event, SOUL was also used "frequently with distinguishing adjectives, such as vegetative, sensible or sensitive, rational or reasonable."

The foregoing tour among definitions has been necessary to establish two factors regarding ANIMA and SOUL that are often overlooked, but which are important to the several contexts of this book.

Both words define not THINGS per se, but TWO functions. The first has to do with the life principle that distinguishes between the inanimate and the ANIMATED. The second function establishes additional or inherent factors of the animating life principle, such as the sensitive and sensible qualities.

Temporarily leaving aside the rational or reasonable factors associated to them, the sensitive and sensible qualities are SENSATE ones.

Since sensate factors are not particularly identifiable with matter, which is usually considered inert, it must be assumed that sensate factors are inherent and inseparable extensions of an animating life form that, by virtue of the animating factors, is endowed with faculties to sense whatever is important to sense.

For example, the sensing of invisible, intangible influences, such as sexualizing influences whose existence almost anyone can sense.

Indeed, it is exquisitely necessary to sense influences. After all, it is rather too late to avoid effects AFTER they have come down on one. Thus, any animate life form that is not sensate regarding the sensing of influences will probably and promptly be clobbered into extinction.

With all of this, it can now be suggested that it is possible, in somewhat vulgarized versions, to consider and discuss the animate and the soul WITHOUT necessarily including the sensate influencing attributes of either or both. Indeed, except in a usually gross material manner, knowledge about what animate life forms can and do sense is almost NON-EXISTENT.

Also during the modern period, it became possible to drop the concept of ANIMATE and simply refer to life forms only as life forms. This neatly disposed of the inconvenient difficulties arising out of the enigma posed by the nature, essence and energies of the animating life principle.

ANIMAL

The term ANIMAL is derived from the Latin ANIMA and which basically referred to animating breath.

Today, ANIMAL is principally utilized to distinguish whatever is alive but which, on the one hand, cannot be identified as a plant, or, on the other hand, is not to be identified with MAN, and most certainly never with WOMEN.

In its earliest and most original Latin meaning, however, ANIMALIS specifically referred to "anything living," which is to say, anything alive, breathing, and "having the breath of life."

In this sense, then, the term ANIMAL was associated with such terms as ANIMATING and ANIMISTIC.

Later concepts of ANIMAL SPIRIT or ANIMAL SOUL had to do with "the supposed 'spirit' or principle of sensation and voluntary motion, and answering to nerve fluid, nerve force, or nervous activity."

Please note that the definition of ANIMAL SOUL given just above is considered obsolete, largely because the idea of soul as animating energy was also declared obsolete.

All of these factors having been declared obsolete, it was then possible to consider that the sole energy aspect of a life form involved only what it consumed as nutritional substances acquired from some source external to itself.

At this, the concept of a formative, indwelling energetic principle could be abandoned, together with the ideas of indwelling nerve fluid, nerve force, and nervous activity.

Thereafter, concepts having to do with indwelling energies arose only with regard to human creative energies, human power, and human sexualizing energies. It cannot really be said that these types of energetic activities exclusively arise from nutritional substances alone.

It seems that at some point, probably in early Medieval Latin, the term ANIMALIS was sometimes treated as originating from ANIMA, but at other times treated as originating from the Latin ANIMUS.

ANIMUS, suggestive of aggression and aggressive force, referred mostly to "brute force," "brute beasts" and, as time advanced, to "inferior animals."

So, in this way the term ANIMAL was detached from its earlier meanings of animating force or energy, and also from the concept of "animal soul"- which likewise referred to animating energetics but gave those energies something of an entity-like form.

Since this shift in meanings regarding ANIMAL is entirely relevant to the topic of this book, it is necessary to identify more precisely how and why it came into existence.

The eight volumes of THE ENCYCLOPEDIA OF PHILOSOPHY (1967) is a wonderful compilation of just about everything philosophical. The encyclopedia carries a rather extensive entry for ANIMAL SOUL. That entry is well worth reading, if only because, all things considered, it is one of the most amusing, if not outright hilarious entries in the eight volumes.

In the context of ANIMAL SOUL, we again encounter the personage of Rene Descartes (1569-1650), the famous French philosopher and scientist. As is stated in many authoritative sources, Descartes was chief among the founders who designed the contours of modern thought and among the most original philosophers and mathematicians of any age.

In its essay on Descartes, the Encyclopedia points up that the "concept of the animal soul did not give rise to any serious problems until the seventeenth century, when Cartesian dualism brought out distinctions which had been latent in the dominant Aristotelian tradition."

However, as a result of Descartes' concepts, debates increasingly surrounded the animal soul or mind, and they became "sensitive indicators of a number of fundamental issues in modern philosophy and science."

The debates are traced back to Aristotle, had postulated gradations from inert, inanimate matter to plants, and then to animals. Plants had the functions of nourishment and reproduction, but animals were also endowed with sensation, motion, and all degrees of mental functions except reason.

Aristotle reserved reason for man, but his gradations from inert to reason precluded a sharp discontinuity between physical and mental functions in man.

To help resolve various resulting theoretical complexities, Descartes advanced the concept that "animals are pure machines, while men are machines with minds."

Further, if biological phenomena could be included in the domain of Descartes' idea of a universal physics, "then a boundary would no longer lie between inanimate and animate beings."

Physics would then include all of nature except the mind of man. Note that it is somewhat of a wonderment to consider what an inanimate being might consist of.

The Encyclopedia goes on to state that after the discovery of the circulation of the blood, Descartes "was encouraged to attempt a general mechanistic physiology in hydraulic terms."

He argued that most human motions do not depend on the mind, and he gave examples of physiological functions and reactions which occur independently of the will—functions such as digestion, reactions such as sneezing.

Descartes went on to stipulate that in man the mind could also direct the course of the fluid (or animal spirits) which controls movements. However, to attribute minds to animals would threaten traditional religious beliefs, "since the psychological concept of mind was conflated with the theological concept of soul."

To help resolve THIS problem, Descartes argued that it would "be impious to imagine that animals have souls of the same order as men, and that man has nothing more to hope for in the afterlife than flies and ants have."

Similarly, "God could not allow the sinless creatures to suffer. Without souls, animals would not suffer, and man would be absolved from guilt for exploiting, killing and eating them."

One of the longer-term results of Descartes' ideas, many of which became modernist doctrines, was that the distinction between man-mind and animal-beast became more recognizable, largely because, in a philosophical sense, the distinctions tended to inflate men's appreciation of man, and relegated animals to a lower order.

The encyclopedia points up that the debate of the animal soul controversy was enormous. The central issue, however, did not actually focus on the animal-machine and man-machine-with-mind hypotheses, but concerned the adequacy of mechanistic explanation to account for all biological and psychological phenomena.

Prior to Descartes, the search for mechanistic explanation had incorporated the concept of Final Cause and Purpose, i.e., with regard to the origin especially of animate life forms and their purpose of their existing.

In other words, is mechanistic explanation adequate to account not only for the mechanistic (hydraulic) workings of biological and psychological phenomena, but also for origin and purpose?

Descartes coped with this difficulty in an expeditious and surgical manner: he excluded explanation-by-purpose from physics and from biology.

This was very comforting to societal mainstreams, since they no longer had to worry about THEIR Final Cause and Purpose. Thus, purpose has remained excluded from the modern mainstream sciences ever since. Indeed, the exclusion of Purpose is convenient to the elimination of conscience.

In any event, the nature of Purpose (the Why of things) was an issue of enormous antiquity, in all pre-modern cultures, and was inextricably bound together with the Life Principle.

Eliminating Purpose from the science of physics and from biology served quite well in also eliminating the difficulties of admitting the existence of a life principle.

So, these theoretical maneuvers had the long-term effect of setting science free of metaphysical contexts, and free of the mysteries of how and why matter came into existence and how it became animated.

Thereafter, as the Encyclopedia indicates, "adherence to the animal-machine doctrine in physics and biology became the crucial test of loyalty not only to Cartesianism, but a test of loyalty to the formats of the modern sciences."

One of the principal fallouts of all this was the widening of the gulf between man-machine and beast-machine—with the term ANIMAL thereafter being associated with beast-machines having no souls.

This ultimately resulted in ANIMAL being dissociated from contexts of animate, organized, living, and redefined the term exclusively as "one of the lower animals—a brute, or beast as distinguished from man."

As stated in the Encyclopedia, "there has been no peace" since Descartes' theories became science doctrines. The doctrines "have proven inadequate" in the light of the theory of evolution, the methods of modern psychology, and of cybernetics, and the emergence of Soviet and Chinese bio-energetics.

This somewhat extended discussion of ANIMATE and ANIMAL has been necessary since it sets the ground for the next chapter dealing with the energies studied by the Renaissance magnetists, and the following chapter on animal magnetism and its direct association with sexualizing energies.

Chapter 5
MAGNETISTS OF THE RENAISSANCE PERIOD

The specific phenomena of profound interest to the magnetists of the Renaissance period was later erroneously lumped into one or another of three categories: occultism, spiritualistics and hypnotism.

This indiscriminate lumping served to erase the early contours of energetic magnetism, and subsequent work of its kind, as a clever societal maneuver to place the topic of energetic magnetism into the unscientific category of modernist thought.

DEFINITION OF RENAISSANCE MAGNETISM

To the Renaissance thinkers, MAGNETISM was identified as a vital effluence radiating from every object in the universe, in a greater or lesser degree, and through which all objects might exercise a mutual influence on one another.

From this concept the idea of the "sympathetic system" was formulated. In the case of organic systems, the idea roughly meant that those systems were subject to being influenced by transmission of "vibrations"—although that term had not yet come into the full popular usage it was to acquire much later.

The eventual unfolding of the contrasts between the scientific and the unscientific consigned the Renaissance ideas to the latter category until they were recovered in vague part by the 1960s concept of the interconnectedness of everything working via sympathetic systems.

Since the early magnetists experimented and worked with magnets, especially with regard to healing, it is generally assumed that the term MAGNETISM was derived from the term MAGNET. This derivation is certainly possible.

But it is more likely that the term came from the concept of MAGNES MICROCOSMI, which in Renaissance thought referred to Man as a microcosm of Earth itself, and as such having poles and magnetic properties.

THIS concept also incorporated the MAGNES MACROCOSMI the planets, stars, and cosmos—from which came "subtle effluence" that influenced and affected man's body, energies, mind and intellect. These macrocosm effluences combined with "earthly substances radiating a grosser emanation," and the mixed whole of which affected the body.

The MAGNES MACROCOSMI and MAGNES MICROCOSMI concepts in principle are magnetic-energetic concepts, and as such can easily be incorporated into the contexts of influences and energetics.

THE SYMPATHETIC SYSTEM OF THE RENAISSANCE EPOCH

The venerable Swiss-born physician, Paracelsus (1493-1541), is probably the best remembered of the Renaissance magnetists. He may have originated the "sympathetic system" concept, and certainly was its most energetic proponent.

But in the modernist historical sense he is more usually pointed up as an alchemist, which attribution tends to stigmatize the whole body of his work. More correctly described, he was a researcher of energetics and sympathetic energy systems.

However, his whole body of work was extraordinarily large. It encompassed many other topics such as chemistry, metallurgy, herbal remedies, and what later came to be known as homeopathic healing.

Paracelsus was noted during his times by his "egotism" and contempt for traditional theories, earning him large doses of enmity from certain of his contemporaries. In the last analysis, however, he had great influence in his own and succeeding centuries. Upon his death, a statue was erected to him in Salzburg.

A later influential magnetist was Jan Baptista van Helmont (1577-1644), a Flemish physician, chemist, and natural philosopher (natural philosophy being later dubbed as physics). By any measure today, Helmont was a substantial thinker and researcher.

He discovered carbon dioxide, distinguished gases as a class of substances, and is credited with introducing the term GAS in its present scientific sense.

He attributed physiological changes to chemical causes, but, as most official modernist sources stipulate, his conclusions "were colored by his speculative mysticism."

This "mysticism" is an oblique, stigmatizing reference to the fact that Helmont was an energetic proponent of magnetism and of the sympathetic system.

As he wrote: "Material nature draws her forms through constant magnetism from above and implores for them the favor of heaven; and as heaven, in like manner, draws something invisible from below, there is established a free and mutual intercourse, and the whole is contained in an individual."

Further, he established or embellished the concept that magnetism was either composed of a "subtle fluid," or that the subtle fluid was the medium via which magnetism affected whatever it did.

He then proceeded to offer up an observation of the type that has, as we will see, consistently proved to be a societal faux pas. He indicated that it was possible for the "power of the will to direct the subtle fluid."

Helmont doesn't seem to have been the type to offer remarkable observations like this in the complete absence of evidence, and so there must have been veridical and empirical grounds for him to do so.

In any event, this observation can easily be connected to the modern parapsychological issues regarding psychokinesis on the one hand, and healing by sympathetic manipulation of the "subtle fluid" aura of the physical body on the other.

Helmont went on to make public another observation, one certain to embroil societal concerns even of his times. "I have hitherto avoided revealing the great secret, that the strength [of the vital fluid] lies concealed in man, [and that] merely through the suggestion and power of the imagination to work outwardly, and to impress this strength on others, which then continues of itself, and operates on the remotest objects."

Furthermore, as "proof of the mutual magnetic influence of living creatures," Helmont asserted that by certain manipulations of the vital fluid during the "ecstasy" of the inner magnetic man, "men may kill animals merely by staring hard at them for a quarter of an hour."

With this statement is found one of the earliest references to "ecstasy"—which of course has several formats, but among which is sexualizing ecstasy.

Here is also a very early mention that has to do with "learning how" to manipulate the vital fluids—a prospect being viewed forever after with some kind of societal alarm.

VITAL FLUIDS OF REPULSION AND ATTRACTION

The "work of magnetics" was picked up by others, among which was Robert Fludd (1574-1637).

Identified as an English physician, most official historical sources also describe him as a "mystic philosopher educated at Oxford and on the Continent, and strongly influenced by the mystical doctrines of Paracelsus."

Aside from the misuse of the term "mystical," Fludd was an exponent of the microcosmic/macrocosmic theory of sympathetic systems, and of the magnetic effluence from man.

Fludd indicated that not only "were these emanations able to cure bodily diseases. They also affected the moral sentiments.

For if radiations from two individuals were, on meeting, flung back or distorted, negative magnetism, or antipathy resulted. Whereas if the radiations from each person passed freely into those from the other, the result was positive magnetism of sympathy."

Or, as it might be observed, radiations of REPULSION or of ATTRACTION.

HEALING BY MAGNETIC STROKING

It is somewhat difficult to reconstruct the story of magnetic/energetic applications during the Renaissance decades. Magnetics research has been better remembered by its theories. Not much has survived about its practical applications, especially with regard to healing.

None the less, the evidence is clear that the practical side was by no means neglected, and a large number of magnetic healers emerged during the seventeenth and eighteenth centuries.

Although not the first, but among the most memorable, was Valentine Greatlakes, an Irishman born in 1628. At some point in 1662, he had a dream, several times repeated, that he could cure by laying on of hands, or by "magnetic stroking" as it came to be called.

Although not always successful, he seems to have performed a surprising number of cures in Ireland and then in London where a number of notables attested to his accumulating status as a "divine healer."

News of his healing powers, coupled with news about the invisible existence of magnetic energies, spread far and wide, and patients came by the hundreds to seek the benefits of his stroking.

Somewhat later, during the eighteenth century, another famous stroking healer appeared in the form of a Swabian priest named J. J. Gassner.

Biographical details of Gassner are a little hard to come by, but he is noted as a priest of Bludenz (now in Austria), where his many cures gained wide celebrity for him.

He apparently had deep learning and a noble character, and sometimes made use of magnets, "magnetic manipulation," and stroking or rubbing the affected part. However, according to him, all diseases were caused by "evil spirits," this idea having a tradition extending back to the ancient Greeks.

However he explained causes, not only could he control "sickness" by whatever means he employed, but the "passions" too were amenable to his means.

Among example "passions" enumerated in various literature were anger, patience, joy, hate, and love, and the "passion" of sexual impotence—each of which, by magnetic stroking, could be brought under control by "carrying each to the highest pitch."

"Highest pitch" apparently referred to a type of ecstatic catharsis, a purgation or cleansing release of traumatizing physical and/or mental "tensions"—often, but not always, accompanied by transient types of neuromotor convulsions not unlike the ecstasies of sexual orgasm.

The "ecstasies" released, or purged, the "tensions." And where this worked, Gassner could chalk up another "cure."

In about 1766, the magnetic stroking of J. J. Gassner attracted the attention of Franz Anton Mesmer, and whose name ultimately was to tower over all others.

Chapter 6
MAGNETIC FORCE—ANIMAL MAGNETISM

The saga of Franz Anton Mesmer was exceedingly dramatic and extended far beyond his death. It resulted in a veritable Age of Mesmerism, the vitality of which took on international interest and fascination that endured for about 140 years.

Indeed, such was the strength of Mesmerism that it came to constitute one of the first international movements of any kind. And its international vivacity was such that the anti-energetic sentiments in the mainstream modern sciences did not succeed in deconstructing it until about 1920.

Even then, Mesmerism left three long shadows of itself: the first in the guise of hypnotism; the second in the guise of psychical research; the third in the guise of the energetic mysteries of sexual energies.

FRANZ ANTON MESMER

France Anton Mesmer (1733-1815) was born in Switzerland at Weil, near the city and lake of Constance. By all accounts, he was of copious intelligence and a somewhat high-minded individual, whose thinking was completely in keeping with his times.

Modern historians seldom consider him as a person within his times but assess him according to modern standards as they later developed. And by those later standards, Mesmer's activities consisted of one strange folly after another.

He was educated in Vienna where he took a degree in medicine. As his doctoral thesis he produced a study entitled DE PLANETARUM INFLUXU (the influence of the planets on the human body).

In modern contexts, this document is mistakenly condemned as Mesmer's "astrological thesis." But in his times, and as we have already seen, the thesis examined magnetic energetic influences that were thought to be universal in nature.

Mesmer observed that the action of the magnetic influences "consists of alternating effects which may be considered as fluxes and refluxes" of sympathetic systems.

The effects manifest "in the human body with properties analogous to the magnet; there are poles, diverse and opposed, which can be communicated, changed, destroyed and reinforced; the phenomenon of inclination is also observable."

In later summarizing his thesis, he indicated that "the property of the animal [read ANIMATE] body which renders it susceptible to the [magnetic] influence of the celestial bodies, and to the reciprocal action of the environing [local environmental] ones, I felt prompted to name, from analogy to the magnet, animal magnetism."

As discussed in chapter 4, please bear in mind that the contexts Mesmer was using referred not to "animal" magnetism, but to ANIMATING magnetism, and that, during his times, this usage was understood and accepted.

MEDICAL USES OF MAGNETIC "PLATES"

Mesmer was one of the many physicians who were exploring cures and healings via magnets. Mesmer apparently innovated, designed, and constructed his own version of such plates. By applying his magnetized plates to a patient's limbs, he effected his first cures in about 1773. Unfortunately, what these plates consisted of has been lost.

But probably analogous to them are various magnetic plates designed in Japan during the 1980s, which also produced cures.

Further, the application of weak electromagnetic currents to bone fractures and ulcerous infections has been confirmed as speeding up healings and cures. [See, for example, THE BODY ELECTRIC by Robert O. Becker, M.D., and Gary Selden, 1985.]

Mesmer came to special public attention because of a bitter, and quite public, controversy involving the invention of his plates.

The priority of this invention was claimed by a Jesuit priest having the curious name of Maximillian Hell, a professor of astronomy/astrology at the University of Vienna. Mesmer won this claim but was quickly involved in another controversy involving his cure of a blind girl.

At some point between 1770 and 1775, Mesmer was among the many physicians and intellectuals who witnessed a number of cures effected by the strokings of J. J. Gassner without the use of magnets.

Because of this, Mesmer correctly conceptualized that the human body possessed a magnetic "field," and that such fields could affect each other. Mesmer thereafter disposed of the magnets.

For a fresh start he abandoned Vienna as well and traveled to the Paris, the City of Lights.

MAGNETIC "VATS"

Installed in Paris, he quickly developed novel techniques and equipment to effect cures. The exact nature and materials of the new equipment have again been lost to posterity. But not their impact, resulting scandals, and the extraordinary controversies that came to surround the very name of Mesmer.

The equipment Mesmer designed consisted of several versions of a large circular vat (in French, BAQUET), filled with "certain substances" that apparently consisted of mixtures of various metals and shards of glass. Whatever the substances consisted of, they served to "collect animating magnetism" and transfer it and its sympathetic qualities to the sympathetic systems of the patients.

The theory was that the "certain substances" collected and amplified the magnetic forces, and then, via hand-held connectors, the forces were transferred to and resaturated the sympathetic systems inherent in the bodies of the patients.

The methods utilized to effect the transfer tend to boggle the imagination.

The patients sat around the baquets in communal groups, each holding a metal or glass rod, or a mere copper wire or string of thread, the other end of which was pushed into the substances in the vats. Mesmer erected several circular vats, each about a foot high, and experimented with a number of hand-held "connectors" that served as conduits for the animating (or re-animating) magnetisms.

There is no doubt that some cures were attained for ailments strictly physical in their cause, but even more cures were obtained regarding illness mental (psychosomatic) in origin. Even Mesmer himself indicated that his "techniques" better dealt with what we today would refer to as conditions psychosomatic in origin.

Indeed, as a physician, Mesmer usually, and correctly, first sent physically ill patients to other doctors, and otherwise accepted them only if physical remedies were of no effect.

THE ENERGETIC PHENOMENA OF THE VATS

Although the exact material constituents of the circular, communal vats have been lost, the nature of the energetic phenomena experienced by the "patients" has not.

As described (usually too briefly) in most sources, these phenomena consisted of "violent convulsions, cries, uncontrollable laughter, and various physical symptoms" — followed by "lethargy" after which the "cures" became apparent.

WHAT was cured, and WHY it was, has always remained an historical mystery, confounded by expressions of awe, shock, and professional hysteria. On the face of the brief descriptions of the phenomena, it is difficult to know what was actually meant by "violent convulsion." Later scientific criteria established "convulsions" as consisting of quite serious and very painful involuntary contractions of the muscles during which the nervous system goes haywire, sometimes resulting in coma.

It is also difficult to understand what was meant by "various physical symptoms," or even what was meant by "cries" and "laughter." However, the sum of all of these phenomena quite clearly falls into the category of catharsis of the ecstatic, or ecstasy, type. And obvious clues regarding this can be comprehended not by studying the phenomena, but by examining WHO attended upon the vats. Many had no visible ills to cure. If this particular issue is examined, it will be seen that they came just for the thrill of experiencing the animating, magnetic energies.

THE SOCIAL BACKGROUND REGARDING THE VATS

Mesmer's reputation preceded him to Paris, and once installed there he acquired numerous supports. Principle among these at first was Charles d'Eslon, medical adviser to the Count d'Artois, brother to King Louis XVI. This was high patronage, indeed.

In September of 1780, d'Eslon asked the Faculty of Medicine to confirm Mesmer's ideas and techniques, a request that was rejected.

None the less, public enthusiasm and high patronage support had grown to impressive heights.

In March 1781, on behalf of the King, no less a personage than the powerful Minister de Maurepas offered Mesmer 20,000 livres (a significant amount) and a further annuity of 10,000 if he establish a school and agreed to divulge the "secret" of his "treatments." Mesmer at first refused, but later accepted a subscription of 340,000 livres for lectures to pupils.

With this financial arrangement, Mesmer increased his vat-facilities, and surrounded them with rather impressive environments. These consisted of large rooms noted for the opulence of their furnishings, with enormous reflecting mirrors everywhere, the whole being dimly lit.

Mesmer and his vat-facilities were mobbed with applicants, among them vast numbers of the aristocracy and royalty. Many memoirs of various members of the aristocracy establish that the mob included even Queen Marie Antoinette and the whole of her court.

SPONTANEOUS SEXUAL ORGASM AT THE VATS

It is from some of these memoirs, not consulted by biographers of Mesmer, that a complete picture of the "convulsive" catharsis is revealed. There is no doubt at all that those holding the connectors often experienced an aspect of ecstatic catharsis known from ancient times—some kind of involuntary auto-orgasm in females and auto-ejaculatory release in males.

Hence, the connection among the "convulsions," "cries," "laughter" and the subsequent "lethargy" tend to fall into place—since these taken altogether are recognizable and familiar constituents of sexual orgasm.

And, indeed, if the "convulsions" had been painful, it is quite unlikely that applications to sit at the vats would have been any more numerous than the cases of those willing to try anything and everything to ameliorate their ills.

MESMERIC TRANCES

Also known from ancient times, ecstatic catharsis engendered dramatic and empowering shifts in "levels" of consciousness of the kind we today would refer to as heightened "altered states"—and during which many kinds of so-called "paranormal" trance phenomena were experienced.

Such phenomena also came to light within many of Mesmer's vat participants. But a perpetual confusion has settled in regarding this matter, in that Mesmeric trance phenomena have been historically confused with hypnosis. Hypnotism can easily be confused as an extension of Mesmeric trance, since it, too, is a type of altered state.

But in actual historical fact, hypnotism as such was not identified until about 1842 by the English surgeon, James Braid (1795-1860). Braid first termed the phenomenon as "neuro-hypnotism," a phenomenon that also sometimes aroused involuntary sexualizing activity.

Types of hypnotism, however, had earlier been identified in ancient Persia and India, with probably even more ancient antecedents in Egypt.

In any event, Mesmer's stay in Paris was cut short, leaving Mesmeric trance phenomena to be investigated by later of his followers.

MESMER'S EXPULSION FROM FRANCE

Although a great deal has been written about Mesmer's expulsion from France, it remains unclear as to why and how the expulsion was instigated.

The official story holds that in 1784, the "French government" charged the Faculty of Medicine, the Royal Society of Medicine, and the Academy of Sciences, to examine "animal magnetism."

Considering the high patronage of Mesmer, which included

the King, many of his ministers, and significant personages of the Court, it is difficult to determine exactly what happened.

In any event, and whatever the real reasons, nine Commissioners were convened under the presidency of no less than Benjamin Franklin, then in Paris, and included the astronomer, Jean Sylvain Bailly, and the chemist, J. K. Lavater, both esteemed scientists of the time.

The Commissioners were restricted to the activity of attempting to establish evidence of a new physical force that was claimed as the agent of the cures. But it is clear that the actual target was Mesmer himself, and the actual purpose was to get rid of him.

The Commission produced two known reports, but between them the consensus among the Commissioners is quite garbled.

Franklin, for example, recommended further examination of the issue. But King Louis XVI, not known for much in the way of certitude, was somehow stampeded to order Mesmer's expulsion from France, and which was quickly effected.

Mesmer removed himself to Meersburg, Switzerland, were he lived a quiet, unobtrusive life until he died in March 1815. How it was that Mesmer, a veritable supernova, thereafter consented to obscurity, remains something of a mystery.

THE CONTINUING SAGA OF MESMERIC PHENOMENA

Even so, and even if he "retired," the continuing impact of Mesmerism was itself phenomenal. It is fair enough to say that any written account which might do justice to him, and to the remarkable phenomena of Mesmerism, must necessarily fill a number of volumes.

In the twentieth century, something along these lines was attempted by the redoubtable Eric John Dingwall, Ph.D., a Director of the Department of Psychical Phenomena at the American Society for Psychical Research (1921-1922), and Research Officer at the Society for Psychical Research (1922-1927).

For many years, Dingwall collected papers published between 1800 and 1900 recording Mesmeric research and phenomena in France, Belgium, the Netherlands, Germany, Scandinavia, Russia, Poland, Italy, Spain, Portugal, Latin

America, the United States, and Great Britain. He ultimately edited these papers into four volumes which he published in 1967-68.

As he described via a masterful understatement: "Accounts of alleged paranormal phenomena occurring in the mesmeric and hypnotic states have been omitted by most writers on hypnotism and details, generally speaking, of this aspect have not so far been published. The aim [of the four volumes], therefore, is to raise the curtain on the almost unknown and forgotten activities of the mesmerists of the nineteenth century, while concentrating on the paranormal aspects of their work."

Dingwall gave the four volumes the general, and quite misleading, title of ABNORMAL HYPNOTIC PHENOMENA: A SURVEY OF NINETEENTH-CENTURY CASES.

Dingwall appears to have been either somewhat ironic, or politically cagey, since, as he well understood, mesmeric and hypnotic phenomena were never quite synonymous. As it was, hypnotic phenomena were scientifically acceptable, but just so.

In any event, Dingwall's four volumes give some idea of the enormous extent of the saga of Anton Mesmer and of the GLOBAL scope of mesmeric phenomena encountered and documented by his successors—ALL of which, by 1920, had outrageously been caused to vanish into the modernist landfill of the unscientific.

The Mesmeric phenomena, as so called, were not really to reemerge until the Soviet bio-energetic research referred to earlier, and the Chinese CH'I energetic research of the 1980s-1990s still to be referred to later on.

Chapter 7
ODIC FORCE

Four years after Anton Mesmer was run out of France, Baron Karl von Reichenbach (1788-1869) was born in Wurttemberg, not far from Lake Constance near which Mesmer had been born. In 1788, Wurttemberg was a city in the autonomous state of Wurttemberg having its capital at Stuttgart, the whole of which was later incorporated into modern Germany.

Reichenbach appears to have been something of a political activist during his student days. By the time he was sixteen, Wurttemberg was under the military control of Napoleon, and the young Reichenbach had formed a secret society with the goal of setting up a Germanic state in the South Sea Islands.

For this visionary effort he was duly arrested by the Napoleonic police and for some months held in detention as a political prisoner, after which he continued his education in natural science, political economy, and law, ultimately receiving his Ph.D.

REICHENBACH—INVENTOR-INDUSTRIALIST

Reichenbach proved to be of scientific and industrial substance. After his education, he traveled in Germany and France investigating the operations of ironworks, and in 1815 (when he was twenty-seven) he built and operated his own plant at Villigen in Baden.

He also diversified and built a beet-sugar factory, several blast furnaces and steelworks, and a large charcoal furnace.

He discovered kerosene, paraffin, and creosote. Kerosene, a coal-tar product earlier known as coal oil, quickly became of enormous importance throughout the world because of its wide use, before commercial electricity, in kerosene lamps.

Today, kerosene is mostly used as a carrier in insecticide spray and as a fuel in jet engines. Paraffin and creosote were to have equal importance in other areas.

By 1835, Reichenbach had accumulated considerable wealth

and a widely respected scientific reputation as a brilliant chemist, inventor, and industrialist, as well as a noted authority on meteorites and magnets.

He had also taken a deep interest in "physico-physiological research on the dynamics of magnetism, electricity, heat, light, crystallization, and chemicals in their relation to emanations of vital force."

Reichenbach's name would be erased from most modern histories because of this particular interest. So it is difficult to ascertain when the interest began or under what circumstances it did.

Almost certainly he would have been familiar with mesmeric research. But it also seems quite likely that he had independently encountered magnetic phenomena both inorganic and organic of a type which, in his mind, did not exactly equate with the so-called animal magnetism of the Mesmerists.

OD

In any event, Reichenbach detached his work from animal magnetism by designating the "emanations of vital force" as OD.

He derived this strange term from Odin (or Woden), the chief Norse god who established the laws that governed the universe and controlled the destiny of man. Odin also was kept busy as the god of war, learning, and magic.

As a word, Od seems to have presented verbal difficulties, so it was later elaborated more clearly as Odic force, or Odyle energy. However, since the "magnetic force" of Mesmer and the "Odic force" of Reichenbach both refer to "a force which permeates the whole of nature," it is difficult to discern differences, if any, between them.

REICHENBACH'S EXPERIMENTS IN ODIC SENSITIVITY

A major characteristic of Reichenbach's work illuminates the scope of his interest in what sensitive humans are actually sensitive to. With regard to this, it is quite possible that Reichenbach was attracted to magnetic sensitivity by examples of water-witching (water dowsing), the successes of which he had observed on many occasions.

An impressive line-up of experiments along the lines of sensitivity became visible at about 1839 when Reichenbach was fifty-one and had achieved the status of a matured and respected scientist.

Between 1839 and 1850, Reichenbach designed and conducted experiments involving some two hundred "ordinary people drawn from all walks of life" who had demonstrated some kind of sensitivity.

Some of these experienced "specific reactions to the proximity of other people" in the form of "feelings of pleasant coolness" or drowsiness, or disagreeable, or numbing, or "exciting feelings."

Most of the individuals also "manifested a special right-hand/left-hand polarity" which affected their reactions to other people standing, sitting or sleeping near to their right of left sides.

A disproportionate number of the sensitives demonstrated sympathy with the color blue, an antipathy with yellow, particular food fetishes, and sensitivity to certain metals, and were unpleasantly affected by mirrors.

Quite a number of such sensitives could "see" emanations from crystals and magnets in total darkness and detect alternations in electric current. They could also perceive an aura (energy field) emanating from and surrounding the physical body.

With empirical precision still acceptable today, Reichenbach conducted hundreds of experiments involving crystals, magnets and the human body. His principle goal seems to have consisted of examining his Odic force with regard (1) to its relationship to electricity, magnetism, and chemistry; and (2) to what extent the force was perceptible to sensitives.

ODIC LIGHTS

The Od, Odyle or Odic force was perceptible to sensitives. Reichenbach's experimental sensitives usually sat in totally dark rooms in which he also placed another completely silent individual, a type of crystal, metal or chemical. These experimental procedures resulted in both quantitative and qualitative data such as enumerated below.

1. Various substances radiating the Odic force were perceived via vague or strong feelings of heat or cold.
2. Sensitives possessing more refined or greater sensing/perceiving capabilities might perceive "the odic light" described as a clear flame of definite color issuing from metals, crystals and chemicals and poles of magnets.
3. The Odic force could also be seen issuing from the main parts of the human body, the fingertips, mouth, hands, forehead, feet, and BLEEP! The Odic force could also be seen surrounding the body entire as a colored "mist" or "smoke."
4. The Odic force could also be seen over new graves.
5. The force could be conducted to distances by all solid and liquid bodies.
6. Bodies, however, could be "charged" with greater or lesser amounts of Od at given times, but the Od was apparently transferred from one body to another by contact with inorganic, crystalline and metallic substances, and physical touching of organic bodies. However, mere proximity, without contact, was sufficient to produce influencing charges between bodies.
7. Reichenbach noted that the "odic tension" (charge, as in a battery), varied during the day, diminished with hunger, increased after a meal, diminished at sunset, and increased before and during daybreak.

Reichenbach worked with colleagues who ensured the designs and controls of the experiments, and with sensitives who were also "persons in perfect health."

In one such case, the sensitive Prof. D. Endlicher of Vienna saw "unsteady flames forty inches high" on the poles of an electromagnet, the flames exhibiting numerous colors, and ending in a luminous smoke, which rose to the ceiling and illuminated it.

Reichenbach, a chemist, attempted to evolve a nomenclature for the odic force regarding which source the energy radiated or flowed from: "crystalod, electrod, photod, thermod," and so on.

He also insisted that the "odic flame" was a material something, and that it could be affected by breath or a current of air.

Some sensitives perceived more complex odic phenomena regarding the human body, including rays, beams and undulating lights. Some of Reichenbach's sensitives could tell whether a female was premenstrual, menstrual, or pregnant, and how the mother's odic forces were interacting with the unborn child.

As one description along these lines, "the mother's pores are open," and from them exude an odic emanation.

The emanations develop themselves into "electricity" upon their exit from the body. Objects or events making "violent impression" on the mother's mind are incorporated in the mother's outgoing Odyle force. The mother's Odyle force now contained an "odic image" of the object or event.

If Reichenbach's terminology is understood correctly, the odic image is somehow reverse-projected into the developing Odyle of the fetus.

In any event, some of Reichenbach's sensitives quite easily could distinguish between the Odyles of the mother and the fetus.

One of the situations Reichenbach occasionally had to deal with involved increases of erotic manifestations in the presence of "strong Odyle force." Such manifestations brought "disturbing" physical effects to some of his sensitives, some of his witnesses to the experiments, and apparently sometimes to himself.

Indeed, it seemed not uncommon that others besides the sensitives felt "odic electricity" because "disturbingly aroused," and some of his sensitives fell into "temporary convulsions" and "were depleted" afterward. Some also lost weight.

Some male and female sensitives could tell whether males were horny by special features of their odic energies and magnetic auras. However, the nature of the special features was either left undescribed or have been bleeped.

Reichenbach's records, however, indicate in delicate terms that some female sensitives refused to work within the proximity of a horny male because of the "disturbing nature of their odic energies." Male sensitives were apparently not bothered with active female odic energies and seemed to enjoy their presence.

Chapter 8
ENERGIES PHOTOGRAPHIC

Subsequent to Reichenbach's work, a full part of the saga of energies, magnetic or otherwise, then commenced in Boston, Mass. Therein resided one William H. Mumler, who, in 1861, was head engraver at Bigelow, Kennard & Co., a firm dealing in jewelry. Like many designers of the time, he had become interested in photography.

One day, in a friend's studio, he tried to take a photograph of himself by focusing the camera on an empty chair and then leaping into the chair after uncapping the lens.

When the plate was developed, an extraneous figure was discovered sitting in the chair, a young, transparent girl with her lower parts fading into a dim mist. Mumler recognized the transparent figure as a young cousin who had died twelve years earlier.

SPIRIT PHOTOGRAPHY

The experiment was repeated several times. A number of Extras could be discerned—faces, transparent figures or parts of them, and other luminous "lights" appearing in many but not all of the photographs.

Mumler and several others became satisfied that the extras on the plates were spiritual in origin. This gave birth to the concept of "spirit photography," and which quickly became a hot and emotional fashion, eagerly joined in by this or that scam artist.

A great hubbub immediately followed. Many professional photographers made the most scrupulous examination of the materials Mumler had used.

As it turned out, it didn't matter if Mumler used his own materials or those of others, or even if fresh materials were introduced at the last moment before the photographs were taken.

Good spirit photos were achieved in the presence of professionals quite prepared to doubt their authenticity. But it seems that the spirits were themselves prepared to be photographed, some of whom were recognized by some of the doubters.

With no identifiable fraud detected, Mummer's authenticity was established—immediately after which he became vogue and did tremendous business.

Eventually, an unproved accusation of fakery was brought against him. A scandal developed, and Mumler transferred his activities to New York City where he prospered until another accusation of fraud was raised by a newspaper.

This time Mumler was arrested by order of the Mayor of New York. However, at the trial a number of professional photographers testified on his behalf and Mumler was acquitted. Even so, he died in poverty in 1884.

Mumler's photographs had created a sensation that many wished to duplicate or get in on. Many professional and unprofessional photographers set about experimenting, and some, of course, set about creating wildly ersatz fabrications.

Even if not provided by newspersons themselves (as some were), fake photos exposed as such made for good mainstream news copy declaiming against the authenticity of all such photographs.

BIO-ENERGY PHOTOGRAPHS?

Even so, many enthusiastic photographers obtained nothing unusual for their efforts. Others not obtaining recognizable spirits had to settle for the unexpected appearance of weird lights, illuminations and emanations streaming from sitters' fingers, heads, or other body parts, or "auras" wavering around their bodies, and etc.

Some photographs revealed swoops of lights that had no apparent connection to the sitters being photographed and seemed to originate from a source outside the photographic frame. Sometimes there were mists" or "fogs" wandering to and fro.

When such phenomena, appearing on the photographic plates, could not be accounted for by fraud or trickery, they were interpreted as representing such things as magnetism, radiations, subtle fluid, digital effluvium, ectoplasmic flow, auric light, astral body, thought waves, and N-rays—and lastly, lights in areas not mentionable in print.

N-rays (now forgotten about) were a type of ray thought by some to be unceasingly emanating, whether strongly or weakly, from the physical body, which could interact and interpenetrate both inorganic and organic matter.

It was also somewhat determined that the person of the photographer was somehow involved as having special kind of "energy" that permitted the strange luminous phenomena. Indeed, something like this had occasionally been noted throughout history in the cases of people that attracted or convenienced energetic events.

As an aside, in the early twentieth century there was the case of the famous Austrian-American physicist, Wolfgang Pauli (1900-1958), who in 1925 was awarded the Nobel Prize in Physics for enunciating the Exclusion Principle, and who in 1931 was the first to postulate the existence of the neutrino.

Pauli, however, hardly ever worked in or near a laboratory because his mere presence, even if 200 feet distant, caused equipment to act up and not perform as expected. Then there are those individuals never permitted in an X-ray lab because something about them exposes the X-ray film.

Although the pro and con polemics of spirit photography grew heated, both sides generally agreed (albeit for different motives) that the photographed phenomena were emanations unknown to physical science.

With science to back them up, critics ponderously declaimed that since the emanations were not known to physical science, they obviously "could not exist" and were thus unscientific.

To this, proponents of the emanations indicated that science had not yet discovered everything.

But in the light of mainstream cohesion, this was considered a weak argument, since a fairly large proportion of scientists and their sycophants held to the view that at any given time science HAD discovered everything that was important.

This, of course, was merely a fallacy within the social aspects of science—and, however empty of substance, social aspects can always be smoothed over and made to look okay.

As it was, photographs of emanations, etc., began to pile up in the United States. The exciting vogue for such photos reached England, the first on record there being produced in 1872 by one

Frederick A. Hudson. The photographic excitement swiftly reached France, Germany, Italy, and even Russia.

While all this sensational, and now international, hubbub was cascading around Europe, in England PSYCHIC FORCE was identified and named at about 1869, as we will review in the next chapter. But if the world did not yet comprehend what psychic force was (it was a new term), the world DID know what photographs were.

THOUGHT PHOTOGRAPHY

At some point in all this photographic furor, and to further complicate the already complicated issues involved, it began to be observed that images of individuals STILL LIVING sometimes appeared in photos taken miles away.

Indeed, a short report provided by the Comte de Bullet, dated December 10, 1874, was published in the periodical entitled HUMAN NATURE—to the effect that the Comte had obtained on a plate in Paris the double of his sister who lived across the Atlantic Ocean in Baltimore, Maryland.

After more of the living appeared in spirit photographs far and wide, the concept of "thought photography" came into existence. But it was not at all understood how the "spirit" of the living could translate across distances as great as oceans.

So it seemed most sensible (to some anyway) to assume that the images came from the thoughts of the photographer, although no one had any idea how or why they should translate to the photographic plates in the photographer's proximity.

With this development, a situational crisis subtly arose that was rather frightening within the larger contexts of the societal status quo.

That spirit photography might have relevance to the actual existence of spirits was bad enough. However, the emergence of thought photography was far worse. It created a crisis that has never been given the attention it deserves.

It could be reasoned, and it was, that if the thoughts of a person could actually effect the chemical molecules on a photographic plate, then, from an easily recognized scientific principle, there was little standing in the way of a person's thoughts affecting the chemical molecules in the brains of other people.

In other words, here was direct physical evidence that thoughts, via some as yet scientifically unknown energetic activity, could be transmitted, at least to photographic plates.

But the implications beyond this were clear enough, and they once again cracked open the tightly shut doors of what we today might call mind-influencing.

Indeed, such a prospect had been of modernist societal concern ever since Paracelsus.

That Renaissance luminary had indicated that: "By the magic power of the will, a person on this side of the ocean may make a person on the other side hear what is said on this side . . . the ethereal body of a man may know what another man thinks at a distance of 100 miles or more."

Since the time of Paracelsus, the mechanism of this transmission, whether oceanic or merely 100 miles, was thought to be a magnetic fluid that interacted with "sympathetic systems" of consciousness, and which fluid had the power to "conquer time and space."

In this sense, then, one could bet one's bottom dollar that the modern societal mainstreams, very much maintained on ensuring the privacy of thoughts, wanted nothing along such lines to be demonstrated or proven by any form of veridical evidence. And, as but one preventive measure, mainstream funding was, by common unspoken mainstream consensus, to be withheld from any who proposed to proceed gathering such evidence.

Thus, even though scads of photos were tested again and again by photographic experts, ultimately including those of Kodak, etc., any veridical evidence the photos conclusively demonstrated was simply ignored.

Even so, various daring researchers set about making even more remarkable escapades regarding the energies photographic.

Most notable (for a while, at least) among these was one Hyppolite Baraduc (1850-?), described as a "psychic" researcher who made "interesting experiments in thought photography."

However, he made excursions beyond mere thought photography by constructing Baraduc's biometer, an instrument that indicated the action of "a nervous force and other unknown vibrations outside the human body."

In 1895, Baraduc addressed a communication on these subjects to the French Academy of Medicine, although the Academy had not at all changed its view of magnetic fluids, etc., since the time of Anton Mesmer's expulsion from Paris about a hundred years earlier.

Undaunted, Baraduc then published, in 1896, announcements of his work, observations, and photos in a book entitled IMAGES OF THE COSMIC OD VITAL FORCE.

He quickly followed this, in 1897, with PHOTOGRAPHS OF HYPERVIBRATORY STATES OF HUMAN VITALITY, and in the same year yet another astonishing publication entitled HUMAN RADIO-GRAPHIC SYSTEM. (In French, the term RADIOGRAPHIE refers to X-rays, and so it is probable that N-rays are actually implied here.)

Apparently, Baraduc had earlier trekked into a project yielding photographic evidence he claimed proved that "something misty and vaporous leaves the human body at the moment of death."

This evidence was provided in yet a THIRD 1897 book rather daringly entitled: THE HUMAN SOUL: ITS INVISIBLE FLUIDIC MOVEMENTS, ILLUMINATIONS, AND IMAGES. (An updated version of this was later published in English in 1913.)

With little to suggest much in the way of catching his breath, Baraduc's photographic enthusiasms seemed to have escalated.

He soon went on, in 1904, to publish fresh photographic evidence in a book entitled: VIBRATIONS OF HUMAN VITALITY.

This was immediately followed, in 1905, with THE VITAL FORCE: OUR VITAL FLUIDIC BODY, A BAROMETRIC MODEL.

When Baraduc's young son, Andre, died in 1907, he apparently was able to transcend at least some of his grief. When the young body was laid out in its coffin, Baraduc successively photographed it, with the result that "radiations of a formless mist" were shown extending outward from the coffin.

Then, when some six months later Baraduc's wife lay dying, he set up his cameras at her deathbed and photographed her as she died. The photos revealed "three luminous spheres emitting thin fingers of light" just above her body.

Another photograph taken fifteen minutes later showed the three globes united and "concealing the corpse's head." Further, "luminous cords" could be seen around them.

Three and a half hours later, the united globes while emitting "cold breezes" then separated from the body and eventually floated away from it and finally disappeared.

The photographic plates of these two sad events were examined and reexamined with the certitude they would be debunked. No professional was ever able to do so, and so they remain among the most dramatic photographs ever taken.

Meanwhile, at about 1908, experiments with thought photography were taking place elsewhere, and as far away as Japan.

Dr. T. Fukurai, Professor of Kohyassan University, and formerly Professor at the Imperial University of Tokyo, was conducting thought-photography experiments with Mrs. Nagao, Miss Tetsuko Moritake, Mrs. Sadako Takahashi, Mrs. Tenshin Takeuchi, and a Mr. Kohichi Mita, all of whom had demonstrated "mediumistic" capabilities.

Dr. Fukurai published a report showing photographic evidence of emanations, and then went so far as to declare that "clairvoyance is a fact."

He was thereupon forced to resign from the University in 1913. Eventually his reports were translated into English in 1921 under the title CLAIRVOYANCE AND THOUGHTOGRAPHY. Thereafter, this early Japanese effort passed unnoticed into historical obscurity.

SEXUAL ENERGY PHOTOGRAPHS?

This author has it on very substantial authority that many sexual energy photographs were acquired, and ultimately found their way into private collections especially in Europe, and which, alas, have not been viewed by me. But it is easy enough to accept their most probable existence.

For one thing, researchers wishing to capture energies on photographic plates could not have been completely unaware that sexual activity produced ecstatic energy states and that these might be suitable for their photographic attempts.

For another thing, even though polite decorum was superficially maintained on social surfaces between 1875 and 1914, Paris, Berlin and London were noted for their fabulously vivid pornographic activities behind and beneath the prim social surfaces.

In Baraduc's case, anyone who had the equanimity to photograph his dead son and his dying wife clearly could have faced up to the rigors of photographing all types of erotic situations, including copulation and orgasm, this, of course, in the hope that some kind of invisible energies would become photographically apparent.

In any event, several knowledgeable researchers claimed that such photographs were achieved by Baraduc, and there seems little reason to doubt it.

Chapter 9
PSYCHIC FORCE

In reviewing the tales of Anton Mesmer and Reichenbach as briefly as we have, it is easy enough to get the mistaken idea they represent two isolated sets of unimportant circumstances.

This is how they have been treated by modern historians, scientists and psychologists alike, and so it seems that societal forces have properly established their non-importance.

However, if one draws together any and all past work that might have bearing on the nature of human energetics, it will soon be seen that the literature in this regard is massive, and that Mesmer and Reichenbach were not isolated examples of it.

The totality of such work is so massive that it cannot conveniently be incorporated into a book such as this, or in fact be incorporated into a single book unless it would consist of several thousand pages.

Indeed, when Eric J. Dingwall, the stalwart historian of psychical research, attempted to collect and publish the work of the nineteenth century mesmerists who carried on after the death of Anton Mesmer, he ultimately needed four volumes to do so.

Those four volumes, published in 1967-1968, establish that serious and careful work took place in France, Belgium, the Netherlands, Germany, Scandinavia, Russia, Poland, Italy, Spain, Portugal, Latin America, the United States, and Great Britain.

Although Dingwall's four volumes are given the title of ABNORMAL HYPNOTIC PHENOMENA, the actual topic is along the lines of unusual energetic phenomena brought to light via various kinds of altered states of consciousness.

Dingwall also brought together, in private, a large collection of sexual materials. Behind the more public scenes of Psi research, this is referred to as his "pornographic collection."

He kept this collection quite close to his chest. But in correspondence to me, he indicated that a good portion of it included documents regarding sexualizing energies encountered while conducting mesmeric and psychical research. In fact, it was Dingwall who suggested that a book should be written by "some daring soul."

Because of the scope of past energetic research, it is to be wondered why the whole of it has been ignored and excised from modern history, science and psychology. In any event, the scope of it establishes that Mesmer and Reichenbach were NOT isolated examples. In fact, within an even larger picture, they found themselves dealing with phenomena that modern anthropologists associated with shamanism.

The verifiable history of shamanic phenomena, including their sexualizing overtones, is found in most pre-modern cultures, and indeed dates back to before recorded history, and which phenomena are still recognized by contemporary Siberian Russian, Mongolian, Chinese, and Amerindian shamans and "medicine" persons.

Thus, it would seem that anyone seriously investigating human energetics would soon come to face phenomena not all that different from what Mesmer, Reichenbach and many others encountered.

MODERN PSYCHICAL RESEARCH

On the noble surface of modern psychical research, it would seem that its workers never encountered sexualizing phenomena. But such is not the case at all. Indeed, it might be said that psychical research, and later parapsychology, possess quite large "closets" in which were hidden various phenomena not tolerated by societal mainstreams.

The first Psychical Research Society (SPR) was founded in London in 1882. Several histories of the SPR exist, and from them it can easily be determined that it was established under excellent leadership.

Its work commenced under the general idea that psychical research was an important science within whose scope numerous phenomena rejected otherwise could be studied within the parameters of systematic organization.

However, in actuality the SPR was founded principally to examine various unusual and astonishing phenomena encountered in Spiritualism. And so a brief background review of Spiritualism is now required.

SPIRITUALISM

The full story of Spiritualism which, in the modern West, rose and fell between 1845 and 1932, is a strange tale of epic proportions, so much so that few have ever managed to do it justice.

Public interest in it went into decline during the 1930s. But during its earlier history, many astonishing mental and energetic phenomena associated with mediums often made headline news, sometimes on a daily basis.

There are two ways to remember Spiritualism: the simple and the complicated way.

The simple way identifies it as a belief involving spirits and departed souls, who, via a living medium, provide compelling evidence of their continuing existence and give messages to those yet living.

However, had conversations with the departed been all there was to Spiritualism, then it is unlikely it would have obtained the enormous and long-term celebrity it did.

It is therefore quite clear that other exceedingly dramatic phenomena associated with Spiritualism triggered its high profile. Getting a grasp on the "dramatic phenomena" is a somewhat complicated task, especially in brief form.

ASTONISHING PHENOMENA OF SPIRITUALISM

As distinguished from communicating with spirits, the phenomena of Spiritualism fell into two main categories, rather loosely defined as MENTAL and PHYSICAL.

The mental phenomena might have been discounted as such. But the physical phenomena were another matter.

The list of such physical phenomena is quite long and varied, and in many cases thoroughly documented by numerous researchers of high repute and working in different decades and in different countries. To itemize but a few examples:

- Movement of objects without contact, vibratory effects, increases and decreases in weight

- Levitation of the human body
- Materialization and dematerialization
- Biological phenomena: influencing the growth of plants apparently by vital bodily emanations or by other unknown means
- Chemical phenomena: unexplainable lights, perfumes, catalytic action, production of water, production of photographs of invisible energies
- Electrical phenomena: discharge of electroscopes, phenomena suggestive of human energy radiations
- Thermo-dynamic effects: variations of temperature, increase of heat in apported objects, the penetration of matter through matter, detectable currents of wind and air, touches of invisible energies
- Perception of auras, energy fields, energy flows or streams
- Clairvoyance in all of its variegated forms
- A long list of various kinds of magnetic and biomagnetic phenomena
- A long list of energetic phenomena transferred across spaces, around impediments, and through material obstruction

Faced with these phenomena, at about 1858 early researchers began to recognize that the human organism was somehow bound up with a "force" that operated beyond the periphery of the physical body—and yet had impact on physical matter.

The "force" needed a descriptive name, of course, and one of the earlier suggestions was "exo-neural action of the brain" —"exo" meaning outside of.

This suggestion was immediately resisted by many scientists, especially by brain researchers, who scoffed at such research and had no desire to become involved in any exo-neural prospects.

In explanation of this, the approved scientific view took it for granted that nothing existed outside of the body's skin, and thus exo neural activity was not possible in the first place. Indeed, it was not until about 150 years later that the real existence of bio-electromatic fields outside of the skull was confirmed.

In any event, the term "exo-neural" was conceptually and phonetically difficult, and it is understandable why it never caught on.

PSYCHIC FORCE

In about 1861 in France, the then famous astronomer, Camille Flammarion (1842-1925), may have been the first to suggest the term PSYCHIC as a replacement for exo-neural. However, it didn't catch on in France until decades later, and never caught on in Germany.

In England, though, Edward William Cox (1809-1879), a lawyer by profession, seems to have been the first to suggest the term in English. Cox may have been interested in phenomena earlier, but his concentrated research seems to have taken place only in the last decade of his life.

Cox was a member of the London Dialectical Society, formed in 1869 to examine and report on the alleged spiritual communications of mediums whose population was definitely on the rise.

The members of the Dialectical Society originally intended to do away with the "Claims of Spiritualism." But in the end, their famous report on SPIRITUALISM published in 1871 noted substantial corroboration, especially as regards the physical phenomena.

Cox did not accept the "spirit" hypothesis, and instead argued for the existence of a "force" that would explain many forms of the physical phenomena.

His idea regarding the nature of this force was first presented, in 1872, in a booklet entitled SPIRITUALISM SCIENTIFICALLY EXAMINED WITH PROOFS OF THE EXISTENCE OF A PSYCHIC FORCE, and later he enlarged his ideas in a book entitled THE MECHANISM OF MAN (1876).

Cox is best remembered in the literature for his work with Sir William Crookes and their first experiments with the already internationally renowned Spiritualistic superstar, Daniel Dunglas Home (1833-1886).

So extraordinary where the phenomena emanating in the presence of Home that he certainly deserved the high acclaim given him as the "greatest physical medium in the history of modern spiritualism." And, perhaps more aptly put, in the history of anything anywhere. For example, he was thoroughly documented as floating in a horizontal position in and out of third floor windows.

Sir William Crookes (1832-1919) had taken deep interest in physical phenomena. After earlier witnessing remarkable demonstrations by other mediums, and then by Home, Crookes arranged to conduct some experiments with him.

Crookes was already recognized as one of the greatest physicists of his time and had received many honors. He had been president at different times of the Royal Society, the Chemical Society, the Institution of Electrical Engineers, etc. He had discovered thallium, was the inventor of the radiometer, spinthariscope, the Crookes tube, etc. He was the founder of the CHEMICAL NEWS, and editor of the QUARTERLY JOURNAL OF SCIENCE.

When Crookes indicated that he would enter into investigation of the phenomena of Spiritualism, the press and many important scientists received the announcement with jubilation, since it was taken for granted that Crookes would clearly show the phenomena as "humbug."

A somewhat complicated series of experiments with Home then followed, usually in the evenings in a large room illuminated by gaslight.

One of the principle objectives was to discover if the force had properties capable of impacting on physical matter. This involved a number of different kinds of apparatus, some more simply constructed than others.

Among more elaborate equipment designed to measure the physical existence of the invisible force, one end of a long mahogany board was placed on the edge of a desk, the other end supported by a spring balance and strain gauge hanging from a substantial tripod stand. The board was supported in a way that prevented movement of it by hand pressure.

Home would sit at the desk and place his fingers lightly on the end of the board and focus his "force" into the board causing the other end to move up or down. The strain gauge would indicate the motion, indicating the measurable existence of the "force."

Cox was an observer of the experiments with Crookes and Home, and as a result he was able to write as follows:

"I noticed that the force was exhibited in tremulous pulsations, and not in the form of steady, continuous pressure, the indicator rising and falling incessantly throughout the experiment.

"The fact seems to me one of great significance as tending to confirm the opinion that assigns its source to the nerve organization, and it goes far to establish Dr. Richardson's [another researcher] important discovery of a nerve atmosphere of various intensity enveloping the human structure.

"I would recommend the adoption for it [the "force"] of some appropriate name, and I venture to suggest that the force be termed Psychic Force; the persons to whom it is manifested in extraordinary power Psychics; and the science relating to it Psychism as being a branch of Psychology."

SENSATIONS ASSOCIATED WITH THE PSYCHIC FORCE

Along with other researchers corresponding with Sir William Crookes about their own experiments with the psychic force, a Dr. Crawford soon reported at least four different forms of it and described the sensations it could produce both around the medium and persons nearby.

1. A sensation of cool breezes, generally over the hands.
2. The sensation of a slight tingling in the palm of the hands, and at the tips of the fingers, near the mounts.
3. The sensation of a sort of current through the body.
4. The sensation of a "spider's web" in contact with the hands and feet, and other parts of the body, notably the back and the loins [loins being the Victorian code word for genitals.] The sensation of the passing through of a current is feeble, but the interruption is easily felt.

The research with the physical aspects of the psychic force went on for some time, and ultimately the highly respected Sir William Crookes prepared his report. If the mainstream scientists and the press were hopeful that Crooks would trash the phenomena, they were to be disappointed. For, as Crooks concluded in the introduction to his final report:

"Of all persons endowed with a powerful development of

this Psychic Force, Mr. Daniel Dunglas Home is the most remarkable and it is mainly owing to the many opportunities I have had in carrying on my investigation in his presence that I am enabled to affirm so conclusively the existence of this force."

Here it now must be recalled that Sir William Crookes was ranked as of the top scientists in England at the time. Therefore, he was not a gullible idiot, and he should have been accepted with some attention.

He submitted his report to the Royal Society on June 15, 1871.

But in that "Crookes had not demonstrated the fallacy of the alleged marvels of Spiritualism," the report was refused and even the inscription of the title of the paper in the Society's publications was denied.

It was only in the July, 1871, issue of the QUARTERLY JOURNAL OF SCIENCE that the public became acquainted with the first account of Crookes' observations.

The scientists of the time might have rejected the implications of Crookes' work. But not the public. A rash of well-attended "sittings" with mediums exploded everywhere, perhaps not so much to witness the phenomena, but to obtain first-and experience of the tremulous pulsations in "the vicinity of the loins."

SEXUALIZING ENERGIES OF THE PSYCHIC FORCE

Unlike Crookes' experiments, clearly illuminated by gaslight, most psychic force mediumistic sessions were held in completely dark rooms. This enabled many sitters to report seeing various kinds of luminous energies not only coming out of the mediums but arriving through the walls from elsewhere.

As a caution, though, numerous of the "mediums" involved were opportunistic frauds and tricksters, bent on profit taking from the gullible. Most of these were exposed as such, but there remained a large number of experiments set up by individuals of high repute and conducted under exacting controls.

One distinction that separated the real medium from the fake ones had to do with energy sensations felt by those attending the seances. Such energy sensations could become quite powerful regarding the real mediums but were generally absent in the presence of the fakes, no matter how dramatic was

72 | Psychic Sexuality

their trickery otherwise.

A real seance seems to have been a trying affair. It was not unusual for the medium producing the psychic force to end up exhausted and depleted. However, they were prevented from falling onto the floor because their hands, feet, arms, and torsos had been firmly tied and taped to their chairs to prevent trickery.

In any event, we are not so much interested in what the mediums did, but what the witnesses reported experiencing. What they mostly reported were energies, either felt and/or seen.

All sorts of descriptions of the energies abound in the literature, such as "we could all see a stream of pale gray matter, like fog or steam from a kettle, oozing from her [the medium] fingers. It was shaped like rods, about a foot long and an inch thick. The gray material could extend and contract."

There is little reason to wallow in doubt about this kind of thing, because in later years many reported much the same while drunk or enjoying recreational drugs.

A Dr. Crawford (whose biographical details are not well recorded) subsequently produced a theory about the psychic force emanations. This theory is slightly complex, so you have to follow it slowly.

"Operators [the mediums and/or their excarnate guides] are acting on the brain of the sitters, and thence on their nervous systems. Small particles, it may even be molecules, are driven off the nervous system, out through the bodies of the sitters' arms, wrists, hands, fingers, or elsewhere.

"These small particles, now free, have a considerable amount of latent energy inherent in them, an energy which can react on any human nervous systems with which they come into contact.

"This stream of energized particles flows around the circle [of the sitters] probably partly on the periphery of their bodies. The stream, by gradual augmentation from the [combined] sitters, reaches the medium at an high degree of 'tension' energizes her [the medium], receives an increment from her, traverses the circle again, and so.

"Finally, when the 'tension' is sufficiently great, the circulating process ceases, and the energized particles collect on or are attached to the nervous system of the medium . . ." [from whose body now extended the psychic energy forces which could be felt/seen by

others.]

Aside from the fact that the above took place in a mediumistic seance, and that the energies were often seen in a literal sense, it seems useless to doubt much in this regard.

The reason is that even under usual circumstances, many people report sensing or feeling energies of others. This is especially the case if the situation involved has become highly charged, such as in combat and sexual situations.

SEXUAL ENERGY DISPLAYS DURING SEANCES

During the seances, many strange phenomena sometimes occurred which were not generally discussed or put officially into print.

Sometimes, female mediums or sitters achieved spontaneous orgasm, which left them "exhausted." If male, they suffered erections of the male appendage, and sometimes spontaneously ejaculated in their undergear or trousers.

Thereby, the concept of "tremulous pulsations of psychic force" took on new, if unofficial, potency, such as "tremulous pulsations of sexual force" that can rattle not only boards hooked up to strain gauges, but also erotically stimulate, to the point of achieving sexualizing ecstasy, the autonomic nervous systems of bio-bodies as well.

Indications of this kind of thing are present in many reports, but in a way most people today will not recognize.

During Victorian times, proper people did not refer to sexual energies, and they seldom utilized the word "sex." But large numbers of sitters confessed themselves "disturbed" by the psychic force. "Disturbed," of course, was a Victorian code word for what we today would call horny and/or sexually aroused.

In any event, certain researchers tried to estimate physical effects of the psychic force on the mediums and sitters. It was soon discovered that both the medium and sitters lost "dynametric force"—meaning that their muscles became lethargic and somnolent.

Instantaneous weight losses also occurred. Dr. Crawford reported putting his experimental sitters on the scale and found that their loss of weight at the end of the seance was greater than the weight lost by the medium. The sitters lost, on average, five to ten ounces "and were more exhausted than the medium."

An Admiral Moore, a sitter, complained of a "drain of vitality." One of the reasons that Lord Adare earlier retired from sittings with the famous male medium, Daniel Dunglas Home, was because he became so "disturbed" that he couldn't concentrate and was soon physically exhausted.

A Colonel Rochas described a case of levitation by psychic force with the famous female medium, Eusapia Paladino (1854-1918). He indicated that "we ought to add that one of the persons who was quite close to the table almost completely fainted away, not from emotion, but through disturbed weakness."

Rochas also said that "he felt drained of his strength as the result of Eusapia's efforts." A supply of smelling salts was usually kept handy for psychic force seances.

Eusapia Paladino frequently insisted she be nude for her seances, and in her trances demanded sexual insertions from those males she sensed had achieved psychic force erections.

Naturally, male researchers and sitters were eager to be at her seances, always held behind locked doors. It is on record that the wives of the male attendees hated Eusapia with a hysterical passion that sometimes escaped Victorian decorum.

A certain researcher (or sitter) named Frere wrote that "The operators [the spirit guides of a medium] often speak of lines of force, of a vibratory synchronization. All our sensations are accompanied by a development of potential energy which passes into a kinetic state and externalizes itself in motor manifestations."

"Motor manifestations" referred to excitatory, but involuntary, physical activity, such as muscle spasms. But in many cases of sitters and observers, it also referred particularly to involuntary sexual arousal and climaxial experiencing in the vicinity of the "loins."

SEXUALIZING AROUSAL SIMILARITY OF ANIMAL MAGNETISM, ODIC FORCE, AND PSYCHIC FORCE

At this point, the similarities of sexualizing arousal so far discussed hardly need much further elucidation except to elaborate a bit more about why they occurred within the particular circumstances they did.

While it is true that sexual arousal can occur because of mental associations to erotic stimuli, this kind of arousal by itself seldom ends up in spontaneous or involuntary climaxing.

Thus, the sexualizing similarity involves the occurrence of the spontaneous/involuntary climaxing. In any feasible sense, such would not take place except if some kind of energies were physically affecting the autonomic nervous systems of the experiencers.

This would suggest, in turn, that animal magnetism, odic force, and psychic force are merely different names for the energetics involved.

Chapter 10
ORGONE ENERGY— BIONIC ENERGY

Information regarding sexualizing energies is hard to dig out of the histories of animal magnetism, odic force, and psychic force. An assessment of the large literature establishes the existence of powerful societal suppression regarding their phenomena and any research of them. The sexualizing energy aspects are further concealed, this most probably in keeping with the taboo regarding sex prevalent during the nineteenth and early part of the twentieth centuries.

However, anyone patiently and knowledgeably sifting through the enormous literature can find the evidence regarding energetic sexualizing phenomena. The evidence found is cumulative and taken altogether is highly supportive of the real existence of such energies.

As it is, though, the evidence is really not all that necessary, in that most people, probably from time immemorial, physically experience and mentally realize not only that sexual energies have some kind of real existence, but that they interact over distances if they are strong enough.

A far greater mystery, but equally based in copious evidence, has to do with WHY research along the lines of human energetics has been condemned and suppressed by powerful societal factors.

Mesmer, Reichenbach, the photographers of energies, and psychical research were all attacked (best word) by powerful societal forces.

This resulted not only in their historical condemnation, but established serious barriers against ANY examination of the topics they represented.

Further, the attacks frequently were vicious, so much so that even reputations of highest eminence could be destroyed. For example, the positive interest of Sir William Crookes in the physical phenomena of Spiritualism damaged his high scientific standing almost beyond repair.

A calm and lengthy survey of this negative situation reveals that it is not the people involved, but the topic of human energetics as a whole, under any label or format, that is being suppressed by powerful societal forces. And this by methods resembling overkill with the ultimate goal of complete erasure.

All possible explanations considered regarding the societal suppression, the actual source of its origin and reasons for it remain arcane, especially if compared to the concept that the more that is learned and known about human potentials, the better off everyone would be.

THE FIRST DELIBERATE RESEARCH INTO SEXUALIZING ENERGIES

With many similarities to the saga of Anton Mesmer, and to the scientific deconstruction of Karl von Reichenbach and later psychical research, the story of Wilhelm Reich demonstrates yet another revolting example of societal overkill regarding any knowledge about the actual existence of human energetics.

Wilhelm Reich (1897-1957) was born the son of a farmer in Dobrzcynica, Galicia. He showed high promise in his early tutoring, so much so that his poor family worked to provide him with higher education.

After World War I, in which he served in the Austrian army on the Italian front, he studied law at the University of Vienna, and then went on to study medicine, obtaining his M.D. in 1922. After graduating he undertook further studies in neurology and psychiatry.

No less a personage than Sigmund Freud recognized Reich's excellence. Reich was soon appointed as the first clinical assistant in Freud's Psychoanalytic Polyclinic in 1922, and later became vice-director in 1928. These positions held by Reich were of no mean importance, and they contributed mightily to his growing reputation as an excellent thinker and scientist.

Reich joined the Austrian Socialist Party in 1924, and the Communist Party in 1928. These early affiliations with Socialism, Marxism and Communism were later to be held against him in the United States. But in Europe at the time, such affiliations were rather standard fare, and almost an unavoidable intellectual necessity.

The socio-political intensities in Europe had little in common with how Americans understood politics. It could be said, in general, that Europeans were preoccupied with socio-political theories in much the same way as Americans were fascinated with movies and moviemaking.

In any event, it was de rigueur for intellectuals to consider at least the social (as differentiated from the political) promises of these growing theories.

Competent biographies of Reich make it quite clear that he was principally interested not in political issues but in social health and well-being, and in reforms that would cure mental and emotional factors upon which social ills were founded and perpetuated.

Reich had become convinced that much neurosis was caused by poverty, bad housing conditions, and various other social ills. Essential Freudianism, Marxism and European Socialism had been set up to improve the human lot in this regard, and so it was logical for Reich to involve himself in all three. In the sense of all this, Reich completely fitted into the times and developments of Europe.

However, much like Freud, Reich had early on become convinced that social ills principally arose from neuroses based in blocked and distorting sexual urges. He early advocated the establishment of "health centers" in which the blocked sexual urges could be unblocked and once more take on their natural expression.

Europeans were quite prepared to discuss and debate social ills, the traditional basis of which was perceived as resulting from the unfair distribution of economic wealth on behalf of the wealthy and the politically powerful.

Reich, however, advised that the more actual basis of social ills arose from blocked sexual urges brought about by confusions inherent in social conditioning that resulted in faulty functions of energies involved with sexual orgasm. Not only was society as a whole guilty of maintaining the conditioning, but the basic family unit also.

Reich made his views known by publishing papers, and then in his first book entitled THE FUNCTION OF THE ORGASM (1927). This book addressed three issues:

1. the biological function of orgasm;

2. the release of pent-up emotions and energies; and
3. the sexual frustrations of the working classes.

In 1927, socialists of all waters were quite prepared to undertake the curing of social ills by the most radical political and economic means possible. However, they were not at all prepared to deal with faulty sexual orgasm.

Indeed, the nature of sexuality was still taboo within science and the new psychoanalysis, and within Socialism, Marxism, and Communism as well. The working classes, firmly rooted in the meaning and identity of the family unit, did not consider themselves as being sexually frustrated.

In this way, Reich managed to step on just about everyone's toes, and he was ushered out of the developing "orthodox" mainstreams of psychoanalysis, doctrinaire Marxism, and all versions of European Socialism.

Reich, however, was made of rather stern stuff. Undaunted, he moved to Berlin in 1930. To begin the process of "the sexual education of young people," he helped establish an organization on behalf of sexual-politics—the VERLAG FUR SEXUALPOLITIC (SEXPOL-VERLAG). (In English, PUBLISHING HOUSE FOR SEXUAL POLITICS (SEXPOL-PUBLICATIONS).

In this undertaking, he followed the logic inherent in the original Freudian concepts regarding the overriding importance of the sexual urge in human affairs, but with a slight difference.

Freudianism held that sexual problems were mental in nature. But Reich was convinced that actual "bio-physical" energy was involved, energy which could be physically blocked, and thus lead to the mental distortions.

As it turned out, however, Berliners were not amenable to Reich's orgasmic ideas that had to do with sexual education of young people, and soon increasingly vicious smear campaigns began appearing.

The smear campaigns ultimately resulted in Reich's being expelled from the Communist Party in 1933 because of his advocacy of sexual politics. He was unbothered by this, since he had visited Russia in 1929 and confessed himself disappointed with Russian bureaucracy and bourgeois moralistic attitudes toward sexuality.

A short while later, the International Psychoanalytic Association expelled him, ironically because of his Communist membership. That Association apparently being unaware that the Communist Party had already expelled him.

Undaunted by these various, and conflicting expulsions, Reich published his first monumental book in 1933, entitled CHARACTER ANALYSIS, a profound and basic tome still utilized by analysts.

In it, Reich held that "bioenergy" which "normally travels through the body in a specific circuit gets trapped wherever muscles are tight."

He went on to explain that this kind of situation, if chronic, inhibits and reduces the body's bioenergy flows, affects the immune system and leads to sickness and other dysfunctional discomforts often ending up as debilitating neuroses.

Also in 1933, Reich had taken critical interest in the emergence and dangers of German fascism which he correctly foresaw as a rising tide of political influence.

He blamed the rise of Hitler on "the sex-repressed German family" and explained the intricate details of this in his book MASS PSYCHOLOGY OF FASCISM (1933). First published in Scandinavia, it took a few years for it to be translated into German, and to be comprehended by the Hitler Movement.

None the less, smear campaigns against him began emerging in the Scandinavian countries, Austria, and Germany, not so much as regards the rise of fascism, but because of moralistic outrage about the function of the orgasm, and because of Reich's blasts about sex-repressive family units.

Again, undaunted by smear campaigns and media abuse, Reich did not defend himself but rather escalated HIS attacks on the "perverse character of the Hitler regime." Since Communism paraded itself in Western Europe as a form of Socialism, the propaganda sections of the Communist Internationale were affronted by Reich castigation's of "sham Socialism."

Since the whole of this developing situation had to come to a head, it did so in 1939. Reich was by that year a targeted enemy of Communism, the Nazi's, and of moralistic outrages regarding orgasm energy blockages in the family unit.

He first strategically evacuated to Norway where he planned to continue his work. Uneasily established there, however, the Germans began their invasion of Norway in April, 1940, and Reich barely made it out with his life. He then headed to the

United States of America.

Once there, he set up shop in Forest Hills, Long Island, but shortly removed to "Orgonon," Maine, "Orgonon" being the name of his "estate" and orgone research laboratory, and which included an observatory.

As a result of this judicious move to the U.S.A., Americans were now somewhat surprised by having to learn about such electrifying matters as:

- Armor in the genital character
- Basic life processes
- Biological energy
- Biopathic contractions
- Control over irrationality
- Emotional expression of the body
- Emotional plagues
- Energy blocks and energy fields
- Eye contact
- Field excitation of orgone energy
- Genital disturbances, excitation, and gratification
- Orgastic convulsions, impotency, and potency
- Orgonotic energy charge, pulsations and streamings
- Radical approaches to liberating creative energies

The Americans soon became alarmed and distressed by Wilhelm Reich as the European communists and fascists had been.

ORGONE—A SEXUALIZING ENERGY

The vast bulk of Reich's work is quite difficult to summarize. The best, and so far the only competent source for Reich's saga can be found in Myron Sharaf's monumental biography entitled FURY ON EARTH (1983), which should be required reading for anyone interested in human energetics.

Beyond that, and with apologies to the followers of Reich's work, we can get at the central gist of it for the purposes of this book.

As pointed up in FURY ON EARTH (p. 276), it is difficult to pinpoint the exact date for Reich's formulation of orgone energy. The general chronology of his workplaces it at about 1940.

But this most certainly refers to the term ORGONE, not to Reich's awareness that such an energy existed, and which awareness obviously would have taken place even quite early in his life.

His earliest usage of ORGONE seems to have evolved in 1939 in relationship to "orgone radiation," but this radiation was established by Reich in a context having to do with "bions."

It is difficult to grasp what was meant by bions, but visual evidence of them could be observed "in the dark basement room" as radiations from heated ocean sand.

The bionic radiations, or the bionic light, visible to the naked eye, was described as bluish light emanating from the walls and from various objects in the darkened basement room.

Reich explained that he could not exclude "subjective impressions" with regard to the light phenomena. There is no record that Reich's bionic light was ever compared to Karl von Reichenbach's luminous phenomena, although it too was perceived in dark rooms by sensitives in touch with their own subjective (or clairvoyant) impressions.

Very roughly put, orgone energy was considered a non-electro-magnetic force, a life force, which permeates all nature, and in some way is closely associated with "orgastic potency."

If heightened by physical or therapeutic means, orgastic potency results in phenomena not unlike the cathartic phenomena associated with Anton Mesmer's vats that accumulated some kind of energy and then transferred it to those holding the wands.

If one can directly perceive the energy of orgastic potency (presumably by some direct and/or clairvoyance means), it is of the color blue.

The orgastic potency is composed of radiating bions which, Reich stated (and later demonstrated), can be transferred to objects and other human bodies for therapeutic (cathartic) purposes.

Reich derived the term ORGONE from ORGANISM and/or ORGASM or both and stipulated that it was an energy that normally traveled through the body in a specific current but could get blocked up and result in any number of undesirable phenomena.

As Reich's research with orgone energy continued, he was ultimately to divide it into three chief characteristics: visual observation, thermal measurements, and the electroscopic effect.

The sexual aspects of orgone energy were often played down later, but in the end, they are unavoidable, since the sexual apparatus of the human body cannot be detached, rationally anyway, from the energies of the human body.

The evidence is quite compelling that Reich quite early envisioned possibilities of interacting with orgone energy. This energy is foreshadowed in Reich's 1922 paper entitled THE SPECIFICITY OF FORMS OF MASTURBATION, and in his first 1923 version of what was later to become his major thesis entitled ON GENITALITY." Sexual energy, later renamed orgone energy, is considered in depth in his book THE FUNCTION OF THE ORGASM.

ORGONE ENERGY ACCUMULATORS

The existence of orgone energy was to Reich a good thing, capable of many different kinds of applications, if it could be "collected" and intensified.

Therefore, the next step in the study of this energy radiation (whether orgonic or bionic in nature) was to build an apparatus that would collect and contain it.

As described in FURY ON EARTH (p. 277), metal reflected the energy whereas organic material absorbed it. Since metal did reflect it, Reich designed a box-like "collector" that had metal walls on the inside backed with organic materials on the outside.

One panel of the collector had a porthole through which the presumed energy could be seen from the outside by researchers and witnesses. As originally intended, the collector was designed not to treat illness, but to visually study the bionic radiation.

With this collector which intensified the energy, it was possible to observe two kinds of "light" or luminescent phenomena, the bluish, moving vapors, and sharper, yellowish "points" and "lines" that flickered.

Thereafter, Reich began experimenting with different kinds of accumulators, and found that the energy seemed to accumulate in just about any old container.

If Reich had not had the idea before (which he certainly had), he now concluded that the energy he was studying was "everywhere." He also concluded that the energy "came from the atmosphere."

After research on the visual, thermal and electrostatic effects had sorted out at least some basic questions, between 1940 and 1948 Reich turned his attention to the "medical effects" of the orgone accumulators.

His reports on these effects were stunning and began attracting profound interest of many important researchers in a number of fields.

Although the following brief statement may be over simplistic, he had begun to demonstrate:

1. that organisms suffused with bionic-orgone energy were highly disease resistant, and
2. that organisms weakly suffused could be brought back into a more healthy state by being subject to accumulated infusions of the orgone energy.

SEXUALIZING EFFECTS OF ORGONE ENERGY

However, trouble had begun pushing into view when individuals discovered that sitting in the accumulators often enhanced sexual potency, even to the degree of occasionally effecting spontaneous thrills.

While the general public would have no precise idea of what bionic energy meant at the cellular and molecular levels, almost anyone could clearly understand the wonderful enhancements of sexual potency.

With this news, excitedly promulgated by wide press coverage, Reich's reputation (and following) increased immensely, and copies of his JOURNAL OF ORGONOMY and ORGONE ENERGY BULLETIN were much in demand.

Additionally, it is clear that Reich hoped to achieve "cures" of awful diseases via orgone energy, especially, but not only including a cancer cure.

Here was a "hope" that finally galvanized certain societal forces in reaction to Reich. Reich also ran into problems regarding his announced attempts to collect bionic energy into types of "guns" or "cannons" in order to transmit it, among other possible practical uses, for weather control.

However, these events only increased the "furors" that had accumulated not in the bionic accumulators but around the person and name of Reich himself.

THE SOCIETAL TERMINATION OF WILHELM REICH

Because of a wide, invisible web of vested interests, the FDA proceeded against Reich as if he were a common charlatan peddling a worthless cancer cure.

During 1952, the FDA and the Justice Department issued a court injunction banning not only the construction of orgone accumulators but demanding the sanitizing of the word ORGONE from all his paper, books and other materials. Reich's "inalienable rights" guaranteed by the Constitution and the Bill of Rights were simply cast aside, while this kind of activity at such high levels implied that he was something more than a harmless kook.

During 1953, and before an official hearing could take place, the FDA, assisted by the FBI, confiscated all of Reich's documents, books, research papers. These were finally fed into the Gansevort Incinerator, New York, on August 23, 1956. With his First Amendment rights shredded into the wind, Reich somewhat noisily refused to comply with the court order, and when the proceedings against him were finally heard in 1954, he again refused.

He was thereupon found in contempt of court and was sentenced to imprisonment. He first sent to Danbury Federal Prison for ten days where he was subjected to "psychiatric examination."

He was then moved to incarceration in the federal penitentiary in Lewisburg, Pennsylvania, where he died on November 3, 1957, with the actual circumstances of his death remaining unclear. Why Reich should have been imprisoned for nearly three years on the mere charge of contempt of court is, by any rationale, not readily comprehensible.

At this point, we might assume that various phenomena human energetics are real, and that they have been touched upon by numerous researchers. The sexualizing element within these phenomena is consistently encountered.

While many of the phenomena encountered might be readily experienced upon average, the essence of the sexualizing energies is entirely real and tangible within the scope of usual human experiencing.

We can now turn our attention, in Part II, to the ways and means such energies, usually invisible, can be seen by clairvoyance. Here we encounter a truly rich and wonderful panorama and history.

PART II

THE TREMULOUS PULSATIONS SEEN BY CLAIRVOYANCE

Chapter 11
PREVENTING KNOWLEDGE OF SEXUAL ENERGIES

In Part I we briefly reviewed some historical instances in which extraordinary human energies played a central role, and did so in very active and surprising ways. In the contexts of each of the instances, the energies were given a number of different names, such as vital fluids, animating energies, sympathetic vibrations, magnetic, fluxes, effluents, animal magnetism, odic, psychic, and orgonic, etc.

However, in sequentially comparing what the different names were referring to, it is obvious that they collectively identify human energetics.

Thus, in the historical sense beginning in the Renaissance, we have a sequential profusion of names, but all of which get back to human energies.

At first sight, the profusion of names might appear as merely a semantic difficulty. It is at least that, to be sure. But a deeper examination as to how and why the different names came about reveals another more important factor.

This factor now needs partially to be brought to light within the overall scope of this book, because it has a great deal to do with societal factors that prevent and defeat the accumulation of verifiable knowledge regarding human energetics.

In turn, the lack of the knowledge has impact on individuals and how they can or cannot sense or perceive the energies.

THE SOCIETAL CONDEMNATION OF KNOWLEDGE OF HUMAN ENERGETICS

We have seen that the whole of the research reviewed in Part I spans almost five centuries. Further, we have seen that each aspect of the research emerged in different time periods and under different researchers.

We have also seen that all of the research in any form was almost immediately condemned and put down by strong societal measures—condemned so vigorously that the research was in fact effectively erased from all mainstream scientific, philosophic, and academic histories of those five centuries.

The condemnations not only deconstructed the research of given individuals. They also acted as preventives with regard to accumulation of knowledge of human energetics. And they additionally acted as warnings to others that might drift into the magical directions of human energetics.

All of these societal measures to discourage and prevent research of human energetics are still generally active today. There are various kinds of energetic research going on here or there. But it goes on outside of mainstream parameters, and none of it is accepted or integrated into the mainstream lines of science, psychology, or philosophy.

Of course, the mainstream forces cannot really prevent such research if it is undertaken individually and without mainstream approval. But the mainstream forces can ignore the existence and implications of such research, and ultimately can find ways and means to discredit any possible validity of it.

To return now to the profusion of names. When the work and phenomena of Anton Mesmer was condemned by the mainstream forces of his time, the essence of his work was in fact continued by many researchers in many different countries.

But none of it had much chance of being recognized as acceptable by the societal mainstream.

To escape being painted with the same tar brush as Mesmer, many subsequent researchers avoided utilizing the terminology associated with animal magnetism and mesmerism.

Such was the case with Baron von Reichenbach, and whom indeed WAS considered as an important mainstream researcher, and in fact discovered much that could be fitted into conventional mainstream parameters.

As a thorough and exacting researcher, it is unthinkable that Reichenbach had not studied all available information regarding the phenomena and procedures of mesmerism.

However, in trying to avoid the anticipated societal condemnation of his work if he presented it along the lines of mesmerism, he opted to use entirely new and different terms: OD and ODIC FORCE.

This is a socio-political ploy quite common among scientists and philosophers, a ploy utilized to ESCAPE from the societal condemnation of earlier work.

As we have seen, Reichenbach's work did not escape, and when the portents and implications of his work were recognized, not only was his work condemned, but he himself was subjected to personal humiliation.

After Reichenbach, no researcher hoping for a modicum of recognition by mainstream powers dared to utilize mesmeric or odic metaphors, since such rubrics had been vigorously condemned both in name and as regards the substantial topics they represented.

The term PSYCHIC FORCE came into existence for much the same reasons, and with much the same societal outcome.

This outcome forced the psychic researchers to formulate their organizations outside of acceptable mainstream sciences. And such work, even if later renamed PARAPSYCHOLOGY, continues to exist outside of even a hint of mainstream acceptance.

As it turned out, the psychic force research was very substantial and persuasive. But this fulminated even more vigorous societal condemnation of it. Psychical research did not actually cease, but the fulminations caused the term PSYCHIC to be taboo within the modernist mainstream sciences and philosophies, and within their workings it remains taboo to this day.

A careful study of Wilhelm Reich more of less suggests that he never intended to enter into psychical research.

From the start of his work, his interests focused precisely on sexual energies, especially those associated with orgasm.

In this instance, he needed a new term, and ORGONE, or orgonic energy, was derived from orgasm. Indeed, there can be little doubt that orgasm IS a form of energetic transaction, one with multitudes of side effects and by-products.

But, as we have seen, Reich did not escape condemnation either, specifically because his work intruded into the category of human energetics. In demonstrable fact, he and his work were terminated by mainstream officials, and with a viciousness that can be seen as little else than hysterically deadly.

The factor that links the different names has to do with

human energetics. It is this factor, under any name, that appears to be the special target of mainstream societal suppression.

This, to say the least of it, is very mysterious, and exceedingly illogical IF the bigger goal regarding acquisition of knowledge per se is considered.

But in some sense at least, there is a comic side to this five-century-long story of suppression.

THE EXPERIENCING OF SEXUAL ENERGIES CAN BE PARTIALLY DEADENED

The real existence of sexual energies is universally experienced by people in all cultures and in all stations of life.

The experiencing (or sensing) transcends language barriers, social strata, and even educational conditioning designed to install emotional and mental deadening against such sensing.

But human organisms, having the superlative sensing equipment they do, seldom become so dumbed-down that they altogether cease from such experiencing.

In considering the above, however, it must quickly be pointed up that there are strategic differences between sensing sexual energies and the many formats of behavior that can download because of them.

Herein lies a great difficulty, in that the knowledge gap between sexual energies per se and sexual behavior per se is not only enormous but gargantuan.

One element of this great difficulty obviously proceeds from the fact that the energies are invisible while the associated behavior is visible. This causes attention to be focused on behavior, but only because it IS visible.

Another element is that while the energies are invisible, they are none the less tangible.

This invisible-but-tangible aspect is confusing, often resulting in messy situations not only regarding sexuality but other factors that can be sensed in spite of their essential invisibility. Even many great minds, least of all those philosophic and scientific, have not been able to come to terms with what is involved.

The entire realm of intuition, for example, is a good example of this, in that it is entirely composed of sensing invisible but obviously real factors. But intuition moved quite close to energetics, and so research of it is avoided by mainstream science and psychology.

THE EXPERIENCING OF SEXUAL ENERGIES UNDER SPECIAL AND ORDINARY CIRCUMSTANCES

As we have seen via Part I, sexualizing energies have been rather uniformly and somewhat dramatically encountered in all vital-energy research. As described, they have been encountered as a current through the body, sensation of a slight tingling in the palms of the hands, and other significant parts of the body, notably in the back and the "loins" (i.e., the genital regions).

Within those research encounters, a number of those involved observed that whether weak or strong, such effects are not simply imaginary, because whatever is involved results in tangible experiencing.

But as can be recognized, such phenomena are encountered not only in vital-energy research, but in general human life at all levels. And such general experiencing can sometimes be as dramatic as that encountered in the special cases of vital-energy research.

Indeed, the real existence of invisible, sexualizing energies universally experienced as having tangible qualities is the one ethereal wedge that drives rather deeply into societal responses seeking to suppress knowledge of human energetic phenomena.

One of the more obvious reasons for the societal suppression is that the phenomena are indicative of BIGGER hidden resources of human-energy powers. And it is apparently those powers that, for some mysterious reason, the suppressive mainstream forces feel must better be left unexamined in order to prevent their enhancement.

To reiterate for purposes of emphasis, this is the same as saying that knowledge of invisible sexualizing energies must be suppressed, since they point in the direction of opening up knowledge of other invisible energies, such as telepathy, clairvoyance, psychokinesis, and so forth.

All of those items are closely related to energetic powers,

and as such the central key to their development would consist of more complete knowledge of human energetics overall, and which knowledge would include information about sexual energetics.

As it turns out, though, and rather comically, the suppression of human energetics cannot, at the individual level, also entirely suppress the universal experiencing of sexualizing energetics.

But dumbed-down information about that particular kind of energetics can be achieved by social conditioning that directs focus not on formative and vitalistic sexual energies, but rather misdirects focus upon sexual behavior, the genitalia, and various moralistic containment policies.

Thus, to the degree this misdirecting, dumb-them-down attitude is accepted and reinforced, the farther away is any real cognizance of not only sexual energetics, but the whole of human energetics as well.

THE BASIC SOCIETAL WAY OF DUMBING DOWN HUMAN SENSITIVITIES

A thorough examination of this "problem" reveals that there is a time-tested societal way to prevent this sensing.

This simply involves NOT teaching people how to expand, refine, and hone their innate sensitivities beyond what is needed to fit them into average societal formulas.

TWO DYNAMICS OF SOCIAL CONDITIONING REGARDING PERCEPTION

Most people eventually realize that they may be some kind of victim to social conditioning, and anyway most people realize that social conditioning agendas do exist.

But there is very little real information publicly available as to the METHODS utilized to effect such conditioning.

There is a really big, and complicated story in this regard. But a full part of it is that social conditioning cannot take place very well unless the quite excellent and remarkable perceptions of each human organism are first dumbed down in certain strategic aspects.

After all, any individual who can perceive a whole lot also will become enabled to know a whole lot.

With regard to perception, there are two identifiable dynamics of social conditioning that are worth considering, and certainly so within the contexts of this book and its topics. Very briefly put, it is more or less true that human perceptions can be conditioned by social, cultural, and environmental factors.

There seem to be a number of reasons for this, but one is that the effectiveness of social organizing depends a great deal on uniformity of perceptions among those belonging to the social grouping.

Since most social structures are built up in direct support of some kind of doctrinal ideas, the perceptions of the inhabitants of the structures are educationally conditioned to reflect the doctrinal ideas.

As but one example, the philosophical doctrines of the modern sciences denied the existence of human animating energies. This doctrinal denial resulted in two rather deplorable spectacles:

1. the necessity to trash evidence of the energies to keep the doctrine sanitized; and
2. educational conditioning to deaden perception of the animating energies, or at least to condemn them to high levels of social intolerance if they occurred spontaneously in people.

Another reason, however, is more basic. It has to do with the reality that people need to know what something does or should look like in order:

1. to trust their perceptions when they do occur;
2. to recognize what they are perceiving when and if they do perceive it; and
3. to have some kind of agreement that everyone is seeing the same thing more or less in the same way.

This is perfectly understandable in the light of overall human nature. But there are a few quirks involved.

As but one quirk, it doesn't seem to matter very much if the "same way" is actually the wrong way, or if the same way is completely of illusion in the first place. In either case, uniformity of perception is achieved.

Another quirk is that perceptions are stronger if they are socially tolerated, and weak or non-existent if not tolerated. Indeed, large groups of people can "agree" not to perceive this or that—and they usually don't thereafter.

For example, within science proper exist many topics that scientists have "agreed" not to acknowledge as existing. One of those topics, of course, is human energetics. Thus, a mainstream scientist would not perceive a vitalizing human energy field even if thousands of lives depended on doing so. Further, since agreement not to perceive any factor redolent of human energetics, many such scientists could attack and deconstruct any evidence of them and feel justified in doing so.

As already mentioned, another forbidden topic intuition, and most mainstream scientists have denied the substantial evidence supporting its real existence. This, even though intuition is otherwise credited and documented as saving lives and enabling new inventions.

One of the admitted reasons for the avoidance of intuition is that it ranges too close to a topic utterly forbidden in the mainstream sciences and philosophies, the topic of clairvoyance. Indeed, any serious substantiation of clairvoyance is put down with a vicious enthusiasm at least equal to that pertaining to the wholesale condemnation of human energetics.

Still another quirk involves the fact that people cannot recognize what they are perceiving unless they already know what it is and what it should look like. Indeed, these two very subtle criteria are exceedingly important.

For one thing, people often simply don't perceive something they have never seen before. If they do perceive it, they usually will have to ask someone else what it is. This more or less means that even if someone is sensitive to something, it might not be recognizable in any cognitive sense at all.

THE SOCIETAL TACTIC OF DESENSITIZING SENSITIVITIES

Here we encounter a boon with regard to societal conditioning agendas. All human organisms, in their natural state, are actually equipped with extensive arrays of sensing mechanisms and faculties.

Various formats of societal conditioning would require an

artificially induced desensitizing of entire categories of those sensing mechanisms and faculties.

Indeed, and logically considered, cognitive perceptions are largely dependent on sensing faculties, and if the latter are artificially desensitized, cognitive perceptions must suffer likewise.

There is much more that can be discussed regarding societal conditioning, especially when it comes to both the conventional and psychic force aspects of creativity and power.

Those aspects, however, need to be presented within the contexts of creativity and power, and so we can now segue back into energy phenomena, especially in relationship to the sexualizing energies.

A NOTE ON PERCEIVING SEXUALIZING ENERGIES

While it is possible to think of PERCEPTION as a singular thing, in actuality there exist many different form and qualities of it. Even so, two general categories of perception can be identified:

1. the first consisting merely of sensing or feeling in the absence of images; and
2. the second consisting of sensing, feeling and images combined.

In that the sexualizing energies are invisible, any sensing, feeling or imaging of them qualifies as a form of clairvoyance.

If we return briefly to the five centuries of various kinds of energetic research, one of the more remarkable aspects was that many observers stated that they could not only sense the energies, but literally see them as well.

Those who merely felt the energies described them much as any person would who experiences them as invisible charges, heat, stimulation's in various body parts, especially in the region of the loins, and as having horny or "disturbed" repercussions.

The seers of the energies, however, described them as consisting of rays, protrusions, extensions, fluid-like circulating fields, and beams, and as having lights, colors, and so forth.

Direct perceptions in this regard of the fluid-like, circulating fields, are entirely consistent with many descriptions of the "auras" surrounding and interpenetrating the physical corpus, and the real existence of which has been acknowledged since earliest recorded antiquity.

SOME PRELIMINARY DISTINCTIONS BETWEEN AURA AND ENERGY FIELD

In the chapters that follow, the modern term "energy field" and the ancient term "aura" will be utilized as nearly synonymous, with certain distinctions.

There is a rich tradition regarding what is meant by aura, but hardly any tradition regarding what is meant by energy field. In fact, the use of the energy field metaphor came into existence to escape the modern societal condemnation of the aura metaphor.

But there is another nuance to the distinction. Basically speaking, an aura is what clairvoyants can see. An energy field is what can be measured by instruments designed to do so.

In any event, in the traditional lore the aura is basically conceived of as a luminous radiation and typically composed of different colors.

An examination of the colors as usually described reveals that they correspond to the colors of the visible light spectrum. This can lead to wonderment as to why the colors of the subtle radiations are confined only to the colors of that spectrum, in that the visible light spectrum is only a very small segment of the entire electromagnetic spectrum.

It is quite possible that many of the subtle radiations might not even belong to the electromagnetic spectrum, which reflects the existence only of physical electromagnetic energies —but does not reflect basic animating life-force energies, and which have not been discovered so far.

The point being made here is that because of the lore the aura is conceptualized as being made up of colors. Thus, potential aura-seers can easily be conditioned to expect to perceive the radiations as colorful—when indeed many energies within the aura are colorless.

So, the single concept of colorful radiations does not lend

itself to perceiving aspects of the aura that are colorless, but dynamically present.

In respect of the above, it is probably appropriate to keep in mind the well-known adage that what you expect to see is what you do see, and what you don't expect to see is what you don't see.

But there is a workable clue here. Colors don't produce themselves, but energies as motional vibrations can produce colors. Hence the first goal of the would-be aura seer is to perceive energies.

ARTISTIC REPRESENTATIONS OF THE HUMAN AURA

Regarding the human aura and the astral-aura light realms, artistic representations of them occasionally can be found dating from antiquity onward through the centuries and up until today.

All of these artistic representations deal with or attempt to portray luminosity and light as well as energetic shapes that are usually invisible to the physical eyes, but not to the perceiving, image-making mind.

Among the best-known of the many examples portraying the aura-light-shape realms are the art works of William Blake (1757-1827), the English poet and artist. But there are many other very beautiful examples.

The personal human aura is USUALLY portrayed as a self-contained envelope, or full-body nimbus, around the physical body, usually shown as oval or ovoid in its mistlike contours.

The full-body nimbus is usually shown as extending about two to three feet outside of the physical body.

It consists of fluctuating colors, color layers, and variously shaped energy structures and which sometimes can extend far beyond the margins of the mistlike properties. Good clairvoyants can detect "damaged" areas within the energy body, which are associated with illnesses or with dysfunctional emotionality.

The colors seen are also associated with many kinds of qualities and activities, although there is no general agreement on this matter of colors—except in the case of the color dull black—which clearly and unequivocally portends approaching death. In all cases in which I have seen this kind of dull-blackening aura, even among some of my dearest friends, all have died shortly or within the year or so.

If death is imminent, the aura disintegrates altogether and disappears, although the bio-body might live on for a few days with artificial life support assistance.

It's also worth noting that the aura often turns dull black regarding those who will shortly meet premature or accidental death, as if the energy "intelligence" somehow knows of this in advance.

The historical descriptions of the aura are very important, of course, and very compelling as well, and they certainly have a place within this book.

But leaning too heavily on them tends to obscure another important factor. The traditional concepts portray the aura as light, luminosity and color, while the concept that auras also have SUBSTANCE is marginalized.

Indeed, if the elements of human energetics did not possess substance, then they could not be tangibly FELT, as is particularly the case regarding the sexualizing energies.

So the substance aspect of human energetics must be restored for the purposes of this book, and we will utilize the next chapter to do so.

Chapter 12
THE PSYCHIC FORCE AS AFFLUENT SUBSTANCE

Before reading this book, almost everyone will already have some kind of idea about what the term PSYCHIC means. Such ideas can be exceedingly different among individuals. But it is quite likely that a large proportion of them hinge on the general concept of PARANORMAL mental activity and which is distinguished from normal mental activity.

This is a psychological distinction which began to flourish rather late in the history we have been reviewing. It appeared during the late 1920s, and only during the 1940s did it take on broad usage.

It arose not in parapsychology, but in psychology proper when, during the 1920s psychologists and sociologists sought to identify and establish the characteristics of normal and abnormal behavior.

One of the widely stated motives behind this effort had to do with the idea that if normal behavior was identified and socially reinforced then more perfect societies could be constructed. In a certain sense, this also called for the elimination, or at least the exclusion, of the abnormal.

This, of course, was a rather simplified and naive utopian concept within the then trendy Modern Progressive Era, and as such was supported in its early stages with extraordinary enthusiasm in science, sociology, and psychology.

As it eventually turned out, however, the idea was quietly retired during the late 1950s. The reason is rather amusing and ironic. While it seemed easy enough to identify the abnormal, and then to condemn it as socially undesirable, it proved increasingly difficult to establish what the normal consisted of.

With this psycho-sociological development, parapsychologists of the time became concerned that their topics of study and research would be lumped into the abnormal category, and which indeed was soon the mainstream case.

In seeking to escape this danger, they countered by

indicating that psychic activity and phenomena were not abnormal, but PARAnormal: simply and innocently meaning beyond, above or outside of the normal.

One of the important factors that got covered over in all of this was that the original psychic concept had nothing to do with things mental, psychological, or behavioristic.

This original concept now needs to be firmly recovered, not only for the purposes of this book, but on behalf of human energetics as a whole.

THE ORIGINAL CONCEPT OF PSYCHIC FORCE AS AFFLUENT SUBSTANCE

As we have seen in chapter 9, during the 1870s, Edward William Cox introduced the potent term PSYCHIC into the languages of the world. But he introduced the term not as the noun it later became, but as an adjective specifying a particular type of force among all kinds of forces.

The term AFFLUENT doesn't seem to be used very much anymore. It has two principal definitions, the second of which has to do with being financially wealthy.

Otherwise, it is taken from the Latin AFFLUERE (to flow), and in English came to mean "to flow abundantly," and hence was associated with anything that did so.

Cox, a lawyer, took great care and pains in describing psychic force, and published his descriptions in his 1871 book SPIRITUALISM ANSWERED BY SCIENCE. This is a wonderful book and remains one of the most cogent descriptions not only of the Renaissance concept of vital energies but has direct relationship to the traditional Chinese concept of CH'I energy.

THE AFFLUENT SUBSTANCE

Cox enumerates a number of factors that need to be considered in order to comprehend the nature of psychic force.

He first points up that in Spiritualism it is held that everyone possesses an "amount of animal magnetism," and that animating magnetism is what he, Cox, has renamed "psychic force."

However, whether called animal magnetism or psychic

force, "it" is a "magnetic material" and/or an "affluent substance" that "proceeds from" some kind of human body-matter.

Whatever the affluent substance is and whatever kind of body-matter is involved, it is "projected from the whole or part of the body structure—and, like other forces of nature, is perceptible to our senses only when it meets with some obstacle. All possess it, more or less."

Cox stipulated that the medium who produces physical phenomena "has it more, and thus attracts it from those with whom he [or she] is in communication"—the extended assumption being that those possessing more affluent magnetic substance of whatever kind, stimulate and attract corresponding responses in those who have lesser amounts of it.

The only real problem with the whole of this is that the modern sciences do NOT admit that this kind of magnetism or force exists, even though its existence is continuously experienced by people everywhere.

MAJOR CHARACTERISTICS OF THE AFFLUENT SUBSTANCE

Perhaps on an assumption that Science would come to its senses later on, in his 1871 book, Cox gives a very cogent outline of "The Scientific Theory of Psychic Force."

He itemizes the major characteristics of the force, which I'll try briefly to clarify in order to escape from the complications of Victorian English syntax.

1. There is a Force proceeding, from, or directly associated with, the human organization (read organism, or body structure plus its animating energies).
2. In certain persons and under certain conditions, this Force "can cause vibrations or motion in heavy bodies (such as furniture, other bodies, etc.) external to the person." The Force can also produce audible and palpable sounds in such bodies.
3. The Force does this "without muscular contact or any material connection between" any person present.
4. This Force "appears to be frequently directed by some

intelligence."
5. "For reasons to be specified, we conclude that this Force is generated in certain persons of peculiar nervous organization in sufficient power to operate beyond bodily contact."
6. "There can be little doubt that the Force is possessed by every human being, that it is a NECESSARY [emphasis added] condition of the living nerve, if, indeed, it be not the vital force itself."
7. "In ordinary persons, it ceases to operate at or near the extremities of the nerves; in Psychics it flows beyond them in waves of varying volume and power." At this point in his phenomenological line-up, Cox refers to a Dr. Richardson who also had been examining psychic force, and whom had presented his findings in the POPULAR SCIENCE REVIEW.
8. He [another researcher named Richardson] contends that there is a nerve fluid (or ether), with which the nerves are enveloped, and by whose help it is that the motion of their molecules communicates sensations and transmits the commands of the will.
9. This nerve ether is, he thinks, no other than the vital force. It extends with all of us somewhat beyond the extremities of the nerve structure, and even beyond the surface of the body-encompassing us wholly with an envelope of nerve atmosphere, and which varies in its depth and intensity in various persons. "This [Richardson] contends, will solve many difficult problems in Physiology and throw a new light on many obscurities in Psychology and Mental Philosophy." It might be noted here that the "many obscurities" remain still obscured.
10. "The Force exhibits itself in pulsations or undulations. It is never steadily continuous." However, the tremors caused by the Force in a table, chair, floor, or in organic bodies, are likened to the waves of light or sound.
11. "The differences of the sensation between the operation of the Psychic Force and of muscular force is so manifest as to be palpable instantly to everybody who witnesses [experiences] it."
12. The strength, or power, of the Force is conditional upon

the mental and emotional status of the individual and individuals involved. The Force is "sometimes, but rarely, exhibited when the Psychic is alone. As a rule, the presence of other persons promotes the operations of the Force."
13. The Force "is materially influenced by the electric and magnetic conditions of the atmosphere and of surrounding bodies, by heat and cold, by moisture and dryness, and still more by the nervous conditions of the persons present."
14. As will be examined in the following chapter, characteristics of the Force can be perceived by a variety of clairvoyant means. But if the manifestations of the Force are powerful enough, they can be witnessed by normal perceptions. Exposure to the manifestations sometimes temporarily increases the clairvoyant faculties of individual's in their proximity, faculties which otherwise lay dormant.
15. "The attention of the Psychic" regarding manifestations of the Force is not necessary. This is suggestive that the manifestations of the Force arise from "an UNCONSCIOUS action of the brain, the ganglion, or the nerves."

UNCONSCIOUS CEREBRATION

Cox stated that the manner in which this unconscious action is effected "is undiscovered because it has not been examined scientifically." Then, or now, it might be added. But Cox refers to the matter of "unconscious cerebration."

In order to illuminate the Force as being "frequently directed by some intelligence," Cox next refers to Carpenter's theory of "unconscious cerebration, or, in less learned language, the capacity of the brain, under certain conditions, to work, not only without the will, but without the consciousness of the individual."

"Unconscious cerebration" is identified as "hitherto mysterious mental states which scientific men, unable to explain, have contented themselves with denying or ignoring, [while] unreflecting persons have attributed [the mysterious mental states] to supernatural influences."

In more contemporary terms, unconscious cerebration is probably equivalent to preconscious processes that take place in the subconscious before emerging into consciousness or mental perception.

Indeed, in some fashion, sensory systems ORGANIZE data BEFORE it is forwarded to the conscious intellect. In this sense, then, unconscious cerebration can be thought of as a type of Intelligence functioning beneath conscious awareness.

This matter is not as complicated as it might first sound. Although Cox utilizes sleepwalking and trance states as examples of unconscious cerebration, riding a bicycle or driving a car without consciously thinking about doing so are other examples.

IS PSYCHIC FORCE A FORCE?

After Cox had identified the major characteristics of "the Force," he then goes on to mention: "The term PSYCHIC FORCE has been employed to describe the power or influence that either proceeds from or is intimately associated with the human organization." The term is used "for want of a fitter one, but we call it a FORCE because many of the phenomena present the results of a force."

He compares psychic force to the forces of heat, light, magnetism, electricity, and galvanism as consisting of energetic "particles in motion, making themselves perceptible to our senses when they strike against some opposing matter.

"But it does not follow in this particular [regarding particles in motion] that Psychic Force should resemble those other forces. We call it a force for convenience, but it is doubtful if, strictly speaking, it be a FORCE, but having more the nature of an INFLUENCE than of motion of particles projected and impinging on other bodies."

The term INFLUENCE has several definitions, all associated with "flow" or "flowing." The definition Cox apparently was using is "the act or power of producing an effect without apparent exertion of force or direct exercise of command."

A very early definition of INFLUENCE, however, referred to "an ethereal fluid thought to flow from the stars," or inherent in the universe, "and to affect the actions of men."

THE DIRECT SIMILARITY OF PSYCHIC FORCE TO THE CHINESE CH'I ENERGY

One of the major, but subtle, situations regarding the forms of research we are discussing in this book is the rather broad failure of the modernist West to compare the phenomena of their research with the phenomena of the ancient Chinese Ch'i Gong [sometimes given as Qigong].

The literature is quite large regarding Ch'i energies, and many of the most important, and remarkable, disciplines that download from knowledge of them can be found described in detail.

Anyone wishing to discover sources to extend their knowledge beyond the scope of this book can easily obtain a most competent book entitled THE WAY OF QIGONG--THE ART AND SCIENCE OF CHINESE ENERGY HEALING, by Kenneth S. Cohen, and published in 1997.

In that book, QI or CH'I or chi is defined as "Life energy, vital energy, breath of life force, power, air."

Cohen's book is basically about Chinese energy healing by modulations of Qi energy, and which, with some sense of legitimacy, can be referred to as vital fluids.

But for the purposes of this book having to do with sexualizing energies, his Index reveals a category identified as Sexual Qigong.

Itemized under that heading one can discover the topics of Deer Exercise, ejaculation control, ejaculation frequency, exchanging sexual energies, and so forth.

For this, it is clear that CH'I energetics have sexualizing ramifications. It is through those particular ramifications that we can recognize the similarity to CH'I energies of animal magnetism, odic force, psychic force, and orgone energies.

In this regard, one might even be brave enough to suggest that Mesmer, Reichenbach, Cox, and Reich (and even the photographers of energies) had encountered the phenomena traditionally associated with the ancient Chinese CH'I.

As another immediately available source of information about the existence and uses of CH'I energy, one might refer to the recent, and decidedly rather surprising, 1997 book entitled CHINA'S SUPER PSYCHICS, authored by the CH'I master, Paul Dong, and his associate, Thomas E. Raffill.

In this book, the development of Chinese "super psychic" abilities is directly attributed to the utilization of CH'I energies. The development, via CH'I, includes influencing at a distance, and enhanced forms of clairvoyance, as will be described beginning in the next chapter.

The authors give a description of "chi" (on page 131). They indicate that chi gong has a history of 3,000 years, and so the Chinese have developed many interpretations of it.

In its most widespread definition, in everyday life chi refers to the air we breathe (this a metaphor for "breathing energies.") In terms of the body, it refers to energy. In terms of life it refers to vitality. When talking of activity, it refers to abilities. In other words, as the authors say, its meaning depends on the context.

The term CHI GONG in itself means training the body's energetic abilities and bringing them to their optimal level.

Dong and Raffill also point up (again on page 131) that in addition to its medical value, Chinese researchers had discovered, by 1979, that chi gong is a catalyst via which "many people had developed psychic powers." The book gives numerous examples of those developed, and quite impressive, psychics.

Chapter 13
CLAIRVOYANCE— TELESTHESIA

The continuing exploration of the denied science of human sexual energies requires that we continue examining certain terms in order to grasp their deeper meanings beyond the merely superficial. Many of those terms are commonly utilized in a general sense, but without any in-depth idea of what they mean, especially as regards their forgotten historical background.

Other terms that are very valuable have dropped out of use, largely because certain researchers sought to avoid them. Thus, the terminology games researchers played often caused the same phenomena to be referred to one way and then another.

Additionally, some terms have been assigned so many meanings that except in some ambiguous way one can't ever be quite sure what is actually being referred to.

Two of these terms are CLAIRVOYANCE and TELESTHESIA, both of which are meaningful to the sensing/perceiving of sexual energies.

THE COMPLEX NATURE OF CLAIRVOYANCE

The term CLAIRVOYANCE first appeared in French at about 1503, but doesn't seem to have been incorporated into English until more than 300 years later, at about 1847.

It has several meanings in French. But in English it is generally used only with the one meaning associated with it in 1847, which links the English use of the term to mesmeric phenomena.

CLAIRVOYANCE: a faculty attributed to certain persons, or to persons under certain Mesmeric conditions, consisting of the mental perception of objects at a distance or concealed from sight.

This English definition sounds competent enough on the

surface, and it is easy to link it to the "second sight" of the Irish, and to the "seership" faculties of shamans worldwide. But beyond that it doesn't really enlighten one all that much. So it is helpful to survey the meanings given to the French terms CLAIR and VOYANCE.

CLAIR refers to light, brightness, clearness, luminous, transparent, limpid, and to bright or transparent colors, shapes, and forms, and even to invisible clarity. VOYANCE refers to seeing. And so the first meaning of clairvoyance in French is, of course, seeing clearly.

Many people have been socially conditioned to suppose they don't have clairvoyant faculties. But this merely results from mind-conditioning and social reality-making by selective nomenclature.

Everyone possesses clairvoyance. For example, if clairvoyance is defined literally as consisting of mental perception other than by sight, and if one is not utilizing one's eyes while sleeping, then the perception of one's dreams actually is a type of clairvoyance.

Often the eyes remain open during daydreaming, but what the eyes are seeing often disappears from view. It's quite safe to say that the eyes don't really see what is being clairvoyantly seen either in daydreaming or sleep dreaming.

Inventors, artists, architects, engineers, "conceptualists" and so forth are actually very good at seeing their works before they are rendered into physical form so that the eyes can then see them.

Then there are the phenomena of "seeing with the Mind's Eye" or "envisioning" or "intuiting" or "visualizing," and all of which, except for the different nomenclature referencing, are types or degrees of clairvoyance.

Strictly speaking in retrospect, the use in English of the term clairvoyance was probably not a very good idea. It would have been more accurate to refer to the "second sight" of the Scots and the Irish, since clairvoyance more literally refers to a second sight if compared to the first sight of the physical eyes.

In 1920, James Lewis Spence (1874-1955), born and educated in Scotland, published an authoritative ENCYCLOPEDIA OF OCCULTISM, this being the first attempt to sort out the swamp of nomenclature involved.

Spence also published more than forty other valuable works

dealing with mythology, folklore and the occult, and especially elucidating upon the Atlantis theme.

Spence more or less solidified the definition of CLAIRVOYANCE as: "A term denoting the supposed supernormal faculty of seeing persons and events which are distant in time or place, and of which no knowledge can reach the seer through the normal sense-channels."

As such, according to Spence, CLAIRVOYANCE may roughly be divided into three classes:

- Perception of the past
- Perception of the future
- Perception of contemporary events happening at a distance, or outside the range of the normal vision.

Why Spence did not include as a form of clairvoyance the perception of vital energies, auras and energy fields is something of a mystery. Here, of course, we will add this fourth general category.

A number of important subdivisions of clairvoyance had been established earlier, at about 1890 and researched thereafter—albeit under certain strange nomenclature, such as telopsia and telecognosis, which didn't quite catch on for reasons that might be obvious. Others did, however. For example:

- X-ray vision (which did catch on)
- Traveling clairvoyance (which also caught on)
- Medical clairvoyance (which didn't catch on, but is making a comeback today (and in this book, as well))
- Platform-clairvoyance (see below)
- Macro clairvoyance
- Micro clairvoyance
- Hypnotic and trance clairvoyance
- Ecstasy clairvoyance
- Psychometric clairvoyance
- Mixtures of clairvoyance and telepathy
- Telesthesia clairvoyance

A much longer list of clairvoyance types is available, but not needed here, with the exception of sexuality clairvoyance, which before now has never been included in any lists of clairvoyance types.

As a joyous aside, some might wonder what "platformclairvoyance" is. It was the term assigned to the seeing of spirits, incorporeal entities, including ghosts, and deathbed (or near-death) visions which we today refer to as near-death experiences.

The term "platform" was taken from the platforms provided during seances on which spirits manifested to be seen by the sitters. The sensitives and mediums who manifested etherializing force energies also often sat on platforms. The proper term should be, of course, spirit clairvoyance.

Medical clairvoyance is another interesting term. To get at its definition, we should first remember that clairvoyance was defined as a supernormal mode of perception which results in a visual image being presented to the conscious (or dreaming) mind.

Medical clairvoyance was thus conceptualized as the faculty to see the inner mechanisms of the human body, diagnose disease, and perceive the human body aura and its constituents, its shifting colors, shapes, forms, extensions, and etc., its energies.

Excluding the recalcitrant modernist mainstream, that medical clairvoyance exists has been established beyond doubt. So, if medical clairvoyance is possible, certainly mere sexual clairvoyance is also.

The basis for medical clairvoyance was quite accepted in antiquity. Many records describe that medical healers employed clairvoyants (seers) to diagnose or asked their patients to dream about what was wrong with them, or asked oracles, omen-readers, or diviners (all clairvoyant seers) to do the same service.

In this respect, though, the idea of biological clairvoyance might be useful. The best term, however, might be bio-psychic clairvoyance—via which both the physical and psychic factors of the human being can be clairvoyantly seen and described.

TELESTHESIA AS A FORM OF CLAIRVOYANCE

By 1882, it had been found that the clairvoyant communications between distant persons were not only comprised of "seeing" phenomena, but that such phenomena also often incorporated transference of thought, transference of emotions, transference of motor impulses, and of "many impressions not easy to define."

As might be suspected, this latter comment referred to transference of sexual energies at some second-sight level other than the first sight level of the eyeballs.

Regarding the transference of thought, etc., Sir William Crookes had indicated something you might wish to read slowly:

"It is known that the action of thought is accompanied by certain molecular movements in the brain, and here we have physical vibrations capable from their extreme minuteness of acting direct on individual molecules, while their rapidity approaches that of the internal and external movements of the atoms themselves."

Sir William's statement remains one of the best regarding the basis of thought as molecular-atomic activity, and it was accepted as such back during the 1870s.

But when the context of this statement was applied to the problem of clairvoyant transference, it became quite evidential that the transfer also produced certain resonating molecular movements in the brain, and which molecular movements had vibrations capable of acting directly on individual systems. This led to the idea that there were varieties of "clairvoyance" beside the "seeing" kind.

There was, first of all, the thought-transference kind of clairvoyance which was not a seeing kind. To distinguish between the two, the term TELEPATHY was ultimately seized upon to denote the difference between seeing clairvoyance and thought-transference clairvoyance. This term caught on and swiftly became popular because it was easy to think of thought-transference as a kind of "mental radio."

TELEPATHY refers to thoughts across distance. It is an emulation of the radio-broadcasting model. During the 1880s theories abounded regarding utilizing electromagnetic radiation and waves for a cross-distance wireless communication. The term RADIO was taken from radiating. Radio broadcasting was shortly demonstrated in 1901.

There remained, however, the problem of emotions and motor impulses across distance, and which were still incorporated within the general grab-all bag of clairvoyance. The transfer across distance of emotions and motor impulses did not involve "sight" or "telepathy"—and so new terms were needed to denote them.

The transfer of emotions was referred to as "empathy transference;" this term did not catch on for long and has never been replaced. So few of us realize that not only do our telepathic thoughts transfer across distances, but that our emotions do likewise, especially our sexualizing ones.

In 1882, F. W. H. Myers (1843-1901), a leading mind in early psychical research, coined a new term—TELESTHESIA—to denote motor impulse transfers across distances.

The THESIA part of this term is taken from the Greek AISTHESIS meaning perception of sensations. It is most familiar to us when combined as ANETHESIA, i.e., utilizing chemicals to deaden or to cause a loss of the perception of sensations.

There was, and still is, much evidence for the existence of telesthesia. Mothers, for example, when their children are hurt elsewhere at some distance away and out of sight, often feel sensations in the exact same place where the child is being wounded, plus knowing that the "hurt" refers to their children.

There are proven examples of telesthesia in the psychical literature. For example, the case of a Mrs. Fussey at Wimbledon, England, on November 4, 1914, is typical and famous. At home she suddenly felt in her arm the sharp sting of a wound. She immediately exclaimed that "Tab [her soldier son in France] is wounded in the arm. I know it!" The following Monday, confirmation arrived in the form of a telegram.

The most familiar experiencing of telesthesia world-wide, however, is sexual vibe sensing which is a combination of clairvoyance and telesthesia in that telesthesia is a transfer of sensations that affect involuntary motor impulses transferred across distance.

As a term, however, TELESTHESIA did not catch on, even though its sister term, TELEPATHY, did.

TELESTHESIA was meant to denote the clairvoyant transfer across distance of motor impulses, and "many impressions not easy to define." Again, we are among sex-loaded code words of the Victorian age when sex was taboo.

Clearly, many kinds of stimulating motor impulses might be transferred across distance, some of which we are even today quite familiar with, aren't we?

No one in their right mind will deny that certain "motor impulses" are part and parcel of sexual "communicating" and with emotional motor-impulse responses to it.

Indeed, if in some energetic fashion the sexual motor impulses did not activate and gear up, then there would be no responses to sexual vibes whether their source is near or far.

We are now prepared to move on to the next great saga of an earlier researcher of human energetics. The terms discussed in this chapter won't be used, because Karl von Reichenbach's work took place before those terms became fashionable. But you will recognize the experiential concepts of various kinds of clairvoyance and telesthesia.

Chapter 14
BEYOND CLAIRVOYANCE— LUCIDITY

If there was nothing more beyond what has been examined so far, then this book would constitute not much more than a special historical treatment of human sensing factors and sexualizing energies rejected by the modernist mainstream sciences and philosophies of the cultural West.

But there IS something more, a factor so ultra-strange that it has taken the first half of this book to erect a reality approach to it. The ultra-strange factor is identified as LUCIDITY. And this and the next four chapters will be required to provide adequate background materials in order to flesh it out.

DEFINITIONS OF LUCIDITY

LUCID is an adjective, and means suffused with light, luminous, brightness, translucent, having full use of one's faculties, sane, and clear to the understanding.

LUCIDITY is a noun. Two definitions of it are found in Webster's.

The first is given as "clearness of thought or style," and in this sense it is a completely acceptable word even within mainstream workings.

Its second established definition, however, might come as a surprise—and, all things considered, even as somewhat of a shock: "The capacity to perceive the truth directly and instantaneously: clairvoyance."

It is the background history of this second definition that must now be examined for two reasons.

First, lucidity is not merely clairvoyance, but a super format of it, and so the definition above does little to enlighten very much.

Second, there is a very big story involved and which has many complicated aspects.

However, any real appreciation of the lucidity story must begin by making an attempt to bring at least a modicum of authenticity to clairvoyance itself as a necessary human attribute.

THE ABSOLUTE NECESSITY OF CLAIRVOYANT FACULTIES

The general gist of this and the next four chapters can be brought to light via the following brief discussion having to do with the necessity of clairvoyant faculties that enable perception of invisible factors, energies, and forces.

We can get into this by posing an important and larger-picture question about what is actually needed for best chance and optimum human survival.

If one takes enough time to assess the fundamental attributes human organisms need for best-chance survival, those attributes, in the bigger picture, will be seen as two-fold: the absolute necessity of sensing the visible-tangible AND the invisible-intangible.

There is a simple computation involved that helps erect the needed reality here. If one can't sense the invisible, one stands a very good chance of getting clobbered by it. This DOES NOT aid in survival, and there is a fair amount of historical documentation to back this up.

Give or take a little, THIS simple computation was more or less understood as REAL by most societies up until the time the modern mainstream sciences "went" materialistic-only.

This event (formulated at about 1845) erected the five-physical-senses-only paradigm, and whose assumed authenticity thereafter required the deconstruction of clairvoyant faculties that could sense the invisible.

It is abundantly true that the five physical senses alone can usually go a long way toward survival, although what survival is considered to consist of has some bearing on this.

But the five physical senses alone can often be quite notoriously inadequate when, for example, it comes to such matters as foreseeing what is going to happen, and when it will. Since antiquity, this foreseeing activity has been the principal role in all pre-modern cultures for clairvoyance under any format or name.

But in the sense of this small discussion, the consideration is not between the five physical senses and clairvoyance (and various pro and con attitudes regarding them), but more pointedly between sensing both the visible and the invisible.

Thus, all human organisms are naturally endowed with clairvoyant sensing faculties, and this is the principal reason they keep emerging down through the generations in spite of any societal resistance to them.

It might be added that the modern sentiments against clairvoyance have made such an illogical mess of this that it's of little wonder that the simple factors occluded within it are difficult to perceive.

Thus, if it can be stipulated that the human organism is naturally endowed in some way to sense invisibles, then the concept of clairvoyance is authentic.

However, such natural endowments will fall into certain characteristics in respect of all-natural endowments.

Generally speaking, it is broadly understood that all-natural endowments are only of a POTENTIAL nature. And it is understood as well that such potentials need to be actively nurtured, focused, honed, and somehow perfected if they are to achieve any kind of optimum efficiency.

The distinction between natural clairvoyant faculties and lucidity is that the latter comes into functioning only if methods of artificial enhancement are undertaken.

The story of lucidity is therefore the tale of one such enhancement procedure.

TO BEGIN THE STRANGE STORY OF LUCIDITY

The story of lucidity begins as follows. The nature of clairvoyance and other energetic sensing principles are found itemized and explained in ancient Eastern sources.

During the latter half of the nineteenth century these were investigated by a number of Westerners, some of whom had the enthusiastic idea of activating their own extended perceptual powers more or less based on the ancient Eastern knowledge routes.

And among those Westerners we now encounter a particular individual. I will introduce him in the following way.

In antiquity there was a time when it could be said that all roads led to Rome. In much the same way, it can be said that all roads regarding modern concepts of the aura and clairvoyance lead back to the clairvoyant superpowers of one rather startling individual named Charles Webster Leadbeater.

Leadbeater was such a complex, larger-than-life figure that his personality and psychology will probably never be sorted out. Thus, there are many approaches to introducing and discussing his cultural-shaping impacts.

Here, however, we are principally interested only in his clairvoyant faculties, and so first and foremost, it is important to determine if his clairvoyant superpowers were authentic. And there is some startling, but compelling evidence in this regard.

CHARLES WEBSTER LEADBEATER—
CLAIRVOYANT SUPERSTAR

Charles Webster Leadbeater (1854-1934) began his active life as a British clergyman, but soon joined the Theosophical Society in which he was to play a prominent part.

He established a close working relationship with Annie Besant (1847-1933), another prominent Theosophist and eventual successor of Madame Helena Petrovna Blavatsky, the original power founder of Theosophy. It is apparent that Besant was no mean clairvoyant herself, but evidence relative to her faculties is not as clear-cut.

The headquarters of the world Theosophical Movement was in Adyar, India. During the years just preceding 1908, Leadbeater and Besant teamed up to utilize "micro-clairvoyance" to perceive molecular and atomic particles.

Micro-clairvoyance (a modern term) is one of the several super sentient faculties itemized, in the very ancient Siddhi literature of the Indian Subcontinent, as "Knowledge of the small, the hidden or the distant by directing the light of superphysical faculty."

It is not all that clear why the clairvoyant duo took an interest in micro-clairvoyance. But they set about working assiduously at this fabulous enterprise in order to clairvoyantly see and systematically describe the atomic and sub-atomic particles of all chemical substances.

As might be expected, this effort consumed a number of years. But in 1908, the dynamic clairvoyant duo finally caused the Theosophists to publish the results in a rather ponderous tome entitled OCCULT CHEMISTRY: CLAIRVOYANT OBSERVATIONS OF THE CHEMICAL ELEMENTS.

Most Theosophists then seem to have been completely bewildered by the voluminous book and its profusion of graphic illustrations of what molecular and atomic particles looked like. None the less it was revised and added to in a second even larger edition in 1919 by the two authors who had discovered more unknown micro-clairvoyant facts about chemical elements. And, after their deaths, it was enlarged in 1946 and again in 1951. The reason for the postmortem enlargements was most astonishing.

After the invention of the electron microscope (first developed in Germany in 1932,) it could begin to be seen that the clairvoyant drawings of Leadbeater and Besant of the atomic and sub-atomic particles of the elements corresponded almost exactly to what the electron microscopes revealed.

Additionally, the clairvoyants had illustrated some elements which, at the time, were not known to exist, but later were discovered, and had correctly identified their atomic structures.

In 1980, the American physicist, Stephen M. Phillips, in exacting detail pulled this entire story together in a book entitled EXTRASENSORY PERCEPTION OF QUARKS—a "quark" being an elusive elemental particle whose existence was not even suspected until the 1960s.

Had the clairvoyant duo of Leadbeater and Besant identified the structure of quarks?

Yes, indeed, hence the name of Phillips' book.

But they had identified practically everything right down to the spin and electromagnetic valences of the most elemental particles.

"How could two Theosophists, now long dead, identify chemical elements unknown to scientists of their day?" mused Phillips in two popular articles published in FATE magazine of April and May 1987.

Needless to say, conventional physicists ran and are still running for the hills regarding this triumphant clairvoyant success.

But for reasons decidedly obscure, it is perhaps equally

meaningful (somehow) that this success caused not so much as a ripple in contemporary parapsychology, and which otherwise is always on the lookout for proof-positive of ANY Psi faculty.

Due to the remarkable confirmations obtained after Leadbeater's death, there can be no doubt that his micro-clairvoyance was not only authentic (since it WAS authenticated), but also on the order of some unusual kind of magnitude. There is simply no other explanation.

The human species may indeed possess rudimentary clairvoyant faculties. But the remarkable micro-clairvoyance of Leadbeater and Besant can arise only as the result of some kind of very controlled enhancement methods and processes. Unfortunately, what these enhancement methods consisted of have not yet been distilled out from the massive collections of Theosophical documents.

SEXUALIZING ENERGY ENHANCEMENT OF CLAIRVOYANCE

But there IS one essential clue, at least in the case of Leadbeater. It is, however, a clue that no one—repeat, no one—will touch with a ten-foot pole. It resembles something like a forbidden meteoroid obliquely glancing off of Earth's atmosphere and heading back into the dark reaches of space.

As it transpired, Leadbeater caused the Theosophical Society to be embroiled in, of all things, extraordinary (and rather hilarious) sex scandals, the nature of which are usually reduced to the lowest common and standard denominators of moralistic confusions. As it turned out, however, Leadbeater AND Theosophy managed to survive these.

As with even simple sex matters, it is exceedingly difficult to describe the central and entirely complex factors of the most major of those scandals. So the better part of valor here is to attempt to describe what was involved as candidly as possible. It is quite clear that Leadbeater was interested in sexual energies, and that he probably could clairvoyantly see them and their scintillating activities.

His approach to these was probably organized around some kind of esoteric Tantra "exercises" via which the sexual energies could be transmuted upwards (as it might be thought) to invigorate and activate (or empower) other more refined sentient energies that might respond to such triggering.

In fact, there are rich traditions in antiquity regarding the communal ritualizing of this kind of thing to trigger catharsis somewhat along the lines experienced around Anton Mesmer's vats.

But there is another important aspect involved. It was given extensive attention by Freud within the contexts he outlined for the LIBIDO, defined in Webster's, believe it or not, as "emotional or psychic energy derived from primitive biological urges and usually goal directed, i.e., sex drive."

SEXUALLY DERIVED CATHEXIS

However, about 2,500 years before Freud, a quite similar, but much more dignified, concept existed in ancient Greece—CATHEXIS referring to "the INVESTMENT [emphasis added] of libidinal energy in a person, object, or idea."

In the sense used in this definition, INVESTMENT referred to "an outer layer, or envelope" and which in terms of human energetics places us in the proximity of the aura as the energy field that envelopes the physical aspects of the body.

The CATHEXIS concept (giving name to a type of peak experiencing) also draws close to the modern concept that sexual energies can be transmuted into creative ones, albeit the nature of the transmutating steps between the sexual and the creative energies remain conspicuously ambiguous and absent so far.

Another way of putting this, as many have done, is to suggest that there can be connections between sexual orgasm and so-called psychic orgasm. It is helpful, though, to clarify these types of orgasm as sex energy orgasm and psychic force orgasm.

In any event, it is obvious that Leadbeater was attempting to opportune the transmutating investiture of productive cathexis by means historically remembered.

This is to say, to do so via communal, participatory ritualizing of the sexual energies. This, if successfully pulled off, is a little difficult to articulate.

But the idea was that it would "lift" the sexual energies toward triggering the energetic empowerment of "higher" faculties, and within whose scope the faculties of super-clairvoyance, super-lucidity, etc., would be brought online.

Here it can be mentioned that although Wilhelm Reich utilized different terms and concepts, his orgasm-orgone research led toward achieving cathexis much along the same line as Leadbeater's work.

Now, considering the ultra-prudish, sex-freakish Victorian times involved, it might reasonably be expected that ANY format of all this, if publicly known, would undergo extensive censure. Leadbeater's method, though, was certain to get him into deep kimchi or do-do. And so it transpired.

As all achieved Tantric experts do, Leadbeater distinguished between the qualities, functions, and powers of the female and male sexual energies.

Presumably because males and females have somewhat different energy equipment, waves, flows, frequencies, they each have different needs. Thus, there is a logic to the idea that the uplifting energies of the two sexes should be "developed" separately from each other.

Leadbeater's charisma (there can be no doubt that he possessed high voltages of it) was such that he attracted a "court" of youngish males perpetually around him, and which never numbered less than twenty or so.

Leadbeater was an early sex liberationist, indicating that full sexual experiencing within concomitants of guilt had an authentic place in life. Due to the prudery of the times, he covertly advocated the therapeutic advantages of masturbation, teaching it and the best ways of obtaining full therapeutic benefits from it.

His court, however, had an inner circle of students (chelas), numbering about six or so, who were advanced in their studies.

Hoping to achieve the cathexis investiture of the higher energetic envelope, they all reposed in a circle and attempted to utilize synchronized masturbation to trigger the higher powers.

This process required two important provisos, rather strenuous it would seem:

1. that all involved were to time their physical ejaculations to the same precise moment; and
2. that the electrifying jolts of climaxing ecstasy experienced was, by each participant, to be lifted, by

deliberate attention and will, above mere erotic enjoyment in the attempt to transmute that ecstasy "upward" so as to mutually energize the "higher energy vehicles" of all involved.

The exacting, simultaneous coordination among six or so young males required, of course, a lot of practice.

But history had it that the Spartans had succeeded in this, thereby making them a Force to be dealt with, as well as had various elements of ancient Persia, Babylon, Egypt, Macedonia, and of course, ancient India from which the exoteric and esoteric Tantric formulas had emerged in the first place.

When news of these activities gradually became more broadly known, the Theosophical Society was of course embroiled in rather sensational "scandals." One vocal critic indicated that the Society had been "laid to ruin, and by one man."

Leadbeater temporarily retired from the ruin and voyaged to Australia, where he developed an even stronger following, but eventually was received back into the Society as a most honored "Elder Brother."

Those who have attempted to analyze this particular aspect of the Elder Brother's life have not coped with it very well, possibly because they were embarrassed by it. However, the analysts of Leadbeater were probably not well versed in Tantric matters, or in the history of sexual catharsis of Ancient Greece and Egypt.

With those historical factors in mind, it would have been clear that Leadbeater did not completely invent the methods, and that there was a more than adequate historical basis for them regarding therapeutic catharsis and metaphysical cathexis as established in antiquity.

This historical basis revealed the existence of a power-link between unobstructed sexual energies and unobstructed higher creative, empowering functions, concepts of which infused the so-called "Mystery Schools" of antiquity.

And here, it must be said, is a solitary clue as to why subsequent societies (including the modernist ones), which are NOT prepared to endorse wide-spread development of higher powers, have always felt it necessary to erect layers of intolerance and confusion not only around the higher powers but around sexuality issues also.

Put another way, that unobstructed sexual experiencing and realization can, under certain circumstances, lead to activation of the human faculties of high states of lucidity.

Much of all of this seems to have been incorporated into the astonishing persona of Charles Webster Leadbeater. And so it can easily be understood why, on the one hand, he represented several layers of societal "threat," but why, on the other hand, he embodied a super-magnetic charisma somewhat impervious to various machinations of societal denting.

Perhaps as a last analysis, the micro-clairvoyant Leadbeater-Besant duo espied and illustrated (in drawings) the "anatomy" of chemical and atomic particles, and the patterns of their energies, before it became possible to do so by technically advanced methods.

They identified several chemical-atomic particles, the existence of which were only scientifically discovered decades later.

Eighty or so years after their book OCCULT CHEMISTRY several hundred pages in length, their percentage of error has turned out to be so small as to be negligible.

At various points in his life, Leadbeater was very prolific in writing about fluidic vital energies of all kinds.

Ultimately, these will in the future be compared to discoveries, via advanced technologies, of human energetic fields, otherwise once known as AURAS.

Chapter 15
AURA

The term AURA is taken from the Greek word meaning "breeze or air." Thus, breeze-air is a basic metaphor for those kinds of energies that constitute the aura. Implicit in the breeze-air concept are the factors of invisibility and motion but which are tangible. The basic concept for the aura, then, is of invisible, air-like energies that are in motion and are tangible.

This motional aspect must deliberately be carried in mind, because artistic and photographic representations of auras tend to show them as static and motionless. In English, AURA is defined as:

1. a subtle sensory stimulus, or a distinctive atmosphere surrounding a given source; and
2. a luminous radiation; a subjective sensation (as of lights) experienced because of unidentified mental constituents, or before or during various kinds of altered states of consciousness."

Sources other than dictionaries also stipulate that AURA can consist of "a subjective sensation (as of lights) that frequently precedes creativity and visionary experiencing," while "lights" also go off in peoples' heads regarding sexualizing stimuli.

Even though the use of the term aura has become commonplace, the phenomenon the term signifies is actually composed of a number of subsidiary phenomena, each having different characteristics.

The all-encompassing term perhaps should be the one utilized in antiquity: AUREOLE. This denoted "radiant lights around the head or body."

Within the aureole are aural lights and different kinds of transparent "air or breezes" usually seen and pictured as undulating colors.

SUBTLE EMANATIONS OF ANY SUBSTANCE

AURA was first used about 1398 in its ancient context as denoting a breeze or a zephyr.

It was shortly thereafter used to denote a subtle emanation or exhalation of any substance, such as the smell of blood or the color and odor of flowers, but especially regarding "the volatile essence of the soul, that ethereal aura."

ELECTRICAL ATMOSPHERES AND FLUIDIC PLASMA

By 1732, the term was being used, by Benjamin Franklin among others, in the contexts of "electrical atmospheres," not only of the physical kind, but of more subtle kinds.

This, perhaps, could be likened to later concepts of "plasma"—sometimes defined as "a fluidic part" of something as distinguished from suspended part of solid materials.

There is a connection here to plastics (after they were invented) in their sense of solid materials that are pliable, bendable, capable of adapting, and can return to their original formative shape.

MUSCLE JUICES AND AURAS OF THE SEMINAL FLUID

By 1836, aura was also sometimes used in an anatomical sense, apparently with some scientific foresight, in the contexts of "a juice that can be expressed from muscles;" and "the patterns of growth-fecundation are attributable to the agency of an aura from the seminal fluid."

Give or take a little, this, in 1836, is particularly impressive, because advanced genetic research only today is beginning to understand that our genetic materials may in fact be more made up of bio-electromagnetic patterns (or bio-blueprints) which are "carried" by the physical molecular DNA proteins. These are the patterns which are transferred to the next generations.

THE TANGIBLE AND EMOTIONAL AURA

By 1863, AURA was being used in the context of: "On approaching the hand to the whirl in motion, a slight draught is felt due to the movement of the electrified air [in addition to air motion itself.] This draught or wind is known as the electric aura, and which might tingle the skin."

This concept is quite akin to F. W. H. Myers 1882 concept of telesthesia, which was discussed earlier. Telesthesia consists of the transference of emotions and motor impulses that elicit similar responses in those that receive the transference. The electric aura seemingly would elicit such responses.

RODS, UNDULATING BEAMS, AND TRANSPARENT EMANATIONS

As strange as it seems, and even though it is quite an old term, AURA seems NOT to have been vigorously applied to descriptions of the phenomena dealt with by Mesmer, Reichenbach, or applied to the Psychic Force, or to Reich's Orgone energy.

Rather, the phenomena of these, when perceived, were described NOT as auras but as emanations usually transparent, further consisting of lights, rods, undulating beams, fogs, mists, and subtle energies, etc., always in motion.

Here is an interesting clue to something that is difficult to articulate. If one clairvoyantly focuses on trying to perceive an aura, the chances are that it will not be seen.

But if one focuses on trying to perceive energies, lights, rods, mists, etc., the chances of clairvoyant perceptions seem to increase.

WHAT THE AURA SHOULD LOOK LIKE

Perceptions of aureoles during the modern times have undergone several phases, the nature of the phases being determined by influential persons who wrote about the phenomena in ways distinctive to them.

The distinctions as set forth often acted to condition the followers of influential persons, and thus arguments have arisen in various occult and visionary camps as to WHAT the aura really should look like.

Many hearsay descriptions, although not altogether inaccurate, were given something of a jolt with the emergence into the energetics scene of one Walter J. Kilner.

THE HUMAN ATMOSPHERE

Modern descriptions of auras go back to the early nineteenth century. But the first individual to really electrify modern consciousness during the twentieth century was Dr. Walter J. Kilner (1847-1920).

Kilner, a medical doctor, became a member of the Royal College of Physicians in 1883, conducting a private medical practice in London, and at St. Thomas's Hospital where he consulted in electro-therapy.

He was familiar with the work of Baron von Reichenbach, and seems to have worked, behind the medical scenes, with clairvoyants in attempts to distinguish the differences and changes in the auras in sickness and health—and, somewhat to reprise Hyppolite Baraduc, at death.

Around 1908, just as the manuscript of OCCULT CHEMISTRY was being prepared for print in India, Kilner got the idea that the human aura, hitherto usually visible only by clairvoyant means, might be made visible if "viewed through a suitable filter."

After a number of experiments to identify what such a filter might consist of, he found that the substance dicyanin, a coal-tar derivative (a fallout discovery of Reichenbach), was effective for his purposes of revealing the aura.

Unfortunately, the EXACT nature of his "dicyanin screen" seems to have been lost to posterity.

In any event, his "screen" consisted of a solution of dicyanin coal-tar dye between two hermetically sealed pieces of glass, and which solution gave the color green to the filter.

Looking through it first in daylight, either to desensitize or hyper-sensitize the eye, and then turning the eye on a naked man in dim light before a dark background, "three distinct radiations, all laying in the ultra-violet end of the spectrum, became visible."

The first was dark and colorless, and it surrounded the body to a depth of a quarter to a half inch. Kilner called this the "etheric double."

The second, the inner aura (to distinguish it from the third outer aura), extended about three inches beyond the etheric double, while the third, the outer aura, fell a little short of a foot in depth.

Kilner tried various other experiments. He found that the depth of the aura is influenced by a magnet, that it is sensitive to electric currents to the extent of "completely vanishing under a negative charge from a Wilmhurst machine and increasing to an additional 50 percent after the charge dissipates."

The overall auras were "also affected by the vapors of various chemicals, and to loss of brilliance in hypnosis. Illness affects both the aura's size and color. Impairment of the mental powers causes a diminution in size and distinctness. Nervous diseases result in well observable changes in all three of the auras."

From all this, Dr. Kilner concluded that "the higher brain centers" are intimately concerned in the "nerve-aura" and the "nerve atmospheres." He also indicated that "with the approach of death the aura gradually shrinks, and no trace of it is later discovered around the corpse."

He also laid claim to the discovery that the aura may be affected by an effort of will, and that it may be projected to a longer distance from the body and change its shape and colors." This claim, however, is not original to Kilner, since it was understood in China, India, and Mesopotamia as early as 2,500 B.C.

From the differences in the aura, Kilner also drew numerous medical conclusions having to do with defining illness and healing cures. He also found that the auras of different people may show "attraction," that they may "be blended and become more intense by doing so."

His experiments along these lines are not described in detail, but we sense that we are on somewhat familiar and recognizable ground here at least as regards sexuality attracting because of intensification via becoming "blended."

Although not reported in his subsequent books, it was known that his findings also included observations that "sexual arousal expanded the auras, causing them to intensify, and sometimes filling the room."

The logical assumption here is that Kilner and others actually viewed sexual arousal via the dicyanin screen.

Kilner first published a not very large, but quite momentous book entitled THE HUMAN ATMOSPHERE (1911).

This reported on the experiments he had undertaken enabling him and others to see, with their eyes, that "atmosphere." This book turned scientific and popular society on their heads at the time.

And for the next three decades, the human atmosphere revelations of Kilner's books acted like a blast furnace.

Very many undertook to experiment along similar lines, but Kilner and his immediate colleagues seem to have been the best to perceive the aura, indicating that perhaps he had a little true clairvoyant boost in addition to his screens.

Because Kilner had reported that the aura "may be PROJECTED," and that auras could attract, mix, and become more intense by doing so, numerous experiments by others were designed to follow up on these particular aspects.

The seminal reason here was that people might, by "auric will," influence each other's auras, and the advantages of this seemed obvious enough. But this aspect of Kilner's work approached dangerously close to what was feared the most in modernist mainstream enclaves—INFLUENCE from or at a distance.

Thus, the now predicable troubles began. The "exteriorization of nerve-energy" was objectionable to modern scientific thinking, as we have earlier seen since such was entirely redolent of the empowerment of direct mind-influencing concepts.

Although Kilner did achieve many medical endorsements, science in general remained dismissive of his findings.

SCIENCE DISCOVERS THE THERMAL AURA

Scientific resistance to Kilner's aura findings was maintained until the first "thermal auras" near the surface of the skin were photographed with infrared methods during the 1970s.

These auras proved to be about a quarter to a half inch in depth, as reported in SCIENTIFIC AMERICAN and other mainstream sources.

The thermal auras, infrared in nature, and thus darkly shadowed, had been seen by clairvoyants, including C. W.

Leadbeater, as the "dark" etheric double.

The revelations of thermal photography more or less matched the perceptions of clairvoyants, although THAT comparison was not pointed up in mainstream media reporting on thermal auras.

However, the "thermal auras" provided a new mystery. Whereas if only heat were being produced, then it would bleed off into the air around. But the thermal auras had a distinct edge to them, through which body-heat emissions were nowhere seen to escape. Since body-heat emissions do escape, the implication was that some other kind of energy was perhaps involved.

AURAS AS ENERGY FIELDS

Because the early modernist mainstream sciences had unequivocally denounced any possible existence of auras of ANY kind, something of an embarrassing situation arose as various kinds of technical electromagnetic detecting equipment became available.

One way to disarm the increasingly embarrassing situation was simply to adopt terminology that had never been utilized by the clairvoyant contingents.

Thus, the new detecting equipment revealed not aura pulsations, but electromagnetic fields that pulsated.

By 1971, the equipment had detected magnetic (used now in its scientific sense) pulsations regarding crystals, plants, animals, water, air, clouds, storms, wells, springs, various places on the surface of the planet, and the whole human body AND various different parts of it, including the genitalia.

Clairvoyants would, of course, continue to refer to these pulsations as different kinds of auras.

But in their now scientific aspect, the equipment-confirmed pulsations could generically be referred to as "energy fields" — thus neatly separating science jargon from the objectionable aura jargon.

Since 1971, science in large part has maintained that the energy fields can be detected only by equipment — and not by clairvoyant or telesthesia detection.

This scientific insistence rather crudely, but clearly,

downsizes numerous kinds of "human potentials" well-attested to elsewhere in human history.

What is so far true, however, is that the equipment detects only electromagnetic energies, not vital, animating life forces.

And as of this writing the cutting edges of the advancing sciences are more or less agreed, behind the scenes, that the electromagnetic energies alone do not account for animate life forms, much less life entities.

Chapter 16
"THE ENTANGLED MANIFESTATION"

Several elements of the aura energy fields were examined in the preceding chapter. However, those elements were merely a selection of the more simple and obvious phenomena of the aura energy fields.

These simple elements needed to be identified, but they were also presented as background for the additional, highly complex elements discussed in the chapters ahead.

Like most other things that have dynamic importance to life and living, the nature of energetic auras is not a simple matter if one begins in-depth examination.

As a way of getting into what is to follow, it is worthwhile making reference to a bigger picture scenario into which the existence of aura energy fields will logically fit.

The modern sciences of the nineteenth century first assumed that the universe was made up of matter, and that the physical atom was the smallest indivisible particle of matter.

When it became possible to "smash" atoms during the atomic age, it was seen that the atom was divisible into energetic particles.

Roughly speaking, then, the atom was composed of energy, and this clearly implied that the most fundamental "ingredient" of the universe was not matter but energy.

Out of the energies, or because of them, the atoms of physical matter are somehow composed and come into physical or electromagnetic existence.

As this book was undergoing final editing, the January, 1999, issue of SCIENTIFIC AMERICAN magazine published an article entitled REVOLUTION IN COSMOLOGY.

The article indicated that "New observations have smashed the old [scientific] view of our universe. For the past year, theorists have scrambled to make sense of the latest data.

"Either the universe is dominated by a bizarre form of energy...or our universe is just one strangely curved bubble of space-time in an infinite continuum."

If, then, physical matter is not the basic stuff of the universe, but energy is, then a significant question can be posed, at least for hypothetical consideration.

Why should ANY life systems emerge on any planet only in a strictly three-dimensional physical context and with sensing systems geared uniquely and only to perceiving the physical forms of matter?

This question can be posed in a number of other ways. For example, since energy is the fundamental constituent of physical matter, why should life forms consist only of the matter and not the energy?

Or, if life forms are fundamentally erected out of energy, why should they only possess sensory systems regarding matter, and not possess sensory systems regarding energies?

The most comprehensive, and logical, answer is that all life systems have arrays of sensing mechanisms and faculties regarding both matter and energy, and in fact it is understood that all life forms are probably more sensitive overall to energies than to physical matter.

This equates to TWO sets of sensing systems, one geared for perceiving the physical, the other geared for perceiving the energetic.

While philosophic and scientific confusions can arise, as they have, regarding the existence of the double matter-sensing and energy-sensing systems, there is one fundamental area of energy sensing and experiencing that leaves little doubt in this matter.

This fundamental area has to do with the sensing of dynamic sexual energies, a.k.a. sexual vibe sensing, and which are invisible to physical eyesight.

SEXUAL ENERGY SENSING SYSTEMS

There can be absolutely no doubt that our human species possesses sexual sensing systems, although the efficiency of these can be distorted or downgraded by societal confusions.

Of course, in the behavioristic context, this type of vibe-energy sensing is explained away as subliminal responses to "cues" of body language and behavior posturing.

Such cues probably play an obvious role, but the responses often occur over distances when the direct sighting of body cues is not possible.

Subliminal perception of sexualizing aura energies is a far more logical explanation for sensing invisible sexual energies, especially if the human being is energy-based in the first place.

For clarity here, if one senses another's sex vibes, then those vibes are emanating from the other person's aura energy fields. In that one is sensing invisible energies in this case, such sensing is a form of clairvoyance, albeit this term is not usually applied to the sensing of sex vibes.

EMOTIONAL ENERGY SENSING SYSTEMS

People also possess energy sensing systems with regard to emotions radiating from energy fields of others, such as emanations of love, hate, acceptance and rejection, danger, approachability, imminent illness or death, and etc.

Again for clarity, one is sensing invisible emotion-laden energies from another's aura energy fields. This kind of thing is often referred to as empathy, which in itself is frequently being acknowledged as a type of clairvoyance.

THE COMPLEXITY OF AURA ENERGY FIELDS

By considering the two types of aura energy sensing above, it can begin to seem that aura energy fields must be complex if they can emanate sexual and emotional radiations.

Therefore, the aura is not simply an oval energy field around the body but has a multitude of highly complex and dynamic factors.

But this is what might be expected. After all, the physical human bio-body is ultra-complex, indeed marvelously so. Why, then, should its energy aura fields not be at least as equally complex?

EARLY OBSERVATIONS OF THE AURA

Many nineteenth century descriptions of the aura seen clairvoyantly indicate it as "An emanation said to surround human beings and supposed to proceed from the nervous systems. It is described as an oval cloud of light and suffused with various colors. This is perceived clairvoyantly, being imperceptible to the physical sight."

From this description (which has had wide exposure) it can easily be supposed that the aura, in a kind of static passive way, is a thing having prescribed shape, form and contours.

However, backtracking to the Renaissance, the venerable Paracelsus indicated auras of a quite different nature:

"The vital force is not enclosed in man, but radiates around him like a luminous sphere, and it may be made to act at a distance. In these semi-natural rays, the imagination of man may produce healthy or morbid effects. It may poison the essence of life and cause diseases, or it may purify it after it has been made impure, and restore the health.

"Our thoughts are simply magnetic emanations, which, in escaping from our brains, penetrate into kindred heads and carry thither, with a reflection of our life, the mirage of our secrets."

THE AURA AS VITAL FORCE LUMINANT

Here, then, is a description of a quite different caliber. Indeed, the aura Paracelsus describes is not an aura as a thing in itself, but in his view is actually the vital force luminant, extending beyond the body, and which can act at a distance.

The direct implication is that the vital force luminant is not a static cloud of colors, but an active entity in its own right, and one that would seem to have highly active and mobile characteristics.

Modern descriptions of the aura in this sense are rare. This rarity indicates a number of things, major among which is that this kind of aura activity is more difficult to perceive and so it usually isn't.

But if we consider that there are subtle but meaningful distinctions between perceiving and sensing, then it is quite clear that certain types of vital emanations which "penetrate into kindred heads" can be sensed if not actually perceived clairvoyantly.

It doesn't take any great leap of imagination to comprehend

that although the emanations can be clairvoyantly perceived, they can more easily be sensed as "vibrations"—i.e., usually, and frequently, described as "vibe sensing."

To mention again for emphasis, vibe sensing can easily be thought of as a type of clairvoyance without the pictures, so to speak. As it is, a thorough examination of the great accumulation of literature reveals that nowhere has any rule been established that clairvoyance has exclusively to be made up of any kind of sight or images.

Indeed, sensing the vital force luminant doesn't necessarily require clairvoyant pictures. Non-visual feeling of it is quite often enough, such as in the case of sensing sexual or emotional energies. One gets the picture, so to speak, without needing the pictures.

There are many categories of vital energy phenomena that can be sensed, but which do not absolutely need visualizing.

One most probable reason is that the "information content" of the sensing is sufficient enough in itself to convey, or result in, cognitive meaning. As will be seen ahead, and in many different aspects, the concept of energies having information content has wide significance.

THE SCOPE OF THE COMPLEX AURA ENERGY FIELDS

While the existence of aura energy fields has been appreciated since time immemorial, it must be openly acknowledged that the earliest research group in the modern West to examine such energies were the working members of Theosophy, especially between about 1870 and 1932.

Some aspects of Theosophy have already been discussed. There exists a very large literature regarding the nature of Theosophy, and to be sure many definitions of it have been presented.

But as a seldom recognized truth of the matter, it can be stated that the Theosophists, in addition to their philosophical endeavors, were researchers of vital life energies and the larger perspectives of cosmic energetics.

Indeed, the leading researchers of Theosophy pursued the topic of energetics so thoroughly that they eventually could identify aura energy field as "entangled manifestations."

By 1914, just before the onset of World War I, the Theosophists in general had arrived at certain conclusions regarding the nature and constituents of the aura.

It was, first of all, "a highly complicated and entangled manifestation," and altogether consisted of many influences simultaneously operating within the same area.

Far from being a mere luminous cloud around the physical body, it both interpenetrated it AND some of its elements were projected from the body sometimes to great distances.

Some of the auric elements did not belong to the body at all but were emanated from "astral principles."

ASTRAL referred to the first permanent "world" of vital force energies not subject to or changed by physical death.

As had many earlier cultures, the Theosophists indicated that the astral was "material, but of a refined texture" having permanent but quite plastic substance.

The ancient traditions of India divided existence into seven "worlds" or "planes," the lowest of which was the physical.

The astral was itemized as the second lowest of the seven worlds, the world of emotions, desires, and passions, and which have existence with or without the physical body.

The physical bio-body and the astral "body" (as it came to be called) coexist and interpenetrate for as long as the physical body endures.

The emotions, desires, and passions, however, belong to the astral, not to the physical body.

And indeed, upon reflection, it is difficult to attribute emotions, desires, and passions to the physical body.

After all, it is made up only of inert, inorganic particles, and it IS difficult to see how any sum of the inorganic particles could of itself possess emotions, desires, and passions that are otherwise defined by, and only by, their energetic nature.

THE CO-EXISTENCE OF FORMATIVE ENERGY
AND ITS FORMED MATTER

In keeping with traditional Eastern concepts, the Theosophists accepted the concept that since the physical and the astral coexist and interpenetrate, not only clairvoyants could sense and experience the astral, but "also ordinary men"

—inclusive of women, of course.

The cross experiencing between physical and astral happens, as but one example, during dreaming sleep, anesthetics, drugs, or sometimes as a result of accidents during which the astral "body" might temporarily separate from its physical component.

In this sense, the dream world consists of the astral component in process of, as it were, thinking, meditating, or visualizing.

As everyone realizes, the dream world is entirely plastic, as modern surrealist artists have portrayed, while the physical world is solid, as physical realist artists have portrayed.

Although the Theosophists did imply as much, it would be clear that the "astral principles" would have their own sensing systems regarding emotions, desires, and passions. This would clearly be the case if the astral world was the world of emotions, desires, and passions.

In this instance, then, sensing of emotions, desires, and passions (including those sexual) would be a concomitant of the astral energetic principles.

It would also be the case that these energies would have, or result in, "physico-orgasmic" phenomena, especially of the ecstasy type.

But the whole of this would also mean, for example, that a full part of the sympathetic systems researched by Paracelsus and others were energetic in nature, and thus belonged by right to the plastic astral principles.

Extending this line of thinking a little further, the more real human "being" would be composed of the "astral principles" —with the physical body being only their material vehicle.

In other words, energy senses energy. However, for any of this to work, the astral principles need to be possessed of Intelligence, or at least some version of it.

Here it is worth mentioning that although results and effects, and successes and breakdowns, of intelligence can be authenticated, no one has the least idea of what it actually is.

It might be observed, however, that whatever Intelligence is, it is certainly plastic, since it can be shaped and distorted in ways that can amuse and horrify any intelligence watching. Indeed, researchers of intelligence have often become confounded when considering the plastic nature of intelligence.

The NATURE of intelligence is a far more complex topic than merely mapping its various kinds of behavior.

SEVEN KINDS OF AURA INFORMATION SYSTEMS

The Theosophists attempted to categorize different aspects of the "complicated and entangled manifestation." They were moderately successful in this, but there were still some rather tattered open ends.

The categories, "all blended together," were set up along the apparent lines of order of importance, as itemized below:

1. the health auras;
2. the vital animating and energy auras;
3. the emotion, desire, and passion auras;
4. the thought-form auras;
5. the Karmic auras;
6. the character auras; and
7. the spiritual nature auras.

Please note that all of the above-mentioned auras are given in the plural. All of them auras could be broken down into two subsequent categories of the "higher" and the "lower."

But much in this regard depended on certain biases, motives and predispositions of anyone seeking to establish what was higher and/or lower.

And here was a situation that many Theosophists sought to polemically embroil themselves—usually in ways that ended up not being very constructive.

For example, theoretical attempts were made to establish sexual desire as lower-order astral, and creative passions as higher-order astral, or even as belonging to the spiritual nature auras.

But there was one brilliant conclusion broadly shared, and likely to be of some endurance and future enlightenment: that IGNORANCE (whether natural or socially engineered) of these categorized auras contributes big-time to all sorts of human and societal difficulty and misery.

AURA MULTIDIMENSIONAL AND RESPLENDENT

The term MULTIDIMENSIONAL did not really come into vogue until the early 1970s.

However, the "complicated and entangled manifestation" of the Theosophists is entirely compatible with multidimensionality, and especially if the multiplicity of dimensions can be conceptualized as interpenetrating.

And this helps explain, in some part at least, why certain clairvoyants perceive only some of the auras and not others.

This can be elaborated a little by suggesting that clairvoyance (of any kind) is both linked to and relative to different energetic dimensionalities.

Energies, if we might apply them to different dimensions, would in the whole of human sensing systems then have distinct kinds or layers of receptor-faculties that respond only to a given dimension.

So different kinds of clairvoyance or clairlucidity are dimensionally dependent, meaning that if one level of clairvoyance might activate, other levels might not.

One additional and quite special factor needs to be pointed up. While it is hardly mentioned anywhere, it is indicative of why so many never experience a clairvoyant turn-on, so to speak.

If one studies a larger number of artistic representations of aura energy fields, it can be seen that although their differences can be quite remarkable, they none the less have a very special factor in common—beauty, to the degree of being resplendent.

Aside from the fact that the entangled manifestation is complex and complicated, the whole of it from the smallest to the biggest parts is of beauty so extraordinary, so resplendent, that mere words, illustrations, or special effects equipment are quite challenged in approximating it.

In this sense, then, it might be assumed that those not prepared to recognize or deal in beauty are unlikely ever to experience turn-on jolts of clairvoyance.

Indeed, such turn-on jolts might actually be mentally unbearable within otherwise jerkwater realities that exclude or minimize beauty.

Thus, if anyone is curious about what auras (or energy fields) look like, it can be said they are unbelievably beautiful. If this initial proviso does not register, then one probably can forget about ever sighting one, sexual or otherwise.

PART III

THE COPPER MIRROR TRAINING DEVICE OF THE MAHATMAS & EXPERIENCING THE ENTANGLED MANIFESTATION

Chapter 17
PERSONAL EXPERIENCING OF AURA ENERGY FIELDS

In modern Western times, the definition of clairvoyance has been exclusively associated with visualizing the energies. It is true that visualization of the energies is one form of clairvoyance. But that it is the only form is not supported either by esoteric or anthropological literature. It is also not supported by personal experiencing.

The central problem here is one of nomenclature. In the historical aspect of cultures, places, and languages, many different terms were given to special sensing phenomena that are innate in our species, but which could not be attributed to the physical senses.

If the different terms are collectively dissected, it can be understood that their most basic intent was to distinguish between sensing of invisible and visible factors, both kinds of sensing being universal to our species.

For example, in Scotland and Ireland, the concept of SECOND SIGHT traditionally referred to any sensing of the invisible, with special emphasis on foreseeing future events.

But the concept also incorporated all kinds of clairvoyance sensing needed to foresee, and which sensing has existed from time immemorial in practically every part of the world.

The concept of PSYCHIC PERCEPTION came into existence in England during the 1870s, and the concept of second sight fell into disuse. But a comparison of the intent of the two concepts clearly establishes that both refer to the same principal phenomena.

Most African and indigenous American languages have terms equivalent to second sight and psychic perception. Sanskrit of ancient India is rich in having nomenclature refinements regarding second sight, but for which there are no equivalents in any of the modern Western languages.

Thus, there exists a plethora of terms that seem different in an intellectual sense, but which are in fact referring to the same principal phenomena experienced world-wide. The intellectual differences can act as "mental noise" at the personal level with regard to fuller understanding of the principal phenomena involved.

VIBE-SENSING AS A TYPE OF CLAIRVOYANCE

One of the problems with the term CLAIRVOYANT hinges on the general misunderstanding that the VOYANT part of it is taken from the French VOIR, which does mean "to see," and to which was attached CLAIR, meaning "clear," the combination meaning "to see clearly".

However, in French VOYANT is a distinct word, separate from VOIR. In one sense, it means "composed of gaudy colors." But in another important sense, it refers to "signals."

If we use the idea of "signals," then CLAIRVOYANCE easily refers to a clear sensing of signals. In all probability, the nearest literal equivalent in English is clear sensing of vibratory signals.

In fact, vibe-sensing is the contemporary generic term used to denote any sensing of invisible factors, including invisible energies, and such sensing can take place with or without visualizing.

All this means in technical terms, is that the vibe-sensing is incorporating information into awareness systems but is by-passing the visualizing cortex in doing so.

VIBE-SENSING OF SEXUAL VIBRATIONS

If we allow for this correction with regard to clairvoyance, then vibe-sensing is not only a non-visualizing format of clairvoyance, but it is one very broadly experienced.

As such it is most correctly, and very profoundly, used regarding feeling-impacts aroused by sexualizing energies, and with all the empathies and emotions and ecstasies that can go along with them, including such phenomena as sexual charisma and telepathic rapport.

If this is considered as a viable correction to the large scope of misunderstandings, then the statistical base for sensing invisibles is so large as to probably include everyone in some fashion.

After the broad base of sex-vibe sensing, the statistic would begin to narrow depending on what other invisibles are sensed, and in what form. The most narrow end of the statistic would reflect clairvoyants capable of visualizing.

This, in turn, would be relative to what they do and do not bring into the visualizing, for visualizing clairvoyants have existed who "see" one kind of invisibles, but not other kinds.

In the light of the above, the issues of clairvoyance will always be in some kind of a mess, if not because of nomenclature and conceptual difficulties, then because the entangled manifestation IS entangled. With respect to this mess, it is useful to observe that clairvoyance in any format begins with individual personal experiencing that brings up the additional important issues involve, and without which any clairvoyant panorama will remain invisible and unknown.

SOME BASIC ATTRIBUTES THAT ARE UNIVERSAL TO THE HUMAN BEING

To get into the important nuances of individual experiencing, it is ironic that they can best be approached via the topic of universal attributes of the human BEING.

The irony involves the trend within the modernist sciences and philosophies that more or less disposed of the BEING part of the human being because it denoted something too ephemeral to be included in the lexicons of materialism.

The materialist rationale was that all of the constituents of the human organism would be found as solely composed of matter, material interactions, and physico-mechanisms.

The term HUMAN BEING is still used in lay jargon, of course. But in that the human being is thought of as the human body, the historical definitions of BEING have sort of been lost. At any rate, and for clarity, those definitions need to be reprised. BEING is defined as:

1. The quality or state of having existence;
2. Something conceivable as existing;
3. Conscious existence;
4. The qualities that constitute an existent thing or phenomenon; and

5. The essence of something.

To track this a bit further, ESSENCE is defined as:

6. The permanent as contrasted with the accidental or temporary element of being;
7. The property necessary to the nature of a thing;
8. The most significant property;
9. The individual, real, or ultimate nature of a thing, especially as opposed to its existence; and
10. A volatile [or energetic] substance or constituent.

There is an old adage somewhat appropriate to the above definitions: What you see may not be what you get.

In experiential fact, even if the term BEING is detached from the term HUMAN, one can always see the visible matter-body, but one will also get the being-essence part, too.

And it is entirely likely that the visible behavior associated with the matter-body is not being produced by it, but by its being-essence constituents.

SEXUALIZING ESSENCES OF THE HUMAN BEING

There is one area of human activity to which the above definitions seem entirely relevant and which can easily be confirmed, human sexuality.

In the materialistic concept of things, human sexual activity is associated with the genitalia. The genitals are neatly dignified as the reproductive organs, since in the material sense the function of those anatomical organs is to reproduce more material bodies.

But if the whole of human sexual activity is considered, the organs are utilized for reproduction only about 10 percent of the time.

The remaining 90 percent of human sexual activity is devoted to such projects as recreational sex, the release of nervous energy via orgasm not associated with reproduction, and the transmutation of sexual essence energies into creativity.

Additionally, human sexual activity is often utilized on

behalf of increasing the essence of power, making the essence of money, and for participating in the enjoyment of the essence of erotic saturation.

Indeed, if the energetic ESSENCES were missing, then none of them would be pursued.

All of these sexualizing essence phenomena are easily recognized, although one might refer to them as ESSENCE-SIGNALS. And it is clearly recognized as well that material parameters do not even approach an explanation of them.

But the list should include one phenomenon not usually identified for what it is: the therapeutic benefits of exchanging and revivifying lagging energies via physical, empathic, and psychic-force intimacy.

All of the above can roughly be grouped into the concept of vitalizing ecstasy, and which is entirely useful to the human BEING, having, as it does, many beneficial aspects.

To get somewhat of a grip on this, merely consider the concept of vitalizing ecstasy starvation.

The sciences and philosophies downloading from modernist materialism cannot explain the human being's need for vitalizing ecstasy, whether of the sexualizing or any other kind.

DISTINCTIONS BETWEEN PERCEIVING PHYSICALITY AND THE SENSING OF BEING-ESSENCES

On a species-wide basis, very young children experience a lot of things having to do with sensing being-essences. Indeed, many researchers, focusing on how infants deal with information and begin the all-important processes of recognition, are of the opinion that the infants literally "feel-see" the energies characteristic of various kinds of being-essences.

As but one example, it is sometimes noticed that the infant looks at things that no one else can see.

That infants are responsive to vital energies has never been in doubt by anyone observing them intimately, and this kind of responsiveness legitimately falls into some kind of clairvoyant category.

It also indicates the presence of a being-sensing superstructure in all human beings.

In the longer term, however, it is more important that children grow up and turn out to be well-fitted to the particular social and cultural realities in which they find themselves.

Thus, whatever the very young do experience, and how they experience it, the whole of it is quickly to be left behind, with the common result that childhood experiencing is usually of little permanent interest.

It is commonly understood that certain conditioning processes are required in order for the child to become well-fitted.

These obviously differ in various cultures and social settings. But most of them share a commonality in that certain kinds of natural raw-awareness, as it were, need to be detached and subdued from the developmental pathways leading to proper adulthood.

So, if all human infants universally possess sensing of being-essences, this commonality is left behind as their perceptions are compartmentalized by conditioning into different cultural and societal aspects.

Thus, there has long existed a vacuum of information regarding what infants and children actually experience

A significant trek into this vacuum was made by Jean Piaget (1896-1980), a Swiss psychologist, who in 1929 became professor of child psychology and scientific thought at the University of Geneva.

Piaget became especially noted for his theories (since proven out) that the child's experiential, cognitive, and intellectual development proceeds in genetically determined stages and always in the same sequential order.

Piaget's seminal contributions were expanded upon by later research efforts. The sum of these eventually revealed that all children possess factors that are "universal" to our species.

One of these factors, a universal language superstructure, is born pre-existent within the child. This linguistic superstructure can specialize in sensing and copying the formats of given language(s) of the local social environment into which it is born.

Another way of putting this is that babies come equipped with the hardware of a language computer. This hardware is ready to accept ANY language software program. Some researchers suspect that infants learn languages not only by sound, but with the assistance of some kind of telepathic means.

INNER-CORE AWARENESS SYSTEMS

Other research efforts have revealed the existence of universal inner core awareness systems in every child. These systems can specialize in copying the given awareness parameters demanded by various societal and natural environments. The real existence of being-essence sensing systems would be necessary for this.

As a result, we could picture the human as possessed of universally shared, inner core faculties, which eventually becomes cocooned with an outer shell that is formatted because of various kinds of societal conditioning.

All living systems having mobility must at least sense magnetic types of energies if they are to respond or withdraw from them.

It is quite well understood by now that infants and young children do at least sense them via little understood "neuro-sympathies," and often actually perceive them by what amount to clairvoyant means.

With the contemporary emergence of the term "neuro-sympathies," we become somewhat re-linked to the "sympathetic systems" of Paracelsus.

CHILDHOOD CLAIRVOYANCE

That many, or most, young children have some kind of clairvoyant experiencing can no longer be doubted, and most books describing the "natural child" report as much.

In my own case as a child, I still vividly remember watching with great fascination the fluttering forms of color sparkling from people, animals, and objects, from my mother, father, grandmothers, and others, as well as from caterpillars, leaves, rocks, and so forth.

Female breasts, even if yet undeveloped, mostly had white lights. Sometimes a red or green beam shot up out of my dad's head. Blooming flowers had spectacular fireworks-like illuminations, the most dramatic being blooming lilacs. Both my grandmothers kept gardens. I could pick out the dead seeds before planting since they had no lights.

Some lights fluttered about like butterflies. There were some "whirligig" things, especially on bellies. Sometimes I saw streams of lights going off of fingertips, and beams going out of eyes, although this latter seemed rare. The local minister had such beams, especially if he got really worked up.

My family circle was tolerant when I described these things but got nervous when I asked questions no one could answer.

So I didn't get into any real trouble until I asked what the "red light things" were that sometimes stuck out through men's pants, especially the beer drinkers down at my dad's pool hall and at the Elks Club.

So my mother took me to the family doctor to find out if I was having eye trouble. I overhead him say that "it" (whatever "it" was) would go away soon.

And "it" did go away—but not completely—especially after it dawned on me that the seeing was not considered "normal."

Thus, slowly, pervasively, restrained by parents, peers, teachers, and finally by the unyielding social fabric itself, the child is settled into the system where it is supposed to "see" only certain things and not others.

The clairvoyant seeing, however, can reduce back to clairvoyant sensing which is not accompanied by pictures.

And what is sensed can sometimes be articulated in other forms, such as in descriptive literature and via the visual arts.

In my own paintings between 1962 and 1966, expressions of undulating lights and energies kept creeping into my attempts at still life subjects.

I finally gave over to them, and then did a body of work composed of elongated nudes, gigantic males and females, all with blue skin and burning red eyes, all possessing fantastic energy shells and glittering, undulating rainbow auras, and shooting out radiant streamers and bubbles.

This work did not then fit into the New York art scene, and still does not.

I didn't see these things, but I could still sense them, off and on, anyway.

It was impossible NOT to have interest in these matters, and if anything at all, it was this experiencing that led the way into parapsychology research.

THE "KIRLIAN" AURA

In 1958, two Soviet scientists—Semyon and Valentina Kirlian—invented a photographic technique which, as they described it, converted non-electric properties of an object into electrical properties that could be recorded on photographic film (i.e., electrophotography).

Their method was a development of a technique known as early as the 1890s.

For example, in his book THE HUMAN SOUL: ITS MOTIONS AND ITS LIGHTS (1896), Hyppolite Baraduc, included a photo of a hand glowing the electrostatic discharges. (Baraduc was the dramatic photographer of odic and psychic energies reviewed in chapter 8.)

In 1898, a Russian electrical engineer named Yakov Narkevich-Todko demonstrated electrographic photos by using high voltage spark discharges.

The Kirlians combined this earlier work with that of their contemporary, Viktor Adamenko, a Soviet physicist, who demonstrated a piece of equipment called the tobiscope, a device used to detect the acupuncture points of the human body.

During the late 1960s, Kirlian photography had a few years of popularity in the United States.

When in 1967 I first saw such photos in color, I was glad to recognize that at least some of the effects coincided with some of my paintings between 1962 and 1966.

Especially consistent were the rays that sometimes were photographed as radiating from fingertips. The emanations were also consistent with what I had learned about Reichenbach.

The Kirlian photographic evidence was not accepted by the mainstream sciences, and still isn't. The Kirlian effects were dismissed as mere electrostatic discharges, since a mild current of electricity was passed through the hand as it pressed against the photographic plate.

Electrostatic discharges? Well, yes!

Indeed, bio-energetics assumes that the bio-body not only possesses a strong electromagnetic substructure, but also that it is being subjected to energetic inflows all the time.

This can only mean that it IS necessary for electrostatic and magnetic discharges to take place, and these would constitute some full part of the body's aura energy fields.

It is difficult to see how the electrical components of the body would NOT discharge, especially if they became momentarily overloaded by even a small charge.

Mainstream sciences don't have much to say about the tobiscope that locates acupuncture points.

As it turned out, however, neither Kirlian photography nor psychic photography capture the actual dynamic, even astounding, complexity and activity of the energy fields. And what might be called low-threshold clairvoyance doesn't either.

This is to say that nothing prepared me for what I was to experience in this regard as a result of the copper mirror of the Mahatmas, the tale of which begins to unfold in the next chapter.

CHAPTER 18
THE COPPER MIRROR TRAINING DEVICE OF THE MAHATMAS

The entire history of ALL methods and equipment that might extend or enhance human perceptions is very interesting. However, that history is divided into sectors, only some of which have achieved societal support. Some of the sectors are not even recognized as belonging in the same category as others.

So the entire history has never been pulled together into a given conceptual framework that can house it.

One of the factors that links the entire history is the fact that extensions and enhancements of perceptions are highly desirable because many benefits can be downloaded from them. One such benefit is that the sum of human knowledge can be increased, often in single gigantic steps.

However, such increases in knowledge often have serious implications concerning the status quo stability of given societal frameworks. It is therefore not unusual that such increases are resisted, together with whatever methods and equipment might be involved.

Thus, one of the factors that defeats the linking of the entire history of perceptual enhancing methods and equipment has to do not precisely with their discovery, but rather what they portend with regard to preserving a given societal status quo.

BASIC POWERS OF PERCEPTION

For clarity, it can be said that basic powers of perception are conceptually formulated within only the given parameters of the physical senses, and then within mental activities based on them. In this sense, any given enhancement of the basic powers involves factors that increase perception beyond the limitations of the physical senses.

The rough distinction here is between what is visible-tangible via the basic physical senses, and what is invisible-intangible to them. Indeed, what the five well-known physical senses can't "see" is "invisible" to them.

An examination of the structural elements of most societal formats easily reveals that a very large percentage of their "holding power" is closely linked to the management of the visible-tangible.

Although a lot can otherwise be discussed with regard to such societal structures, internal preservation of their holding power is quite dear to their managers, and probably to a large percentage of their followers as well.

Thus, feared difficulties might arise if and when perceptions of the invisible-intangible are introduced into their workings based principally on the physical senses. So the chief prophylactic mechanism is to forestall any emergence of extended perceptions.

If the prophylaxis doesn't work, then more stringent measures can be designed and employed (as, for example, was the case regarding all of the rejected vital force research and developments discussed in Part I).

DIFFICULTIES OF GETTING BEYOND THE VISIBLE

Recorded human history clearly reveals that most discoveries of methods and equipment to enhance perception much beyond the visible had a hard time of it at first, not because what they consisted of, but because of what they portended in societal terms.

For example, the general concept of the CAMERA OBSCURA (dark chamber) was known in ancient Greece and had been mentioned by Aristotle. However, its development during the Renaissance at first resulted in a significant societal brouhaha.

The camera obscura was a device that consisted principally of a dark box large enough for a person to stand in. A very small hole was picked into one side of the box, after which an inverted image of the scene outside the hole appeared on the opposite interior side of the dark box.

At first, the black box had high entertainment value ranging alongside the miraculous. But the idea that external visible reality could, in some invisible way, be reduced to a pin hole and appear upside-down had enormous philosophical and religious implications. Many of the black boxes were seized and committed to the flames, and proper citizens disavowed them.

The reputation of the camera obscura was rescued, in about 1519, by Leonardo da Vinci, who established its principle use as artistic device. He perhaps succeeded in doing so only because of his exceedingly high standing.

About three-hundred years later, in 1826, the Frenchman, Joseph Nicephore Niepce elaborated an invention based on the camera obscura. He achieved the recording of a negative image on a light-sensitive material.

When he coated a piece of paper with asphalt and exposed it inside the camera obscura for eight hours, a permanent image resulted on the paper, and the modern camera came into existence.

The scene outside of the black box had, of course, been illuminated. But when he placed a piece of paper inside the dark box at night when nothing outside of it was illuminated, various patterns of light appeared on it anyway.

When it was understood that only energies could expose the coated paper, what was later to be called psychic-energy photography had inadvertently come into existence, and which has remained a societal super-problem ever since.

The invention of the microscope in about 1590, and the telescope in about 1610, were at first resisted with societal vigor, sometimes to the noise of mob anger against them.

The idea that a micro universe existed, composed of tiny stuff the natural physical senses alone could not detect, was considered heretical not only by religious demagogues, but by philosophers and scientists alike.

The idea that a telescope could see through to the macro heavens confounded the concept of seven spheres thought to hover over the flat earth, especially when another round planet with rings (Saturn) could be espied.

This was enough to inspire various inquisitorial activities, and Galileo, an exponent of the new heavenly device, had his work cut out for him. He survived, but others were carted off to the flames.

There are many other examples of the above, some coming

down to the present. But the point is that societal concerns predominate any inventions or factors regarding any extensions of perceptions by artificial means.

However, one such sector has to do with the enhancement extensions of perceptions of invisible energies discussed in this book. The actuality of various kinds of clairvoyance are perpetually embroiled within this sector.

It incorporates sensing activities that make their appearance during trance states.

The history of this particular sector has been competently written up in a book by the late historian of psychical matters, Brian Inglis, under the title of TRANCE: A NATURAL HISTORY OF ALTERED STATES OF MIND (1989).

The direct implication copiously elucidated by Inglis is that different states of consciousness each possess their special kinds of perceptual systems, something clearly established thousands of years ago by shamans world-wide.

CLAIRVOYANCE AS PERCEPTION-EXTENDING FUNCTIONS OF THE HUMAN ENERGETIC SYSTEMS

In the historical sense, it is safe to say that any and all methods to extend the scope of human perceptions into the invisible have met with societal difficulties, and sometimes to the extreme.

For example, the field of so-called psychic photography is challenged with an enthusiasm that, by now, is entirely questionable. If some energy patterns appear on energy sensitive film, normal, infrared or ultraviolet, in conventional terms the appearance is blamed on fakery, fraud, or equipment failures, and there is a long history regarding this.

MEANWHILE, physicists have become adroit at capturing images and patterns of energetic particles passing through the walls of cloud chambers. Thereby, the real existence of those otherwise invisible energy bits has been made visible to the naked eye, with "photos" of them being published in leading science journals.

However, energetic implications of this knowledge package, scientifically acquired, have not been carried over to the phenomena of psychic photography, a topic that remains camera obscura, without any apertures, in the black box of the continuing rejection.

Likewise, scientifically acquired photos of certain energy structures in association with the human body have not been correlated with clairvoyant perceptions of the same.

CLAIRVOYANCE-ENHANCING TRAINING DEVICES

Throughout Part I, we have seen that the best evidence for invisible energies has occurred in relation to some kind of device or special environment set up.

Such was the case with Mesmer's mysterious vats, the constituents of which have seemingly been erased from history.

The function of Reichenbach's dark rooms is not exactly clear, but that they probably functioned along the lines of black boxes and were apparently supercharged with odic force by his mediums certainly needs to be considered.

Certainly, the concept of an isolated box-room-environment becoming supercharged by orgone energy played a definite role in Wilhelm Reich's efforts.

In the case of the early psychic force experiments of Cox and Sir William Crookes, the medium, Daniel Dunglas Home, apparently carried within his person an energetic supercharge he could activate, after which the amazing effects and phenomena promptly took place.

One of the concomitants of all these supercharges, even if somewhat different, was that they affected those attending upon the situations, themselves becoming supercharged, this resulting, among other phenomena, in sexualizing arousals.

And indeed, even in so-called normal life, those who like to experience sexual arousal, design or gravitate to environments that encourage supercharge arousal along such lines.

The point here is that if sexualizing energy supercharging is possible, then other kinds of such supercharging are also possible.

And if this is the fact of the matter, then human energetics must be involved, with special emphasis on the clairvoyant sensing of them. This sensing results at least in autonomic arousal, even if cognitive understanding of it doesn't actually take place.

This is to say that the physical sensing systems are not, of themselves, responding to the energetics. But that the energy sensings systems are. This easily leads to the concept of an energetic "entity," and which, by ITS phenomena, is somewhat distinct from the mere physical body.

With these observations now in hand, it is possible to suggest that any training device designed to elicit enhanced perceptual systems beyond the merely physical ones must, in some sense at least, first serve to energize the energy-sensing factors of the human organism.

A description of one such "training device" has been in existence since 1927. The source of the description—THE MAHATMA LETTERS—however, is so strange that it of is little wonder it escaped notice.

THE GREAT SELVES

The legendary Mahatmas are said to be Great Teachers living in the Trans-Himalayan vastness of Tibet or Mongolia.

The term MAHATMAN is Sanskrit, a compound word meaning Great Self. As described, the Mahatmans are perfected men.

They are men, not spirit entities, who have evolved through self-devised efforts in individual evolution, always advancing forward and upward until they attain "a lofty spiritual and intellectual human supremacy."

They are not created by any extra-cosmic Deity. Rather, as it might be said, they have achieved intellectual and spiritual supremacy by lifting up themselves by their own boot-strap efforts.

As a result of this self-lifting, they are farther advanced along the "path of evolution" than the majority.

However, they possess knowledge of Nature's secret processes and of hidden mysteries.

The Great Selves are Teachers, because they are occupied in the noble duty of instructing mankind, of inspiring elevating thoughts.

They are also Guardians of wisdom, forgotten or yet unknown. They can be called by other identifiers: Sages, Masters, Elder Brothers, Seers, Immortals, etc.

They are not dead persons, operating from ephemeral realm.

They are alive, with very extended life spans. They possess higher levels of thinking, along with extensive powers of clairvoyance and telepathy, and with abilities to influence minds of mere men, and to bilocate and appear to them.

So, of course, most people, during modern times at least, believe that the Mahatmas don't exist, if they have even heard of them in the first place.

However, the Mahatmas communicated with several of the early Theosophists. As might be expected, the nature of the communicating was often exceedingly strange.

The Mahatmas would cause letters to be precipitated out of the air and fall down to a table or to the floor or cause them to be discovered in unexpected places.

So, of course, the authenticity of the Mahatma Letters was of some concern (and not a little scandal) to the Theosophists. At some point, the Mahatmas began depositing Letters in a shrine at the Theosophical compound in Adyar, India.

When the shrine was later discovered to have a fake rear wall, Theosophy entire was convulsed with Great Doubts concerning the Great Selves and the possible existence of Lesser Selves who might have counterfeited something or other.

All in all, the Mahatma Letters make for interesting reading. But only one of them constitutes the substance of this chapter.

A. P. Sinnett (1840-1921) was one of the three principal, influential founders of the Theosophical Society which came into existence in New York in 1875.

Sinnett had been a long-term CHELA (student) of the Mahatmas, and at some point developed a method of posing questions in his own mind, while answers thereafter would be manifested by the Mahatmas.

THE COPPER MIRROR TRAINING DEVICE OF THE MAHATMAS

When the Theosophists set up headquarters in Adyar, India, Sinnett followed, and during the course of 1882 he was apparently wondering how to develop increases of self-awareness and clairvoyance.

The Mahatmas apparently had telepathically perceived Sinnett's interest, and so he was in process of receiving letters about this from the Mahatmas.

He received a letter which, as most Mahatma Letters were, was immediately circulated among Theosophists, and finally published in THE MAHATMA LETTERS TO A. P. SINNETT (1923), the originals of which ended up in the British Museum.

In answer to Sinnett's wonderment about how to develop increases of clairvoyance, the Mahatmas responded with the following short description of an enhancing device:

"The methods used for developing lucidity in our chelas may be easily used by you. Every temple has a dark room, the north wall of which is entirely covered with a sheet of mixed metals, chiefly copper, very highly polished, with the surface capable of reflecting in it things, as well as [being] a mirror.

"The chela sits on an insulated stool, a three-legged bench placed in a flat bottomed vessel of thick glass – [with] the Lama operator likewise, the two forming with the mirror wall a triangle.

"A magnet with the north pole up is suspended over the crown of the chela's head without touching it. The operator having started the thing going leaves the chela alone gazing on the wall, and after the third time [the guiding Lama] is no longer required."

Presumably, "the thing going" referred to increases of at least clairvoyance, as well as other more refined perceptions, and which at first required a guide to help it get going.

But as soon as the chela got the idea, the guide was no longer needed.

DRS. ELMER AND ALYCE GREEN BUILD THE COPPER MIRROR TRAINING DEVICE AT THE MENNINGER FOUNDATION

I remember reading THE MAHATMA LETTERS during the early 1960s when I was studying the Theosophical literature. I thought it might be interesting to set up the device and see what might happen, but never did.

In 1970 I began volunteering for parapsychological experiments, the successes of which led to working in that field for the next nineteen years.

The work with which I was involved was entirely composed of exploring perceptions and had very little to do with physical developmental "assists" such as the Mahatma's copper wall.

Even so, I could find no information that any Theosophists had ever tested the copper mirror, although it is conceivable that Leadbeater and Besant might have done so.

As we have seen in chapter 14, the reasons or causes of their astonishing clairvoyant powers have never been discussed in any depth.

In any event, the Mahatma training device passed from view until I heard about it from, of all people, Dr. Elmer Green at the Menninger Foundation at Topeka, Kansas.

Elmer Green, together with his wife and co-worker, Alyce, had become famous during the 1970s in the realm of researching brainwave biofeedback and "the image-making faculty."

They had established the Voluntary Controls Program at the Menninger Foundation. The work of the Program focused on the alpha-theta brainwave biofeedback processes and was at first funded primarily by the National Institutes of Mental Health.

At some point the Greens came across the Mahatma Letters and noticed the passage quoted above. Eventually they set up some informal experiments, the results of which inspired them to enlarge their approach by setting up a more formal series, during which some remarkable phenomena occurred.

LUCIDITY

In an earlier research proposal entitled PHYSICAL FIELDS AND STATES OF CONSCIOUSNESS (1 June 1983), the Greens indicated:

"It is clear from a prima facie analysis of those suggestions [in the Mahatma Letter] that both magnetic and electrostatic fields are involved in this elicitation of the state of consciousness called LUCIDITY. Lucidity, whatever its definition, may not develop to a significant extent in three copper wall sessions, but the fact that the teacher, 'after the third time is no longer required, 'implies sufficient progress by the student so that he can continue on his own.

"It is the elicitation and subsequent definition of lucidity with which we are basically concerned...whether it refers to becoming clearly conscious of normally-unconscious psychological processes only in the personal-consciousness domain described by Freud, or

also has significance in the domain of transpersonal consciousness described by Jung."

Elmer Green telephoned me occasionally to describe the work, and to invite me to participate in it. Knowing what I did about the Mahatma Letter and its description of a training device to enhance whatever it did, I was very eager to participate and instantly accepted the Greens' invitation.

However, due to funding problems and research criteria, the written invitation didn't arrive until 1987, five years after his first proposal. During those five years the emphasis of the experiment had shifted from lucidity per se, to different proposal, conceptualized as CONSCIOUSNESS, BODY ELECTRICITY AND PSYCHOPHYSICAL LEARNING. The source of the funding had also shifted.

Despite the proposal's title, the emphasis was actually on "healing," a topic which interested the Fetzer Foundation which had agreed to fund the project with healing in mind.

As the proposal stated, "healers often have unusual electrical phenomena associated with their 'healing' activities. If this is factual, 'healers' of national repute may affect during 'healing' sessions, the ultrasensitive electrometers of the copper wall lab."

For clarity, the emphasis of the experiments had shifted from LUCIDITY to researching whether the "unusual electrical phenomena" associated with healers would interact with the "electrostatic behavior" of the copper walls.

The interest was now focusing on the "Anomalous electrostatic phenomena in exceptional subjects" principally with regard to noted healers.

I felt obliged to explain to the Greens that I was not an "healer of national repute" and probably should not be a part of this particular type of experiment.

My expertise had focused on various modes of extrasensory perception, but which seemed to fall into the category of lucidity. Elmer countered by saying that even so, I had "national repute" as a psychic and clairvoyant, and that he hoped I would participate. So I accepted and became one of the nineteen subjects in the experiments.

Although the initial invitation took place in 1987, setting up the complicated experiment went on for months. I finally went to Topeka during the middle of June 1989 for a week's work in the Voluntary Controls Program.

I found that the Mahatma's copper wall had in fact become a copper ROOM whose four walls and floor were of large copper panels.

The whole experimental situation was exceedingly elegant and splendid. The copper sheets were hooked into several arrays of computer analyzers which recorded their electrostatic behavior.

The chair was not a tripod, but a comfortable padded one, with facilities to hook up the subjects to computerized brainwave and other physiological detectors.

The whole of the copper room was raised up on glass blocks whose function was to detach and insulate the room from Earth's magnetic field.

The all-important 14-Gauss magnet was suspended in the air just over the subjects' heads. The environment was very impressive and thrilling.

Elmer and his several colleagues were nothing if not premeditated, thorough and careful, and altogether an inspiring group. Complete records were kept in the forms of questionnaires, detailed interviews after "sittings" and frequent general discussions.

I was even permitted to design a limited number of experiments having to do with perceptual ESP, all of which went exceedingly well but which, with one exception, are not germane to this book.

I then "sat" in the copper room twice a day for seven days, for periods of about an hour each. As requested, I tried to "influence the electrostatic behavior" of the four copper walls, ultimately with minimal success.

But at about day three, something else began happening. I was about to discover what supercharging was all about. This was both fabulous and wonderful, and ultimately wrecked my life for about the next year.

Chapter 19
UNANTICIPATED LUCIDITY BEGINS

Some discomforts soon became apparent when I began sitting in the copper room for two sessions a day of forty minutes at a time. First of all, it was necessary to sit perfectly still, or as still as possible, because of the leads affixed to the scalp which were conducting brainwaves to the computers.

Body movement, especially of the neck, shoulders and arms introduced "noise" into the brainwave-measuring mechanisms and blotted out the shifting brainwave patterns which were thought important.

Second, I had to keep awake, to keep my eyes open, so as not to reduce the spectrum of the brainwaves to those characteristic of sleep. One might meditate or go into reverie; but with the eyes open so as to prevent descent into sleep. Eye blinking would also distort brainwave patterns.

Part of the technique, if it can be called that, was to focus one's eyes on the vague reflection of oneself in the copper sheet one sat facing. This was interesting for about ten minutes, but soon the eyes watered, and the reflection began wobbling.

However, in the past, dozens of researchers had hooked me into brainwave equipment, and so I was familiar with the requirements.

Yet, on the surface of things there was nothing to do except sit motionless, stare at the mirror image, and do so without drowsing or falling asleep.

MENTAL IMAGES TURN INTO BALLS OF BLUE LIGHT

During the morning session of the third day, which would be the fifth sitting, I found myself reviewing all sorts of things in my mind.

There was no deliberate effort on my part to do so. Indeed, I didn't particularly want to think, but only to notice something unusual as a result of the copper mirrors.

It seemed like strips of movie footage were being run, sometimes at high speed, somewhat as if time was being contracted or compacted. After a few moments of this, several movie strips began running at the same time.

I was not wondering about clairvoyance or lucidity, since that kind of stuff was not the central focus of the experiments. The program was to see if the copper walls showed any electrostatic changes with regard to the sitter.

At some point I began thinking that the images were actually something of a nuisance. So I began wondering about the why of so many fast-moving images, but this seemed to cause them to run faster.

Shortly, they suddenly turned into tiny little balls a metallic dark blue in color. After these buzzed about like bees around a nest, they suddenly disappeared altogether.

At the time I didn't attribute any particular meaning to this. But weeks later I sort of came to the conclusion that the movie strips contained the greater part of what I had experienced in my life.

I felt there was something vaguely "Tibetan" about this, reflective of some kind of meditation method to review one's entire life so as to step outside of those thought-pattern-images.

THE FIRST AURA PHENOMENON

As the blue balls disappeared, I began noticing that something about the copper sheets, which I sat facing, had changed.

A transparent, but almost tangibly "thick" dark orange "mist" had appeared. The mist seemed to be composed of "particles." The copper sheets were polished enough so that one could see one's reflection in them. The orange mist had blotted out my reflection.

Somewhat in surprise, I did the no-no of turning to look at the copper walls on either side and behind me. I found that the entire chamber was infused with the orange mist, and that there were small "waves" going on through it. I also noticed that it was slowly becoming more luminous and more orange.

I naturally concluded the orange field was composed of energies. But since orange has never been one of my favorite colors, I wondered why the energies were orange.

While in process of this wondering, my attention suddenly went to my crotch were, of all things, an erection was in process of manifesting.

Mildly surprised, I then resumed my motionless position. But soon my hands and feet began itching. After about ten more minutes I looked down at my right hand because it had really started tingling and there was no way to scratch it.

To my utter shock, I could see the bones in my hand very clearly, and in more than just a black and white X-ray way. At this, my eyes began blinking a whole lot, and a series of goosebumps invaded my entire body. But the long session was now at an end, and I could scratch my hand.

Immediately after the session I was interviewed about what I had experienced.

I did not yet refer to clairvoyance, because I thought all of this had something to do with the electrostatic behavior of the copper walls.

During the afternoon session, if I remember correctly, nothing particular happened, except I thought I could sense that the magnet suspended over my head had its "north" direction up.

Now, it needs to be explained that the experimental protocols had certain requirements regarding the magnet, which was specially designed and contained in a white cardboard box.

As a control for the experiment, empty cardboard boxes were occasionally substituted for the magnet without telling the subject.

At other times, the magnets were to be placed with the north up or the south up.

Shortly, I could "see" that the north end had a blue glow, the south a pink one, and of course the empty boxes had neither. Knowing about Reichenbach's experiments, I considered the idea that I was merely mentalizing the glows based on what I had read about his experiments.

So I suggested that at the beginning of each session, I should try, by sensing, to identify whether the magnet was north-up, south-up, or whether the box was empty.

The suggestion was accepted by the experimenters, and all of my subsequent calls were correct. At some point, the sessions were then interrupted while an assistant changed the magnet routine several times so as to gather more data about this.

I eventually mentioned that I liked the north pole of the magnet better than the south pole. Although I did not know it then, the experimenters had already accumulated evidence that males "performed" better with the north-up, while females did so with the south-up.

LUCIDITY BEGINS

That night, while watching TV in my motel room, I noticed that the orange luminosity was glowing in my head, or in my consciousness, and that my body was surrounded by it.

The "effects" were now continuing outside of the copper wall chamber. It was at this point that I remember the orange light I had seen as an infant, and forgotten past memories were withdrawn from storage.

These did their accelerated movie thing, and after a while turned into tiny blue balls and disappeared.

BIOLOGICAL CLAIRVOYANCE EMERGES

At the next session, it took about twenty minutes for the orange light to emanate from the copper sheets, which I still thought was its source. I could again see the bones in my hands, but now could also see the larger blood vessels and arteries.

The vessels were dark blue, somewhat glowing, but the arteries were brilliant pinkish-red. I felt I recognized these because of my college training in biology.

But there was also a glowing, blue-green network which infused both of the hands and ran up the arms, whose bones I could now also see. The network was exquisite and very complex, but I didn't know what it was.

At some point, the orange light began shifting to dark yellow as it enveloped the entire chamber. Then it randomly began fluctuating with a number of other colors, like being in the middle of a slowly undulating rainbow.

CLAIRVOYANCE OF ZOOMING LIGHT TUBES BEGINS

Crotch action had again manifested, but I was now absolutely transfixed and had no trouble sitting motionless.

But shortly I was quite startled when, just to my immediate near left, a tubular, slightly undulating beam of purple-lavender light suddenly zoomed up out of the floor and disappeared into the ceiling.

Surprised, I jumped up out of the chair in reflex, hitting my head on the magnet, and causing most of the brainwave electrodes to be dislodged.

So, the experiment was interrupted while these were pasted back on to my scalp.

But while the assistant was replacing them, I could see he was surrounded by a darkish but yet luminous nimbus. And there in the vicinity of his crotch was the tell-tale red radiance sticking out a little through his pants.

I was quite silent while the leads were being reaffixed. The reason, however, had nothing to do with perceiving the energies, but how I now sensed they were being perceived.

I had studied psychic phenomena for many years, and like most people I had adapted to the idea that clairvoyance involved only some kind of mental perceiving. I still think that particular kind of clairvoyance exists.

But the tube had zoomed up and through to my left, and I was convinced that sighting of it had taken place in the parameters of the eye outside of focused vision. This is to say, outside of the fovea, the rodless area of the eye affording acute vision.

To be specific, the rods and cones of the eye surrounding the fovea had detected the tube, much as anyone would detect a motion taking place just outside their focused vision. If, for example, you stare straight ahead at a wall, and move your hand just in back of your shoulder, you will have some kind of vision of that motion, and your eyes will jerk toward it so as to determine what it is.

My cognitive brain was whirling, and I was a little dizzy. Amid my silence, with cascades of goosebumps going on even in the soles of my feet, I now began to grasp what might be happening.

Despite my conviction that clairvoyance was only mental, I now recognized that while I was indirectly mentally "seeing," my eye systems were in fact seeing the energies also.

If this WAS the case, and as yet I had not firmly decided it was, here was a significant distinction between clairvoyance and LUCIDITY.

Before we restarted the session, I asked for a drink of water because my throat was quite dry.

My hands were shaking, and the guy asked why, worried that I was undergoing some kind of bad effect from the magnet. I could only say "Holy Shit, Holy Shit, this is wonderful and unbelievable!"

VISUAL PERCEPTION OF ACUPUNCTURE POINTS COMMENCES

With the leads again firmly glued to my scalp, the session resumed. I again looked down at my hands with my eyes and saw (in addition to the blue network and all else) that the surface of the skin was peppered with small glowing spots.

Of course, I immediately wondered what these were, at which point they somehow MAGNIFIED, and I could see them composed one-half of pink light, the other of turquoise blue light.

Inside of each of them was a transparent lusciously green whorl, or a minute circulating motion and which penetrated through the skin into the muscles, themselves now seen as a kind of liquid light like red Jell-O. I soon realized, with extreme amazement, what these were.

I had always wondered how the ancient Chinese could make maps of the acupuncture points WITHOUT having sensitive instruments which could detect their minute voltages.

It was now quite clear to me that they almost certainly had used MICRO-CLAIRVOYANCE to do so. And at this, I now accepted that what was going on was the restoration and enhancement of my own clairvoyant faculties which had been suppressed since childhood.

At any rate, here was some kind of direct clairvoyance of acupuncture points, or so I presumed. However, there were

MANY more of them than are usually illustrated in the books and on acupuncture "dolls."

Further, all were interconnected by a very minute, glowing, darkish green network, liquid green like the color of deep green water.

I now realized that the blue network must constitute the equivalent of the PHYSICAL neural system which conducts sensations through the physical body, including those of pain and ecstasy.

What I determined to be the lymphatic system was a network of glowing white.

The green network associated with the acupuncture was an energetic one, and thus was distinct from the physical neural and lymphatic networks.

To put it mildly, I was in ecstasy at this point, and the blue network was glowing even more in this ecstasy, so much so that my sensorium itself had gotten aroused, with the result that my membrum virile felt as if it was about to do you know what (although it didn't).

Both the blue and green networks ran almost side by side and were connected to each other at certain points. I could perceive that there was a heavy concentration of both these networks in, yes, the all-important glans or "head" of my membrum virile.

As all this still confusing stuff was going on, I began to get the small idea that this was not merely clairvoyance. And this is a little hard to articulate.

Most accounts of clairvoyant experiencing seem to indicate that there is the object viewed and the viewer of the object. This is to say the object and the viewer are two different things.

But in the copper wall room, I began to get the idea that I wasn't perceiving as viewer/object relationship where boundaries between the two are important.

Something else was happening. The viewer/object relationship had collapsed into some form of integrated "participation." This was the best, but not quite the most accurate term.

In thinking about this later, I began to realize that the term LUCIDITY was utilized in the Mahatma Letter, not clairvoyance, and that everyone, including myself, had automatically assumed that the two terms were synonymous.

With this distinction, it would seem that if the Mahatmas

meant clairvoyance, then they would have used that term. But they spoke of lucidity.

And I now began to comprehend what the Mahatmas had meant by LUCIDITY—something for which the English language does not really have a concept or a specific term.

LUCIDITY

Even so, it's worthwhile once more to review the dictionary definition of LUCIDITY. The first definition is given as clearness of thought or style. But the second is "a presumed capacity to perceive the truth directly and instantaneously, as in clairvoyance."

LUCID DREAMING, for example, may have to do with seeing colors and shapes clearly. But it also refers to dreaming of the truth of things or matters.

Sitting in the copper room, I began to get the idea that the lucidity of the Mahatmas was composed of several layers or levels of clairvoyance functioning all at once. I don't remember having seen anything like all this as a child back in my butterfly-light days.

But here, almost magically so, were "refinements" so absolutely delicate they were unbelievable. And the sense of the trans-dimensional something (no word exists for this) seemed capable of "connecting up" with EVERYTHING EVERYWHERE.

The absolute beauty of all this was, and has remained, indescribable. "Fabulous" doesn't even do justice to the wonderous beauty involved.

I later found color illustrations in a book entitled ENERGY ECSTASY (1978) by Bernard Gunther that came close. Although I had this book in my library for some time, I didn't pay it much attention because it seemed to me that the book's artist was taking liberties.

ENERGY ECSTASY is a book about "human energies, the energy body, and the chakras."

But Gunther's illustrations, although beautiful and in color, still don't do justice, most probably because the illustrations are presented in only the two dimensions of the page.

It is true that the sparkling radiances of all these exquisite energies can be suggested visually on a 2-dimensional page, but their gorgeous fluidic motions have a 3-dimensionality that can't be portrayed.

Someday someone will figure out how to film these energies as motion pictures, and when this happens everyone will be in for an absolute and awesome thrill.

LUCIDITY AT WORK OUTSIDE OF THE COPPER WALL ROOM

The next mind-boggling thing that occurred took place immediately after the session.

There was some kind of heated upset taking place in the computer room regarding the computers, some of which had inexplicably gone down during the session.

When I entered it after being detached from the brainwave leads, the computer room was bathed in red light, with electric-like brighter red beams shooting around here and there. And I, who could now see these, was not even in the copper chamber any longer.

I actually attributed this seeing to my imagination because it would be expected that upsets might produce angry red "vibrations."

Dr. Green was present in the red-lit computer room, and he was busy trying to calm down the flaring up situation. It was then I noticed a circular whitish "light" in the center of his forehead just slightly above his eyebrows.

And THIS I understood to be an important chakra. And it is necessary to introduce the topic of chakras before going on with the Topeka narrative.

Chapter 20
CHAKRA

The term CHAKRA is lifted directly into Western languages from the Sanskrit of ancient India. In its original meaning it signified "wheel," but more precisely the "turning" of anything that turns or revolves. Thus, in ancient India, it also signified a cycle, a period of duration, in which the wheel of time turns once. It also referred to horizon, as being circular or of a wheel-form.

CHAKRA also refers to certain centers of the body having to do with energy, which are said to collect streams of energy of different kinds.

In ancient India, the energy was referred to as PRANA. That term is derived from the Sanskrit PRA, a prefix meaning "before," and AN, a verb meaning "to breathe, to blow, and to live."

PRANA is therefore usually translated as "life," or as the "Life Principle," but it has a more technical description as "the psycho-electrical veil or psycho-electrical field manifesting in the individual as vitality."

As to the numbers and different kinds of pranic energy, various Asian sages have indicated them as three, others as five, some as seven or twelve, and one writer gave the number as thirteen.

The most important distinction regarding the pranic energies is that they do not entirely originate or belong to the biological body or to its own energetic fields but belong more to the natural pranic energy reservoirs of the planet (or as some indicate, of the cosmos).

However, the pranic energies are "breathed in" as life-currents, or vital fluids, to the body systems via energetic apertures in the body's energetic aura—and, according to clairvoyant sensing, are perceived as turning wheels, i.e., as the CHAKRAS.

In the largest sense probable, CHAKRA could refer to any turning that collects energy, or into which or through which energy flows to or out of. So it could include such objects as galaxies, black holes, and the little whirlpools one sees as water goes into a drain. It is the flowing of the energy that sets up the turning.

However, in its most Westernized sense, chakra refers to certain major energy centers of the human body, of which seven are commonly enumerated, although there are many more lesser, but equally important ones.

In any event, chakras are etheric energetic functions that "work" in accord with collecting and distributing the number of vital fluids inflowing and exhaling with regard to the Life Principle manifesting as a physical-electric body.

CLAIRVOYANT PERCEPTION OF THE CHAKRAS

Although achieved clairvoyants sometimes specify ten major chakras, three of these are usually avoided, leaving seven that are usually referred to.

The seven are positioned in the bio-body energy fields at the crown of the head, between the eyebrows, at the throat, the heart, the spleen, the solar plexus, the base of the spine.

As might be suspected by now, the three chakras usually avoided have intense sexual implications.

Thus, most sources indicate that "The three remaining chakras are situated in the lower part of the pelvis and normally are not used" for the reason that these are connected to the astral world of "sexual magic" into which it is better not to make treks and fool around.

THE KUNDALINI ENERGY CHAKRAS

In the larger picture, all of the usually avoided chakras are directly associated to Kundalini energy.

This is defined as a "cosmic energy latent in the human organism responsible for sexual activity and also conditions of higher consciousness." And so here FINALLY is a traditional link between formats of sexual energy and formats of higher consciousness.

The difficulty in integrating ALL of the above factors is that if one wishes to obtain "higher consciousness," then it would seem that ALL of the chakras have to become activated, including the three avoided ones.

While it is true that higher intelligence can be obtained by "working with" only the seven best known chakras, obtaining "higher consciousness" as distinct from mere higher intelligence is another matter.

Higher consciousness, it is said, is achieved only via some kind of Kundalini awakening.

THE LOCATIONS OF THE SEXUALIZING CHAKRAS

The locations of the three avoided chakras are not merely in the "pelvic region."

In both males and females, one of them is directly on the pubic mound, the second is in the cleft between the physical sex apparatus and the anus.

The third avoided chakra is admitted as existing in some sources, but without specification as to where it is located.

Depending on the degree or level of one's clairvoyance or lucidity, different layers or dimensions of the entangled manifestation become apparent. Different aspects of the aura or energy field become visible, and a large variety of different kinds and sizes of chakras become exposed.

It would seem, then, that the existence of the seven chakras is more easily perceived by a form of clairvoyance that is "turned on" more easily than other more complex clairvoyant formats.

However, this does not at all detract from the considerable importance of the seven chakras most usually perceived. The only meaning here is that they are most easily seen, and thus most frequently reported.

If the aura or energy field is a multidimensional affair, then it is reasonable to expect that there are different dimensional forms of clairvoyance and/or lucidity. However, if lucidity is taken as a super form of clairvoyance, then perceptual elaboration would be greater in the lucidity state.

THE CHAKRAS ELABORATED VIA THEOSOPHY

As to written sources concerning the aura and the chakras, there is no getting around the fact that the indomitable and quite prolific Elder Brother of Theosophy, Charles Webster

Leadbeater, put his descriptive stamp on them quite vividly.

Among his numerous contributions in this regard, in 1895 he published THE AURA: AN ENQUIRY INTO THE NATURE AND FUNCTIONS OF THE LUMINOUS MIST SEEN ABOUT HUMAN AND OTHER BEINGS.

Between 1895 and 1925, he published at least six other books along these lines, each addressing different and more complex issues.

Then, in 1927, he published THE CHAKRAS: A RECORD OF CLAIRVOYANT OBSERVATIONS, and which has been reprinted about every eight years since.

This is a quite wonderful and vibrant book, and the seven major chakras are colorfully illustrated, albeit in idealized ways.

It should be noted that the major seven can look quite different from individual to individual.

ENERGIES DENSE ENOUGH TO BE VISIBLE

Leadbeater first indicates that ordinary men have to confine their attention to that part of the body which "is dense enough to be visible to the eye." Therefore, most of them are probably unaware of the existence of a type of matter which is invisible, though still physical.

In quite straightforward English, Leadbeater indicates that the invisible parts constitute the "vehicle" through which "flow the streams of vitality which keep the body alive," and without them "the ego," among other misfortunes, "could make no use of the cells of his brain."

As to the chakras, or "force centers" as he also calls them, these are "points of connection" via which vitality energy from different "planes" flows from one "vehicle" of man to another.

"Anyone," says Leadbeater, "who possesses a slight degree of clairvoyance may easily see them in the etheric double, where they show themselves as saucer-like depressions or vortices in its surface."

He goes on to describe that when the force centers are "quite undeveloped," they appear as small circles, perhaps two inches in diameter "glowing dully in the ordinary man."

If awakened, vivified and developed, they "are seen as blazing, coruscating whirlpools, much increased in size, and resembling miniature suns."

All of these "wheels are perpetually rotating, and into the hub or open mouth of each a force from the higher world is always flowing—a manifestation of the life-stream issuing from...what we call the primary force."

Leadbeater ALSO addresses such issues as the arousing of Kundalini, the awakening of the etheric chakras, various kinds of Yoga, a topic entitled "casual clairvoyance," dangers of "premature awakening," and spontaneous awakening of Kundalini.

All sources considered, Leadbeater's book on the chakras is quite wonderful, concise, and exemplary of invisible consistencies with earlier Eastern sources.

It does NOT, however, include discussions of the three "pelvic" chakras.

Chapter 21
NETWORKS WITHIN THE ENTANGLED MANIFESTATION

For the next sitting in the copper chamber I arrived quite subdued. During the night in the motel room, I had decided to try something which seemed to require some courage, to look into my body at the internal organs.

I had diagrammed those organs time and again back in college in my anatomy courses and sketched them for doctors during autopsies to make a little extra money.

But the prospect of seeing my own organs was another matter. There is a certain fear attached to this.

LUCIDITY OF INTERNAL BODY ORGANS

At some level of consciousness, we know these organs are mortal, that they will ultimately fail, and when they do we will be dead. How would I respond if it turned out I should see something quite dreadful about my OWN organs?

There is a certain insulation when objectively seeing the organs of others; most people, though, are squeamish about their own.

I never thought I was squeamish; but now found out that I was. So there was a certain reluctance to this decision.

None the less I, reclined on the motel bed, pressed my lips firmly together.

When my hands again turned transparent I shifted my attention to the bio-body's heart, to find it either encased in or radiating a soft golden light.

EXAMINING THE HEART VIA LUCIDITY

Because I like rich foods and good wine, I was worried, of course, that I'd see globs of cholesterol usually taken to mean approaching heart problems.

But in moving through this organ, magnifying its interior, I could see very little cholesterol. (One of the first things I did when I got back to New York was to ascertain my cholesterol count—with was considered "normal.")

Strangely, I could hear the rushing of the blood, but not the heartbeat.

EXAMINING THE INTESTINES VIA LUCIDITY

Somewhat relieved, I "did" the stomach, liver, pancreas, etc.—and, biting my teeth, the intestines. All of these seemed okay to me. But the interior walls of the lower colon seemed to be slimy and impacted with mucous and old waste which had hardened and not been excreted.

This had congealed into a rubbery hard substance and was producing a dull black aura.

Here, then, was a "dirty colon" which I had read about. I was later to see that this adverse condition is not unusual when I looked into other peoples' intestines.

Indeed, just as I was preparing to write this chapter, the NEW YORK POST (20 July 1995) published a short article about a forthcoming Elvis Presley documentary entitled "Eating Elvis". Presley's eating habits were awesome and awful. The article quotes the medical examiner who performed the autopsy, who said that Presley's colon was impacted with a clay-like substance which could have been the cause of his death. (I later undertook some rigorous colon cleansing methods.)

EXAMINING THE BRAIN VIA LUCIDITY

Having confronted the stuff in my colon, I dared to see into the brain. Here, seen with lucidity, is certainly a wonder of wonders. But how to describe it?

If the brain is to be thought of only as biological matter, then inside the skull a large part of the biological matters seemed to be some kind of water.

But if the brain is seen as the aura networks of lights and radiances, then the energy-brain extends out through the skull and interpenetrate the entire bio-body, envelope it, and extend at some distance from it.

In this sense, the brain is a "fountain" emitting sprays of light out from the top of the head in the ways magnets have been determined to do.

These then curve downward, like an ultra-fine mist or dew, cascading all around the body and then move back up into the body through, of all places, the soles of the feet.

The whole of this SPARKLES with a wild assortment of colors.

Associated with this are some darker-colored "bands," which, in my way of expressing them, are "more heavy."

These, too, rise up out of the top of the skull, often to a height of three to five feet, and then turn downward.

They then encapsulate the body at about a distance of one to two feet on its exterior and reenter the soles of the feet. They extend into the floor or ground usually about five feet.

I called these "magnetic bands"—but only because of the lack of a more precise term.

These slowly, very slowly, rotate around the bio-body either clockwise or anti-clockwise in different people, and occasionally change the direction of rotation as if some kind of a "polarity shift" takes place.

I really had no idea (and still don't) about what they are. But on average, they do constitute an extended and roughly ovalesque shape, the only ovalesque shape I've ever managed to see regarding personal human auras.

There are never less than five bands, but some people have as many as ten, especially if they are sexually "complicated" as we will see.

Their main source or conduit, however, does not appear to be the brain. They merge in the esophagus and seem to flow through it.

EXAMINING THE SPINE VIA LUCIDITY

From the spine emerges a complex network, usually dark pink in color, which extends through and around the entire body from the skin all the way into each and every internal organ. This network seems to culminate in the nails of the toes and fingers, and the hair follicles, all of which then emit rays of pink and bluish light (as seen, for example, by von Reichenbach's sensitives).

In what I later was told by doctors to be long-term, emotionally depressed people, this network has lost its luster and has darkened. In those taking sedatives or depressants, this particular network seems to have weakened, and in some cases has vanished altogether.

EXAMINING UNKNOWN NETWORKS VIA LUCIDITY

However, most visible are the "networks" of which there are several, while it seems none of them are really known to anatomically exist.

Indeed, the entire bio-psychic organism (a term which by now I am obliged to utilize,) seems to be densely composed of networks of all kinds and which entangle each other.

If these nets are not seen magnified, they altogether can be seen as mists of lights whose combined radiance extends to about a foot or more outside of the bio-body proper.

In this sense, their combined luminosity can look like an oval aura. But when magnified, in fact they are not oval since all of them (or at least all that I've managed to see) more or less follow the contours of the bio-body from the surface of the skin inward and outward.

The skeleton has its own special net, which, to me, seems very strongly and heavily "magnetic" in nature. Any damage to this particular network can easily result in some form of unconsciousness.

What is distinctly emitted from the bio-body, however, are rays, beams, and what I call "bubbles" of energy.

The bubbles can be exceedingly tiny or quite large, and they are like spores or globules of light of many different colors, intensities, and densities.

All of the rays, beams and bubbles can project or drift far afield, and all of them can quite easily be absorbed and disappear into the auras of others. The processes of absorption can take place in fractions of seconds or more slowly.

The various kinds of rays and beams can extend for quite some astonishing distance from the bio-body as we shall see ahead. All of this equates to "medical clairvoyance" which has already been mentioned.

Particularly noticeable are those rays and beams having to do with sexual energies, and the energies of love, hate, desire, and the passions.

Indeed, when impacting into the fields of others, there is a kind of splash of energies, as if a rock hitting water. All of these can quickly be "absorbed" into the energy fields of others.

And so for the first time I really came to understand that those kinds of rays and beams have tangible "substance."

And it all became very real to me, especially when after the copper room session, I told Dr. Green and his associates "Well, I've seen my internal organs."

They were, of course, suitably awed. But no one asked what I had seen regarding my own organs. Rather they all wanted to know what I could see regarding THEIR organs.

So happily at first, I began to look at a variety of internal organs. For example, one of those persons had a liver which looked whitish and sort of "water-logged," and which was considerably different from all the other livers.

I had no idea at all of the possible meanings of this, and was hesitant to tell the person about his liver.

And although I didn't realize it at the time, this kind of seeing into others was an innocent prelude of more vastly complicated things to come. I was shortly to encounter a vast number of things about auras and organs which were completely incomprehensible mysteries to me, factors which I could NOT find mentioned in books.

MY VERY OWN COPPER MIRROR

Even before the working sessions in Topeka drew to a close, I was completely "sold" on the copper mirror device of the Mahatmas. And I wanted my own personal copper mirror.

I couldn't, of course, construct the elegant, four-walled room at the Menninger Clinic. But I could easily build the device described in the Mahatma Letter to A. P. Sinnett.

I asked Dr. Green and Wendell Spencer, the project's biomedical technician, to build an exact replica of their magnet, which had to be constructed because magnet manufacturers no longer build them.

Back in New York I went to a sheet metal supplier and became the proud owner of an 8-foot by 3-foot sheet of copper. This was fixed to a large piece of plywood. After the direction of true magnetic north in

New York had been determined by compass; the copper sheet was suspended in a small room so that I could sit facing it to the true north.

The magnet, reproduced exactly as the one at the Volunteer Controls Program, duly arrived about two months later, together with a bill for $210.

I suspended it over my head, sat down in the chair, which was lifted up on four glass blocks, and was in business. After which, my entire world began to unravel. There were, three reasons for this.

The first was that the LUCIDITY which was so easy to turn on, turned out to be not so easy to turn off.

The second was that the ratio between (1) what I thought I could understand, and (2) what I did not understand AT ALL dramatically increased in favor of the latter.

The third reason was that it shortly transpired that I didn't need the magnet or the copper sheet to turn on the LUCIDITY.

Indeed, it was soon turned on all of the time, twenty-four hours a day, even in my dreams, and nothing I could do seemed either turn it off or even calm it down.

I was living in a realm of lights, rays, beams, bubbles, intermixing auras, traveling "thunderbolts" of wayward energies.

It got so bad that I was seeing the luminosities around door handles and the materials of buildings, the lights emanating from my computer screen, the green and purple emanations of the asphalt streets, and the in-sucking of energies by plastics, and on and on beyond imagination.

So distorting did all of this become that I had to step from the curbs very carefully, not being quite sure where the cement actually ended and where a "luminosity" began. The lucidity of the Mahatmas was getting to be too much!

Chapter 22
TURNING OFF WHAT THE COPPER MIRROR TURNED ON

As has already been mentioned, the auras and energy fields of the human are multidimensional, each dimension becoming apparent to perception only via a different kind or level of clairvoyance. Several levels or thresholds of clairvoyance operating simultaneously seems to be what the Mahatmas meant by LUCIDITY.

SHIFTING THRESHOLDS OF CLAIRVOYANCE

In my experiencing the multidimensional situation became increasingly problematical in that boundaries of the numerous dimensions usually are not distinct, and sometimes often blend into each other.

Several types of clairvoyance have been mentioned in earlier chapters, such as X-ray, medical, micro- and macro-clairvoyance, traveling clairvoyance and spirit-seeing clairvoyance.

To these could be added sensitivity to earthquakes, dowsing, and sexuality, and telepathy, too, which can be described as a kind of extending clairvoyance across distances and through barriers.

If some part of these differing clairvoyant thresholds manifest simultaneously, then a mass (and a mess) of beautiful energies flickering, coming and going, can result.

MIND FILTERS BLOCKING CLAIRVOYANCE

Another situation not identified in any source available to me is that if the being-energy-body "decides," so to speak, to manifest in one or two particular dimensions, then the rest vanish, at least temporarily.

But this vanishing also means that they disappear from clairvoyant view.

In this regard, it would appear that many clairvoyants seeing one or two kinds of dimensional energy activity might not notice others.

This might have something to do with the dimensions, thought systems, or beliefs the clairvoyants themselves are working in. For example, it is quite well understood that mental conditioning (for whatever reason) establishes "filters" in the mind.

These often prevent certain kinds of observing processes. Thus, a clairvoyant who is prudish regarding sexuality might not be enabled to see sexuality manifestations in the auras.

This is to say that the extent of aura seeing may be dependent on what fits into a clairvoyant's given reality and/or knowledge levels.

As it is, an extensive survey of reports and literature regarding clairvoyant perception of auras reveals that sexualizing energies are seldom mentioned.

Considering that sexualizing energies are important, and that if not clairvoyantly seen, they are often sensed and literally felt by others, something here becomes recognizable because of its absence.

THE DOUBLE PROBLEM OF NOT ENOUGH CLAIRVOYANCE AND TOO MUCH LUCIDITY

If human vitalizing energies do exist, and IF our species has the universal capability of sensing-seeing them via various kinds of clairvoyance, then there can be the problem of having too little clairvoyance.

On the other hand, if the multidimensionality factor is incorporated, then sensing-seeing too much via lucidity can also become something of a problem.

For comparison, if ten different movies are shown simultaneously on the same screen, each on top of one another, then the whole might come to look more like a mess of flickering luminosities.

I was not exactly aware that the latter problem of TOO MUCH

could exist as my very own lucidity increased by sitting in front of my very own copper mirror. In any event, I am sometimes a stalwart soul regarding psychic things, and I persevered the best I could.

I was well along into the complex difficulties regarding INCREASES in lucidity when the first real crisis became apparent. This occurred when I had to take a bus or subway somewhere.

Stepping into a subway car now meant stepping into the bewildering arrays of auras of all the other riders, or into a riot of conflicting energies, the whole of which was both breathtaking and sapping. The auras of some people are very "bad" and/or "negative" in an "ugh!" kind of way.

At first I made the best of it, studying the auras of this or that passenger. But then in one young man's aura I perceived, of all things, a rectangular black "bar" complete with 90-degree angular corners, just outside of his body over the solar plexus area. I had no idea AT ALL what this was, and still don't.

Then there were all kinds of energies pumping out of bodies and jumping hither and thither, and into the bio-bodies of OTHERS, including mine. In short, too much of this had, as it were, become really too much.

TURNING LUCIDITY OFF

I tried to turn it off myself. But to little avail. I soon realized I needed help.

I telephoned the clairvoyant healer, Carmen de Barazza, an old friend whom I trusted implicitly, but didn't see very often. All I indicated to her over the telephone was that I REALLY needed to talk to her but didn't explain why.

"Wow!" Carmen said, when I first walked into her office, "all of your chakras are WIDE OPEN!"

I said, "Well, for Chrissakes, let's figure out how to close them down!" I explained everything to her.

She "tested" my lucidity and flattered me by saying that I could "see" many things she couldn't.

With her help, we managed to bring about a kind of SMALLER LUCIDITY that more or less responded to my conscious control, a process that needed about ten visits to the wonderful Carmen.

It's too bad that the Mahatmas did not provide warning provisos in their suggestions regarding how to enhance LUCIDITY.

Meanwhile, I occasionally worked with three medical doctors to help them diagnose difficult patients. However, my lack of detailed medical knowledge about diseases and conditions proved to be a drawback. In this particular work, I sometimes saw the ominous dull black auras.

It was very hard for me to say that these forecast approaching physical death. And I DIDN'T WANT to say it. What if I was wrong?

I also saw a lot of auras with dull black "holes" in them, especially in a number of AIDs patients. I simply didn't have the heart to continue.

EXPERIENCING A SIMPLE EXAMPLE OF MEDICAL CLAIRVOYANCE

However, what I consider to be my most fulfilling example of "medical clairvoyance" occurred when a complete stranger who had heard of me came with the complaint that one of his toes had itched for about six months to his complete distraction.

X-ray and other tests had been taken. But no doctors could say what was causing the itch.

I examined the guilty toe with "medical clairvoyance," at first seeing nothing. Then I did "micro-clairvoyance" and Voila! There was a very tiny splinter lodged in the callous of the toe. It was so tiny you needed a good magnifying glass to see it. We proceeded to dig it out with a sewing needle, after which the itch promptly vanished.

CLAIRVOYANCE OF SEXUALIZING ENERGIES CONCRETIZES

But what I did have the heart to continue was to sit on the front stoop of my building and examine the auras of people walking past. Subway cars were not ideal environments in which to study auras, but from the stoop I could be detached enough to inspect a great deal.

I became particularly interested in the parts of the auras and energy bodies that had to do with sexual matters. And this I was quite up to, as almost everyone is, if only secretly, perhaps.

Thus, I more or less abandoned "medical clairvoyance." Instead, I began focusing on another form of clairvoyance appropriately called, one should think, "the energetics of sexuality clairvoyance." The results of this effort will be described in Part IV just ahead.

Sexuality clairvoyance/lucidity has heretofore remained unidentified in Theosophical or any other sources, but, as we have seen in Part I, had already been sporadically encountered by others.

Along these lines, Manhattan is rich in having real life sources, such as bars and other places frequented by those of different sexual "orientations."

At such places it was very easy to discern the somewhat similar sexualizing energy aspects of those "birds of a feather who like to hang out together."

Everyone, of course, possesses sexualizing energies in their energy bodies and sensoria, this seemingly a mandate of nature, even though some may believe otherwise, or even resent the fact.

With this fascinating clairvoyant project underway, I continued visiting Carmen about twice a week to describe and discuss all of these energies, in the hope that she could help me understand.

And, in good part, she did, although she, too, did not know what the "geometric energies" were, and which I occasionally saw in others in all kinds of different shapes.

PART IV

"ANATOMY" OF SEXUALIZING ENERGIES

Chapter 23
PARAPHERNALIA AND REGALIA OF HUMAN SEXUALIZING ENERGIES

As agreed by everyone, the strictly material aspects of the bio-body are composed of inorganic substances in the form of atoms, elements, and chemicals coming together to form "biological" molecules.

However, as discussed earlier, the question remains as to how the inorganic substances end up as constituting the organic and energetic bio-body—this in the face of the fact that the inorganic substances by themselves cannot achieve this kind of feat or functioning.

AN ENERGETIC MASTER PLAN?

Indeed, the existence of some kind of well-designed energetic masterplan is required which aligns the inorganic substances, and results in the form and structure (morphology) of the biological anatomy.

Thereafter, the morphology is dynamically ACTIVE, resulting in what is referred to as a life organism or life entity.

There is an important characteristic of the life entity I've not yet found distinguished anywhere. This has to do with motion.

If we consider sand on a beach, for example, we know it to be composed of inorganic substances broken down into small particles, or sand grains.

We know that the sand particles get pushed around by the motions of water, wind, and so forth. In this sense, the sand is formatted by motions and influences external to it, in that the sand particles by themselves cannot and do not resist the external motions.

All life forms or life entities, however, are equipped in different degrees to resist various external motions and influences. In this sense, the life entity more or less stakes a claim to existing within external motions and influences.

This can only mean that the life entity must have energies to counterbalance the external motions and energies.

The central idea here is that MOTION of any kind requires ENERGY of some kind.

Furthermore, in the case of animated (motional) life forms, the energy cannot be just diffuse potential, but must itself have rather precise form and structure (morphology).

The existence of energetic masterplans (a.k.a., energetic blueprints) remains problematical in the modern West because its philosophers and scientists are somewhat stubbornly opposed to admitting the actual existence of such an ephemeral masterplan.

However, this stubbornness is beginning to wear down, in that advances in genetic research have begun to suggest that DNA molecules are resonating to something other than pure matter. Additionally, bio-energetics research has quite firmly established the existence of complex energetic fields almost completely denied forty years ago.

ENERGETIC "VEHICLES"

The confusions of the Western situation in this regard have never been problematical within the larger scopes of many pre-modern Far Eastern thought systems.

In those systems, what we refer to as the physical body was simply referred to as the Lesser Vehicle.

With equal simplicity, the combined vital energy masterplan was referred to, usually with considerable reverence, as the Greater Vehicle, and which interacted and resonated with the even far greater vehicle of cosmic energetics.

There is a major and ongoing two-fold point of contention between modern Western and ancient Eastern thinking along these lines, having to do with the matter of clairvoyance.

The Western sciences held that the energetic masterplan did not exist, and that clairvoyance didn't either.

Eastern thinking held that the Greater Vehicle did exist, and so did clairvoyance.

Some recent Eastern thinkers have sardonically observed

that since clairvoyance belongs to the Greater Vehicle, the Western scientists examining only within the limitations of the Lesser Vehicle were unlikely to run across it. And unlikely as well to run across any number of masterplan phenomena and implications.

Since Eastern thinking holds that clairvoyance exists, it also holds that formats and activity of the energetic masterplan systems can be perceived.

The Eastern concepts also hold that different kinds of clairvoyance innate within the Greater Vehicle can be activated, and that some of the kinds of clairvoyance perceive more than others.

A SPECTRUM OF VITAL LIFE VIBRATIONS

One way of identifying these different kinds of clairvoyance is that they are ORDERED along a spectrum of lowest to higher vibrations or frequencies.

In terms of Vital Life, the very lowest of these pertain to vibrations whose nature is destructive and self-collapsing, ultimately even as regards self-tearing-down of the two Vehicles themselves.

The higher of the Vital Life vibrations or frequencies ascend along a scale, from gross to more and more refined mentation, and which is inclusive of different strata of consciousness and awareness intimately coupled with sensitivity, perception, quality and scope.

Along this spectrum of formatted energies, sexual ones are well into the ascending higher scale, their obvious main purpose being the creative proliferation of Lesser Vehicles.

And, as earlier suggested, their activation will also serve as energetic launch pads into other forms of creativity. The concept of sexual energies as being of low and base order is thus the result only of confused societal attitudes.

Most schools of Eastern thinking hold that various aspects of this spectrum can be active or inactive, sometimes distorted or honed, tattered or well-defined, well-greased or rusty, and can have different quotients or caliber of vital energies in terms of weak to strong.

That all of the energies involved have shapes and forms is

clearly indicated in all studies of such energies, even those that are Western in origin. These shapes and forms can be clairvoyantly seen as they are, but something here depends on which dimensional strata of clairvoyance is active.

If not seen directly, the energies can still be sensed non-visually by one's vital energy systems whether the physical awareness of the Lesser Vehicle is aware of it or not.

And they can be given familiar image, literary and even mathematical personifications by various anthropomorphic processes. The well-known artistic presentations of William Blake are but one example of personification of Greater Vehicle energies.

As another example, the female or male sexual energies can be portrayed as Venus or Mars, Yin or Yang, etc. In the West androgynous sexual energies are usually symbolized by Mercury, or visually portrayed as half Venus and half Mars.

The late, great Marilyn Monroe was broadly accepted as Venus incarnate, and the once famous Rudolph Valentino was broadly accepted as Mars incarnate.

ANATOMY OF THE AURA ENERGY FIELDS

That the vital energies of the Greater Vehicle have what amount to anatomical shape and form can be established, for example, by the graphic illustrations of the chakras.

But many other sources ancient or recent also illustrate beams, undulations, rays, tubes, radiations, globules, energies coming and going, appearing and vanishing, changing shape, changing into different forms, etc.

As I chanced to perceive them via my encounter with clairvoyant-lucidity (as I suppose it might be put), the sexual energies of the Greater Vehicle interacting with the physical phenomena of the Lesser Vehicle were quite complicated.

I have not been able to find too much descriptive precedent for these complicated energetic phenomena.

It is true that the all-important pubic chakra was sometimes illustrated as a blob of light over the male or female genitalia, this rather too neatly covering the genitalia with what amounts to nothing more than a glowing fig leaf.

From what I could perceive of the SEXUALIZING energies,

most of them involved formats seemingly consistent among everyone. At one level, these seemed to be closely affiliated with the basic biological body itself, such as the skeletal, neural, acupuncture and other networks, and the organs, including the muscles and skin.

These energies then could extend outward from the physical corpus into the local surrounding energy fields, and then into quite some astonishing distances beyond.

However, the sexualizing energies could be perceived in two general categories or states:

1. there, but not all that active; and
2. aroused, and during which the energetic sexualizing anatomy intensifies and changes dramatically.

In searching my trusty dictionary for appropriate nomenclature (I don't like neologisms), I decided to utilize two familiar terms, and which have the advantage of being carried over into other books dealing with the energetic aspects of creativity and power.

PARAPHERNALIA refers to personal possessions, furnishings, or apparatus. This is normally taken to refer to objects we accumulate or own.

But it is also entirely applicable to matters of sexuality and sexualizing. For example, our genitals are paraphernalia, while "our" paraphernalia can include the whole of our bio-bodies.

REGALIA refers to special finery, usually having to do with outstanding and spectacular costume indicative of office, function, status, and special categories of highly visible ceremonial activity.

Chapter 24
SOME ANATOMY OF SEXUALIZING ENERGY PARAPHERNALIA

As we have seen, the topic of aura energy fields is rather complicated. So, as with anything complex, the topic is accompanied by a fair share of misunderstandings, confusions, and simple mis-information. And, indeed, it may be that the information in this book has not escaped all of them.

But reasons can be identified for at least some of the confusions. So, before going on with descriptions of sexualizing energetics it is useful to clarify two of them, because they have direct relevance toward any fuller comprehension of aura energy fields.

One confusing aspect has to do with how and why the aura energy field exists.

An assumption broadly shared has it that the aura energy fields are being produced by the material aspects of the biological body. In this case, the aura belongs to the physical body.

Contemporary energetic research identifies these as the physical fields of the biological body.

However, although the material aspects of the body might be thought of as producing subtle energetic emanations, it is far more likely that the emanations are a by-product of the various energies flowing and circulating within it.

The confusion here is that the there are two concepts about the aura: that it belongs to the physical body, and that it does not belong to the physical body. Evidence supporting both concepts is offered in many sources.

However, behind this double confusion lurks an idea that obliterates additional ideas that are needed to more fully explain the human entity both as a being and as an organism.

The basic doctrines of materialism that came to characterize the earlier modern sciences held that only matter existed. Thus, the bio-body was composed only of matter.

But there have always been two glitches in this concept, both of which were frequently pointed up by researchers who were antagonistic to the philosophy of materialism.

The first glitch consisted of the fact that even if the body was entirely physical, it still needed bio-dynamic energy to function. It was clear enough that the bio-body ate food, and that the food was converted into the necessary energy that permitted bio-dynamic function.

Thus, the physical body absolutely needed not a continuous supply of food, but rather the energy it could be converted into. In this sense, the human organism was composed of two interacting systems unified as a matter-energy system. The theory of materialism-only was therefore incomplete.

The second glitch, somewhat more serious and fraught with important implications, had to do with how and why the physical-matter elements of the human became ANIMATED in the first place.

This question was a volcanic issue between the exponents of MATERIALISM and VITALISM during the latter part of the nineteenth century and the early part of the twentieth and resulted in stupendous conflicts now largely forgotten.

THE CONFLICTS BETWEEN MATERIALISM AND VITALISM

The vitalists held that the materialists were studying the human body only AFTER it had become animated, and that such after-the-fact studies could not explain the major issue regarding the how and why of essential life animating energies.

And indeed, it is quite fair to point up that how animation of inert physical matter takes place is a question remaining not only unanswered, but mysteriously unexamined.

The term VITALISM is taken from VITALITY, defined as "the peculiarity distinguishing the living from the nonliving," the living having "power of enduring and continuing." The vitalists held:

1. that explanations of the animating functions of a living organism require a vital energetic principle that is distinct from physico-chemical forces; and

2. that the processes of life are not explicable by the laws of physics and chemistry alone, and that life is in some part self-determining outside of those laws.

The exponents of both vitalism and materialism recognized that if a "vital energetic principle" did exist, it would equate to an energetic master plan, or "blueprint," that existed independently of the matter-body, and which activated and energized it as an animated organism.

This not only more than hinted at the existence of an energetic life entity, but that it would logically be independent of and external to the laws of physics and chemistry.

If the existence of the vital life principle was admitted into even a minimum of scientific authenticity, then the dynamic domains of materialistic physics and chemistry were not all they were cracked up to be.

This volcanic issue was finally settled in about 1919, when the materialists totaled the vitalists by denying them any possibility of scientific acceptance.

Together with the issue of life-animating factors, the term VITALISM was shortly expunged and omitted from approved mainstream sources.

It is ironic that today's physicists and those researching morphogenetic fields, morphic resonance, and causative formation are, in fact, various kinds of NEO-VITALISTS—albeit that condemned word probably will not be resurrected.

A particularly informative book in this regard is SYMPATHETIC VIBRATIONS: REFLECTIONS ON PHYSICS AS A WAY OF LIFE (1985) by K. C. Cole.

A DISTINCTIVE DIFFERENCE BETWEEN MATERIALISM AND VITALISM

In an earlier chapter, the ancient Eastern concept of the LESSER and the GREATER VEHICLE was briefly discussed.

The Lesser Vehicle largely corresponds to the animated material body composed of matter and energy.

The Greater Vehicle is exclusively of energy, plus whatever else, and it is this Greater Vehicle that animates the Lesser.

Thus, the materialists have been exponents of the Lesser

Vehicle, while the vitalists were exponents of the Greater Vehicle.

It is now possible to state the main point of the above discussion. The Lesser Vehicle would obviously have its particular aura energy fields, while the Greater Vehicle "overshadowing" the Lesser would have its own dynamic aura-energetic aspects.

To a very large degree, the aura energy fields of both would interpenetrate each other. But in some quite important sense, the energetics of the Greater Vehicle could clairvoyantly become hyper-visible, especially if the double vital energy system became super-energized.

As we have already examined in the case of mesmeric, odic, psychic force and orgone energies, if the animating energies chance to become super-energized then appearance of extraordinary sexualizing phenomena takes place.

This can lead, tentatively, to the surprising observation that the sexualizing energies belong more to the Greater Vehicle than to the Lesser. This is somewhat opposite of what is generally assumed to be the case.

THE ANATOMY OF THE BASIC THREE SEXUALIZING CHAKRAS

Regarding the phenomena of the sexualizing energy paraphernalia of humans, it first needs to be tacitly understood that the phenomena, as I perceived them, apparently DO NOT belong to the physical components of the biological body.

While it is true that the physical components do respond to them, if the sexualizing energy is not present, they don't respond.

Rather, they appear to belong to an extremely complex, highly structured, energy network within which the matter of the physical components is enfolded.

This is to say that the physical body is NOT producing the energy structures, as might be commonly assumed at first. It is more likely that aggregates of arousal energy are flowing into the energy network of the Greater Vehicle.

That energy network is a highly formatted, energy distribution super grid WITHIN which the physical body is brought into existence.

Elements of this super grid penetrate into the bio-body, but its major structural elements are just at the surface of the skin, or just outside of it.

THE FIRST, OR MAIN, SEXUALIZING CHAKRA

Both the male and female versions usually are seen as having three important chakras which, to my knowledge, have not been identified or discussed.

We have already referred to the famous pubic chakra, although Leadbeater and most other sources omitted all but passing reference to it.

In past conventional illustrations, only one sexual chakra is seen, usually placed just in front (hence covering) the vagina or penis, chastely blotting out both.

In fact, though, less prudish Eastern sources place the sex chakra where it is actually to be found: in the crevice between the legs.

In the male it is found behind the scrotum and in front of the anus. In the female it is found between the vagina and anus.

It is almost always reddish in color, even if not active or aroused. If it is any other color, then health or emotional troubles are brewing.

Here, it must be emphasized that this particular chakra has several important implications beyond the sexualizing ones.

It is connected, by a thread-like whorling, up into the body interior. At a certain point, this whorling thread than diverges to connect both to the spinal column and to the esophagus where the whorling then seems to disappear or merge into other energy networks.

It is identically found in all human bodies from birth onward. If this chakra doesn't exist at birth, the infant will not live. A type of this chakra is also found on most mammals.

For lack of a better term, I'll refer to it as the crotch chakra, since there are at least two other sex chakras.

As everyone usually discovers, the crotch chakra is exceedingly responsive to any kind of manipulations, and responds to the rays emanating from the fingertips, if those rays are pink.

It is especially responsive to licking by the tongue, which

itself emits a kind of electrostatic aura which is densely and somewhat "damply" many-colored.

The crotch chakra is also sensitive to sunlight, and many nude sun-bathers have discovered this.

As in other mammals, licking of the crotch chakra especially will render a slightly hypnotic effect, while the eyes will float upward beneath the upper eyelid.

This particular chakra is accurately identified in some texts. Otherwise, it constitutes one of the most "forbidden zones" of the entire human body. For reasons of propriety, the location of this chakra is translated up to the pubic mound. There is another chakra on the pubic mound, but its energies are apparently composed of something else as we will see.

THE ANAL CHAKRA

In actuality, all orifices of the bio-body are kinds of chakras. The crotch chakra is easily distinguishable from the anal chakra, which is usually seen as a transparent darker red color, and which itself will intensify by finger manipulation and licking.

Indeed, a little-known researcher interested in the responsive phenomena of licking has pointed up that among all the mammals, the human species is the only one which does not lick the anus, and in fact cannot because of our up-right standing anatomy. But in fact, the entire bio-psychic anatomy and all of the chakras will respond favorably to the tongue.

The anus chakra sometimes exhibits opaque colors, such as dark red, blue or dull black. These colors seem to indicate some kind of disease of viruses, protozoa, bacteria, or parasites whose own energies cloud up the anal aura.

DIFFERENCES BETWEEN MALE AND FEMALE SEXUALIZING CHAKRAS

Beyond the crotch and anal chakras, the energy anatomy of the male and female versions now begins to differ.

In males, the next sexualizing paraphernalia which seems important is a small chakra about an inch in dimension which is usually deep purple in color.

It is found about half-way between the tail of the spine and the anus, this point being just inside the cleft between the buttocks. The skin covering at this point is very thin and fragile, and so rough treatment is not advised.

When this chakra is lightly massaged or tongued, the male will usually undergo a definite hypnotic relaxation. But conversely, most of his other sexualizing energies will become aroused, and the male will be unable to resist other more strenuous sexual manipulations.

The equivalent chakra to this is found in females not between the buttocks to the rear, but to the front just between the top of the vaginal cleft and the clitoris. It can be seen as being of deep purple, but more usually a dark liquid blue-green.

Massaging or tonguing of this chakra will produce hypnotic and other effects similar to the male responses. However, the female may begin to undergo orgasmic "convulsions," while the male usually does not.

When male and female together are achieving coitus, there can be perceived electric-like, lavender-colored discharges taking place between these two particular chakras.

These discharges appear to increase the pumping strength of the male pelvis and thighs and increase the orgasmic tension of the female pelvic area. These discharges also appear to tighten the muscles of the vaginal area and increase the penetrating hardness of the penis.

Beyond this, from these two chakras can now be seen passing between each other what can only be described as electrical discharges which fan out to incorporate the two bodies entire.

These discharges are very pleasurable, not only galvanizing the entire bodies, but intercommunicating in such a way that a "melding" effect transpires, and the copulating couple feel like they have melted or merged into one.

In the sexology literature, this is often referred to as the "ecstatic union," which it surely is.

The clairvoyant color of these discharges is usually brilliant pink, but also can be experienced as blinding white.

Images or photographs of copulating couples produce stimulations of these two chakras in their viewers, and even some discharges from them, and which is a type of "erotic" ecstasy in its own right.

And here we have our first hint of erotic objects, for a picture of a copulating couple is an inanimate object, but which none the less energetically stimulates both of these two vital chakras. As an aside here, many pre-modern societies "worshipped" images of copulation, and even kept them on altars in their bed chambers. I often wondered why.

But as a result of clairvoyance, although I can't prove it, the ecstatic discharges between these two chakras may have something to do with how the sperm and eggs "agree" to interact. In other words, there may be an "electrical" factor here. If the chakras are sluggish or damaged, an "electrical environment" may not build up and conception might not occur or occur only with extreme difficulty.

Erotic objects indeed help build up the "charges" in these two apparently vital chakras.

In two cases in which I was asked to clairvoyantly examine two males, I espied that in both of them the purple chakras were "dead."

Both then admitted that even though they produced healthy spermatozoa, their wives had never conceived. They also admitted, with my prodding, that while they did ejaculate easily they did not seem to experience anything near what was described in the literature as "ecstatic union." All this for what it's worth.

THE DELICATE CHAKRAS AT THE TIP OF THE PENIS AND CLITORIS

The next of the sexualizing chakras in importance are found at the tip of the penis and at the tip of the clitoris. These are very tiny, to be sure.

In males, this tiny chakra is usually blood red and resembles a glowing ruby. In females it is usually deep green in color and resembles a glowing emerald. If highly energy sexualized, both emit gem-like rays and sparkles.

That these two "gemstones" became, at least in many pre-modern societies, associated with males and females can hardly be by chance.

In size, these two chakras are about 1/16 of an inch in dimension and can easily be missed in clairvoyance.

However, these two points are also deeply embraced by

concentrations of the networks earlier described, and they are part of the larger neural, acupuncture, lymphatic, and other nets of the psychic organism.

Entirely sensitive minute filaments of the major neural networks are especially and densely concentrated in the head of the penis and in the clitoris. Both, then, are very sensitive to pain, even of the most minute kind.

However, when these two tiny chakras are energized or stimulated, they can increase in size to 2-4 inches, and emit beams which extend much further.

In their excited state, the glans of the penis and the clitoris, otherwise exceedingly sensitive to pain, can now undergo very rough treatment, including hard biting and chewing, and all of which will now be experienced not as pain but as highest of ecstatic pleasures.

THE MALE AND FEMALE BENDING BEAMS

For all their small size, these two chakras exhibit some remarkable and potent activities.

As these two chakras become increasingly excited, they can be seen to emit rays of their particular emerald or ruby light. These rays, however, now perform a most extraordinary wonder. For they can be seen to reach out, bend and twist, like snakes, and seek each other out.

Having located each other they now entwine and, even more astonishingly, begin to shrink pulling the two bodies to each other, thus literally drawing penis to vagina. Since this activity has by now also resulted in the intertwining of arms and legs, it is usually not noticed.

It is not too much to say that if and when these two twisting rays have located and entwined, the male and female become somewhat mindless, their intellects go down, as well as their judgment, and some kind of copulation is almost surely to be the unavoidable result.

In this, and from the examples I've clairvoyantly inspected, I believe the female beams are by far the strongest and most vivid. In some cases, the size of the female bending beams is twice or more of those of the male.

In any event, these beams are quite awesome, for they can

reach out at least across a room.

If full intimacy does not take place, or if the entwining of the beams is broken, then there is almost immediately a "slump" of vital energies in both subjects, which often makes people very testy, and psychological scenes can now take place without much further provocation.

In respect of this, I had always wondered why many pre-modern societies were in favor of segregation of the sexes, especially while they were young.

From this clairvoyant viewpoint, such segregating surely cut back on the importune occurrence of these kinds of intertwining, this also for what it's worth.

The male and female bending beams can pierce right though individuals who may chance to be standing in the way —with the result of some kind of sexual arousal, often much to their spontaneous surprise.

The "strength" of these bending beams seems to begin weakening after about the age of thirty, except in certain circumstances.

Pre-menopausal females often exhibit a strong, final display of them, while older males can be temporarily rejuvenated by encountering the bending emerald beams of young females.

THE MINUTE SEXUALIZING CHAKRAS OF THE THIGHS

Now, to move on to other of the sexualizing paraphernalia of the energy body we must turn our attention to the pelvic areas, and the inner sides of the thighs.

No matter what complexities have arisen from the other two chakras, in the female, on the inner thighs closest to the vaginal areas, will be found a series or a pattern of small chakras clairvoyantly seen in the color of glowing white.

A similar grouping of these, but usually red in color, will be found in the male.

In the male, however, the collection of these chakras can encircle the thighs to the outer side as well and extend down to the calves. In some males these collections can ascend up to the hips, and involve at least some parts of the buttocks, usually the lower "cheeks."

Males are usually sensitive to having their thighs and butts touched, while female versions often will keep their legs together, in both cases until a suitable partner has been espied.

These areas are exceedingly sensitive to the rays from fingertips, and often to tongue licking as might be expected.

In both male and female, these arrays of minuscule chakras literally produce heat, and what verges on a slight hypnotic state. Even if an undesirable or importune intruder manages to slip a hand into or onto these collections of chakras, the intruder might expect to soon proceed in other regards.

Conventional sexologists have indeed identified these areas as important "erogenous zones."

The collections of tiny chakras indicate areas of increased sensitivity, and usually protrude about a quarter of an inch above the skin surface.

Practically anyone can locate these by hand if they gently move their fingers a fraction of an inch above the skin and focus on the increase or decrease of "sensation."

Even more arrays of these "sensate" chakras are found all over the genitals, but an especially intense collection of them can be found on the pubic mound, as most people realize without being clairvoyant.

At the pubic mound, however, the collection tends to emit rays which can extend to as much as three inches to a foot when unexcited, but to even greater extent when excited.

Even male and female versions who have not had their clair- voyance reawakened can instantly spot any untoward motion in the vicinity of their public mounds even when not looking down in that direction. It is this collection of tiny chakras which I believe is often mistaken for a pranic one. However, these are not in-take chakras, but out-flowing ones.

Male and female versions will also notice anyone LOOKING at their pubic mounds hidden beneath clothes, even from across a great distance.

There can be no doubt at all that the bio-psychic sensorium, even if only subconsciously so, immediately can detect and identify the meanings and intents of such looks.

This seems to be because, as the ancient Greeks said, the eyes produce beams, and the beams seem to carry "information." These eye beams, though, are virtually transparent even to highly achieved clairvoyants. But if they are magnified via micro-clairvoyance, they can be seen as streams of very minute, fast-moving "particles."

The particles are usually, but not always, greenish in color, and move within what can be called a lavender or purplish "tube" and which can bend as a lot of rays and beams can do.

SEXUALIZING FUNCTIONS OF OTHER ORGANS

Collections of the tiny white chakras can also be found associated with all of the body orifices, the nipples, bellybutton, inside the arms and armpits, on the scalp, and the ears.

All of these have been identified by conventional sexologists as erogenous zones. But what appear to be especially highly refined collections of them can be found on and around the lips, the ears, and the nipples, especially the nipples of female versions and the nipples of many, but not all, male versions.

Many male versions, however, have bands of them encircling the biceps and sometimes even the forearms, and also aligned on the pectorals and sometimes over the shoulders and onto the back.

Many female versions have similar bands or bracelets of them around their ankles and wrists, and almost always on the shoulder and the backs of their necks.

In most cases, both the female and male version have specialized tiny chakras, usually glowing red in the palms of their hands.

Thus, when the pink rays from the fingertips and the collections of sexualizing chakras in the palms, stroke an area laden with similar sexualizing chakras, not only are sexualizing energies exchanged, but other kind of energy as well.

Seen with micro-clairvoyance, this resembles two sheets of electrified copper separated only by a small distance, at which time a profusion of electrical discharges occur between the two plates.

In the case of the erogenous chakras, however, which are usually glowing white (and hence easy to see clairvoyantly), the sexualizing discharges are a delicious purple in color, more towards the magenta.

It has been observed for a very long time that the mouth and lips are the chief erotic, hence sexualizing, organs. In fact, some lips can make others quite "wild," and poems and songs have been written to this effect.

In these cases are to be found a series of chakras inhabiting the lips, usually five in number on the upper lip, and one in the center of the bottom lip.

In some examples of occult art, these are often pictured as tiny five-pointed stars, presumably because others have seen them radiate as stars are perceived to do. They are usually seen ranging from light pink to deep red in color. They tend to "attract" other energy bodies because they glitter. They also can extend rays and beams.

The frequency of these lip chakras, however, is not very democratically spread throughout the species. Some male and female versions do not appear to have them as sexualizing paraphernalia at least in an awakened state—while pink to red lipsticks cannot make up for the lack of them.

But I've clairvoyantly seen them suddenly appear and "come alive" in male and female versions seemingly at first bereft of them.

That these chakras do exist, at least in some people, is clear enough from Kirlian photographs of lips I've seen.

When the chakras are indeed present, they can definitely be seen on the Kirlian plates as small points of white light on black-and-white film, and as pink to red points surrounded by blue lights on color sensitive film.

Male and female versions possessing these six lip chakras usually adore kissing and will kiss just about anything and everything. In today's developing lore, they are often referred to as "mouth freaks" by those who are bereft of these wonderful chakras.

SEXUALIZING ASPECTS OF HAIR FOLLICLES AND THE PORES

It has recently been discovered that the hair follicles and pores possess an absolutely astonishing array of sensors. Their purposes, then, are not just to grow hair and produce sweat.

Among other sensing, for example, these can respond to subtle magnetic changes, as well as magnetic directions. And they can identify chemical odors the nose cannot, or at least usually does not.

Seated in their follicles, the hairs act as antennae, entirely sensitive to "vibrations" of all kinds. The pores emit small rays of light which are likewise sensitive and thus serve as antennae, too.

However, the hair follicle systems seem to be independent of, or at least different from, the white chakras of the erogenous zones, while at the same time being energetically connected.

The hair antennas WILL detect energies invisible to the eye mechanisms and brain and will introduce into the subconsciousness appropriate images (and conclusions) therein.

The hair and pore antennae seem to be sensitive to thought-forms, and apparently can detect their nature or motives.

Thus, when a male or female is being scanned for sexualizing purposes, the hair antennae will respond, inform the follicles, at which time the whole sensorium will become attentive, often with the result of goosebumps or hair standing on end.

The same is true if one enters an environment especially designed for sexualizing encounters, or perhaps not even designed for them.

Seen with micro-clairvoyance, each hair is extended often to about a foot beyond its tip, by a needle-thin ray of intense blue light, but which ray is bendable.

Even if the physical hair part is laying down horizontally to the skin, the ray part will form a right angle to the skin. When something tremendous energizes the sensorium, the hairs themselves will stand up and out from the skin.

These blue rays, in their great profusion, are often thought to comprise the general electrostatic field around the human body which is now known to exist because it has been photographed. These rays are extraordinarily magnetic in nature and can attract or repel just like magnets do.

ATTRACTING AND REPELLING SEXUALIZING ENERGIES

It is well known that the north pole of one magnet (the "negative" pole) and the south pole (the "positive" pole) of another magnet will adhere to each other in the flick of an eye.

The functions of the hairs and their follicles are similar regarding attraction, repulsion, and adhering.

The blue-ray extensions of hairs are incredibly sensitive to what either attracts or repels them.

But when they sense an attraction, they immediately throw out what, for lack of better descriptive words, is like the filaments of a spider's web. The filaments are usually deep blue in color.

Since this web is made of some kind of plastic-like energy, it can be flung out to a considerable distance, and will settle over the source of the attraction and adhere to it.

Thereafter it will either pull the source of the attraction or will actually pull the individual person to that source. If the source is not considered attractive, the hairs will ignore it.

The secret here, even difficult to clairvoyant estimations, seems to be the instantaneous recognition by the whole sensorium of some kind of compatible energies, which altogether are experienced as "thrilling." Whether these consist of animate or inanimate matter doesn't seem to matter.

These nets clearly have purposes besides sexualizing ones. But as a first level of whole sensorium response, they are likely to kick off cascades of sexualizing and erotic repercussions which arouse at least expectancy in all of the other sexualizing paraphernalia.

However, if the hair is too long, or shaved off, this net-throwing function seems to suffer, while shorter clipped hair seems to aid in the function.

This seems to have to do with the fact that the hairs need to grow new tips, and no one has ever been able to tell me how a hair knows what its proper length is and how it decides to grow back to it.

Hairs rejuvenate and recreate themselves, this, it would seem, being the only complete replacement function of the entire human body.

In this sense, the natural shorter hairs on arms, legs, and torsos seem most desirable, and this includes the pubic hairs.

The beard follicles in male versions are especially sensitive as sexualizing agencies and, from the clairvoyant view, shaving of them often appears to be a source of sexualizing energy mismanagement.

In any event, male and female versions can produce the

adhering nets. Female versions don't particularly need this type of net, although most females can and do produce it. As we shall soon see, female versions have OTHER quite impressive energy faculties along this line.

Considering all of the above, it is then not unusual that human bio-psychic organisms are sensitive to sexualizing influences, even if they are substandard when it comes to clairvoyance.

Everyone can demonstrate the above for themselves by carefully and calmly passing their fingers close to, but not physically touching, all or any of the areas defined.

The rays emanating from the fingertips will minutely excite the basic paraphernalia which have now been discussed. One may have to practice a little and refine the focus of sensation. That one has probably already located all, or most, of one's own erotic zones can be taken for granted.

If you then permit your mind to construct the relevant images, you will soon obtain some kind of mental image pictures regarding those energy factors.

Chapter 25
SOME ANATOMY OF SEXUALIZING ENERGY REGALIA

The concepts of sexualizing paraphernalia and regalia have been established for the purposes of the book, and so they are unfamiliar. But there are numerous kinds of vital energies, and in order to increase understanding of them it seems necessary to categorize their differences in some descriptive manner.

The apparent basic function of the sexualizing paraphernalia seems to consist of flowing and circulating energies within the human organism. The traditional Asian metaphor for this has to do with "breath"—breathing the energies in and out.

In rather dramatic contrast, the apparent basic functions of the sexualizing regalia have to do with arousal, the Asian metaphor being "awakening"—flowering or activating into ecstatic life and existence.

The two differences indicate two different kinds of states of the sexualizing energies: a more or less natural state, and an aroused or awakened state.

Another distinctive difference is that most of the paraphernalia can be seen clairvoyantly with regard to everyone except when declines in health and well-being are present.

But the regalia make an appearance, or become visible, only with respect to arousal or awakening.

Thus, they can clairvoyantly be perceived only upon the occasions of the arousal state. Where or how the regalia exist otherwise is a complete mystery to me, since they seem to come out of nowhere and return to the same.

The differences just described are, of course, qualitative ones, but with the proviso that they are MOSTLY qualitative in that they also have some kind of substantive existence that makes impacts on the sensibilities of others.

Even without an excessive amount of clairvoyance, almost everyone can detect and acknowledge the presence of a sexually aroused individual.

Indeed, regalia-aroused individuals are commonly referred to as "hot," "ready," "horny," etc., and so their aura energy fields are communicating this in some kind of way. This can only mean that some kind of information is involved, and this aspect is extremely important regarding the sexualizing regalia.

INFORMATION-CARRYING ENERGIES

If we shift our conceptualizing a little, it is possible to consider that the energies are not just energies pure and simple, but something along the lines of information-carrying energies.

Although this is a concept that can be discussed more fully in the contexts of creativity and power, it can be said that different energies are carriers of different kinds of information. This is in fact quite well understood within the scope of the conventional sciences and the now very important information theories.

For example, if the physicality of the body is formatted because of energetic principles, then the energetic principles must contain the information patterns that result in the developing morphological forms of the physical body.

And indeed, because of recent advances, especially in genetics, it has become necessary to consider that the physical body is composed not only of matter.

Since the matter is formatted along precise lines, resulting in the corpus, some kind of energetic information principle is required to pull off not only the initial formatting, but all developmental vital activity thereafter.

In this sense, then, vital energies are not simply energy, but something akin to energy-information combined.

Attempting a rather grand stride from the above, what is one to conclude if one senses or clairvoyantly perceives a beam or ray jumping from one energetic aura to another? Surely there must be some kind of information purpose involved.

From this, there downloads two fundamental options: That the beam is information delivering; or that it is information seeking.

In either case, generally speaking, this would appear to involve a matter of intent, or intention.

This is to say that if the information-intent of the beam is sexual, then sexual information would be delivered, received, exchanged, sense-emphasized, or sense-modulated.

But the same kind of beam might have other kinds of information qualities as well.

For example, a sexualizing beam might also carry information qualities having to do with love, hate, an entire spectrum of emotions. Indeed, all these qualities are typical of the many confusions that go along with sexualizing phenomena.

The general point being made here is that energetic phenomena of the auras are also information-carrying phenomena, and that the shift, say, from sexualizing to creative-izing affects is but a shift in information-emphasis or information-modulating.

THE PLASTIC-ENERGY CHARACTERISTICS OF THE SEXUALIZING REGALIA

In the foregoing chapter, we have seen that most of the energetic phenomena were local to certain parts of the body. However, some of the rays associated with the aura energy field could extend quite far out, and some of them could undulate and bend.

We also saw that there are several dimensions and purposes within the sexualizing auras themselves. So, the sexualizing paraphernalia discussed in the last chapter is just one of the functional dimensions.

There is another sexualizing dimension having to do with what I've termed the sexualizing REGALIA, and which is clairvoyantly seen only if and when the sexualizing paraphernalia have become active and aroused. If they are not active, then they can't be seen clairvoyantly.

But even if active, and if the clairvoyant thresholds are not sufficient to perceive them, the effects of the aroused regalia are easily sensed far and wide. Indeed, all things considered, there is nothing like a regalia aroused male or female.

PLASTIC ENERGIES

In order to provide a very important background, we need briefly to inspect three needed terms: plastic, stimulate, and horny.

The definition of the word PLASTIC is taken from the Greek PLASTICOS meaning "to mold or to form," and indicates a pliable substance that undergoes molding or formation.

PLASTIC, then, has much in common with its noted synonyms, such as creative, formative, bendable, malleable, adaptable, and especially DUCTILE, meaning "to be drawn out, extended, or withdrawn by will to do so."

The concept of plasticity is exceedingly important regarding the phenomena of the entangled manifestation. When these phenomena are illustrated on a two-dimensional piece of paper, they have to be illustrated in a way that suggests they are fixed or static, not in motion.

However, the different aspects of the entangled manifestation are ALWAYS in motion, always changing, always radiating, always extending out or drawing in. And they are always in process of modifying various aspects to suit what's at hand either in physical, mental, psychic, or energetic ways.

If anything deserves to be called changeling, then the sum of the entangled manifestation is it. It is entirely plastic, shapeable, malleable, pliant, ductile, and adaptable, and always anything but fixed or static.

STIMULUS ENERGIES

STIMULUS refers to something that arouses or incites to activity, to an agent that directly influences the activity of living protoplasm, or to what excites "a sensory organ or evoking muscular contraction or glandular secretion."

STIMULUS is usually utilized only as a scientific or clinical term. But we all know what is meant by it, even though we might not use the word. In the vernacular, its equivalent is what "turns one on."

HORNYNESS ENERGIES

Although a widely utilized word, prudery has caused it to be omitted from standard dictionaries. One therefore has to consult a dictionary of slang terms, wherein it is found (c. 1753) as referring to a policeman, and in Australia (c. 1901) also referred to a bullock.

In about 1889, it was finally accepted, in illegitimate English, as meaning sexually excited and lecherous. However, it is a very ancient concept. Long before the rather deadening term PENIS was conceptualized, the erect membrum virile was referred to as a horn, and few were ignorant of what that meant.

One of the points being made here is that it is somewhat ridiculous to think that the physical atoms and chemicals of the physical body, inorganic and inert as they are, can produce, by themselves, the effect of hornyness.

Indeed, if the formative modern philosophies and sciences of materialism had been forced to deal with this particular issue, then it is doubtful that materialism would have gained such a trenchant foothold.

Indeed, it is rather difficult to see how or why matter itself would or could become horny.

As it is, hornyness is not only an energetic phenomenon, but an AROUSED energetic one. The state of horny is also quite infamous for being non-volitional—with such a mind of its own that even the strongest formats of WILL have a tough time dealing with it.

Seen clairvoyantly, the energetic state of horny can be perceived as an outrageous display of beams, threads, and rays thrusting outward—more or less undulating, extending so as to seek out or stimulate horny states in others, clearly with the intention of melding with them, at least in temporary ways.

ENERGETIC MELDINGS

Hornyness is often described as a "hunger" or a "starvation"—in that having sex per se, even having it repetitively, often does not fulfill that hunger. Thus, it could be concluded that something else is involved.

Something along these lines becomes clear when it can be seen that horny female versions often will not select horny male versions.

What appears to alleviate or fulfill hornyness are complete

energy-body meldings of particular kinds. Although sexual activity is often one of the outcomes, the melding seems to have deeper implications.

Such meldings can be achieved WITHOUT subsequent physical sexual activity, although touching and embracing (and sometimes kissing) always seem to be a needed requirement.

Seen clairvoyantly, hornyness appears to be an automatic, non-volitional, and somewhat cyclical, excitation of the entire energy body (or sensorium) and it begins to produce some astonishing energy body phenomena.

It's worth noting here that there are many types of hornyness besides sexualizing One can, for example, be horny to be stimulated by good or bad art, music, new stamps, climbing mountains, scientific exploration, religious indoctrination, and etc. But we rather refer to these as "fascinations" so as to explicitly preserve the term horny for sexuality attraction matters.

As far as I can determine, the states of all hornynesses appear to occur because the energy body is desirous of modulating or remodulating itself by the use of compatible and sympathetic stimuli.

This "desire" appears to have more to do with the "destiny" of the energy body per se than merely with the genitals of the presently existing bio-body.

In any event, the energy-body phenomena ARE phenomena of arousal mechanisms (if not psychologically blockaded) regarding the male and female versions.

Seen clairvoyantly, the arousals are quite phenomenal and exquisitely wonderful, and glimpsing them is well worth the effort of trying to become clairvoyant.

SEXUALIZING REGALIA OF THE
BIOLOGICAL FEMALE VERSION

In the case of the bio-female version, which is undergoing a horny cycle, the shoulders, upper arms, and back first become slightly illuminated, the color at first usually being an off-white or a slightly light-pinkish one.

This preliminary arousal doesn't necessarily correspond to the female's ovulating cycle, and in fact often occurs after menstrual cycles have ceased altogether, often more profoundly so. So it can't be said to correspond only to bio-reproduction.

This preparatory illuminating might last for about two days, after which "wings" begin sprouting upward from the breasts, shoulders, and upper back. These now begin to take on a slightly undulating, light-bluish hue which is transparent, but somewhat "veined" as in butterfly wings.

Shortly thereafter, the wings begin cascading energies upward, often turning slightly golden at the tops of these undulating "fountains."

I'm almost embarrassed to say it because it's almost too incredible, but these fountains of upward-moving light can extend up to twenty feet above the female's shoulders.

That these sexualizing energy phenomena should be called REGALIA is now perfectly understandable.

At this point in the developing phenomena, the fountains spread out and begin to emit points of light, which are always scintillating white, and which begin drifting downward, somewhat like sparkling dew.

Meanwhile, the breasts have become increasingly sensate, almost to a state of "Painful thrill," something akin to pink "rose blossom" auras have developed with the nipples at their centers, and which by now are at least somewhat blood engorged.

Further down, the red chakra in the crotch has expanded considerably and can ultimately envelop the entire pelvic area. Also, the small green chakra just above the clitoris has begun emitting a bright yellowish green ray or beam, which is bendable and projectable, and which "snakes" out frontward as if trying to locate a "contact."

Meanwhile, the collections of the tiny white chakras comprising the erogenous zones have increased in luminosity, and thus in erotic sensitivity. The female may now rub just about anywhere and experience various kinds of ecstasy.

But now an even more amazing phenomenon occurs. From the pores of the skin begin to emerge microscopic (as seen via micro-clairvoyance) liquid-like GLOBULES of white-light energy.

These emerge from most pores in a stream at about five seconds apart, in so far as I've been able to time them with a stopwatch.

But there are thousands of pores on the skin, and so if micro-clairvoyance is not employed the whole of these floating globules will appear as a field or mist of white light.

Along with these liquid-like globules, a peculiar odor or fragrance now develops. It is often physically tangible. To my nose it is slightly musky and "damp."

This fragrance appears to be easily identifiable to male versions who wander too near. Other female versions will notice it too and comprehend that the female has "gone into heat." The fragrance is effective at least across a diameter of 30 feet, depending on air movements and directions. It will easily fill an average room.

The sparking bits of light drifting downward and the globules emanating widely now fall on everything within the proximity. Most male versions who wander into the perimeter now don't stand a chance.

Whether young or mature, fat, thin, or otherwise, the female now "suited out" in this astonishing and exceedingly beautiful and intensely sexualizing regalia—well, most males will find themselves "disturbed," even though the uninitiated among them might not have a visible clue as to why.

It would appear that OTHER "sensitive" female versions know exactly what is taking place, especially married ones who might hasten to get their husbands and even their sons away, and certainly their boyfriends.

None the less, most male versions, apparently of any age, will find the means to get nearer the female version, and which version now has only to select from among the many who are presenting themselves.

However, in astonishing surprise to clairvoyant seeing, the female version now becomes remarkably selective. The greenish snaking ray or beam energetically extending outward from just above the clitoris will be seen plunging INTO the bodies of the male versions.

If this bending beam doesn't like what it "sees," it is quickly withdrawn and plunges into another male version. The whole of this takes place in an instant, so fast that I've not developed micro-clairvoyance in sufficiently speedy accuracy to perceive what happens at this point.

However, the moment of the plunging and the withdrawing suffices to leave the targeted male versions somewhat temporarily dazed. The pupils of their eyes will widen, however bright the light is otherwise. Usually they have to grab hold of something long enough to recover some semblance of composure.

When, and if, the undulating green beam seems to find what it is looking for, it then proceeds to wrap its flagellating end in convolutions around the testicles of the selectee, also interpenetrating the red chakra between the scrotum and rectum.

The snaking beam now contracts along its entire length, and the male version involuntarily moves very close to the female version.

The pores of the male version will now begin to emit an "oily substance," usually in the color of liquid, dark yellow amber. He may also begin to sweat more than usual, and his tongue and throat will become dry.

However, I've seen female versions "reject" all the males in the perimeter after which the female version shortly leaves apparently to pursue other locales.

If a selection has taken place, few social or moral issues now apply, and ways and means will be devised about how to get around them.

Almost assuredly the anticipated full intimacies will take place even if in the nearest closet, bathroom, or parked car— or, in more permissive environment, right in front of everyone else.

The selected male version will be rendered rather witless, except under the most extraordinary circumstance. Clairvoyantly seen, even without micro-clairvoyance, the reasons are perfectly obvious.

The moment the male version's balls are under grapple, excepting the greenish "snake," the female version instantly ceases producing all of the regalia above discussed, like a switch has been thrown.

Now from the top of her skull rise up a whole flock of the most amazing limpid, liquid green rays. These are entirely extendible and bendable, and they reach out and wrap the entire body of the selected male version in them.

Likewise, apparently to make sure of matters, the two rose-blossom auras of the nipples now produce equally extendible beams which, with strong magnetic force, wrap around the torso of the selected male version.

Indeed, as soon as the couple are in a suitable place to commence the physical part of all of this, the male version almost invariably will rip off the upper garments of the female version and with mouth will "go for" for the rose-flower auras of the nipples.

The clairvoyantly-seen green-rayed regalia headdress of the female version is entirely compatible with the "myth" of Medusa and the crown of "snakes" growing out of this terrible goddess's head. Medusa turns males to stone, which is about the same as saying turning them senseless.

In conventional sexology terms, the whole of what has been described above is referred to as the "seduction of males by females," or "the female conquest." This, it would seem, is somewhat of an understatement.

Fortunately, the energy bodies of a goodly number of female versions are not entirely proficient in manifesting the full regalia. Even so, if they are proficient, even two of them in one room or at a cocktail party can arouse considerable consternation and wreck the otherwise peaceful activities of others in the near vicinity.

Additionally, males that have been "probed" and rejected will thereafter often "pine away" for a long time, so indelibly has the probing been recorded in their sensoriums. I've not yet seen a male version who is completely immune to all of this.

SEXUALIZING REGALIA OF THE BIOLOGICAL MALE VERSION

The full display of the male sexualizing regalia is equally astonishing, but in a number of different ways. In this case, the prelude to the horny epoch is begun when the red chakra between the scrotum and anus begins to expand.

Shortly it will begin forming a plastic shape that encompasses the genitals. In color, this plastic shape is always pink or pinkish red. In males of advancing age, it might be red or darker red.

This plastic shape then commences to protrude directly in front of the genitals like a pseudopodium. It is, in thickness, usually about six inches in diameter.

The idea that this is an energetic "hard on" is entirely appropriate. But the subsequent dimensions of this hard-on soon clearly approach the incredible.

If the hornyness is not quickly taken care of, as it usually and easily can be either directly by auto-release or by the availability of willing females or by paying dollars, then the rest of the regalia can manifest.

One of the first energetic phenomena which then manifests is that from the red crotch chakra will emerge a "tube" of whirling red energy about six or more inches in diameter.

Micro-clairvoyance reveals that this tube forms layers, some of which rotate clockwise, and others rotate anti-clockwise. I've never understood the functions of these rotations.

Soon, the red tube will gradually snake up through the intestines, abdomen, lungs, throat, and brains, and eventually emerge out of the top of the skull. After this, the whirling beam will "grow" upward to about twenty to forty feet.

At a certain point, somewhat horizontally, it will develop "spikes" with curved hooks at their ends. These spikes, however, are rays or beams which are plastic. The symbolic equivalent of these phenomena are red plumes or feathers seen worn on helmets by male versions in many pre-modern societies.

The energy bodies of female versions can spot this red column and spikes from a great distance. Indeed, any clairvoyant can also, especially when examples of them could be seen walking in the street in front of my building's stoop.

If by now the hornyness has not been taken care of, the pink-light, bulging pseudopodia in the genital area begins extending itself in a rubber-like manner, but none the less held horizontally to the ground or floor.

If we can consider anything "normal" in all of this, then it might first extend directly outward to the front by about six to eight feet.

But I've clairvoyantly seen much more extensive examples, the longest being (take a deep breath) about 200 feet, which was noticed by a female clairvoyant friend of mine near Sheridan Square in New York City before I had noticed it. "Jesus Christ," said she, "would you look at that one!"

Any other bio-version, whether male or female, who chances to contact this beam, for example by inadvertently walking through it, will now become "disturbed" (e.g., stimulated), which seems to be the purpose here. In male versions, even chance contact with this beam will tend to arouse non-volitional hornyness in them.

Again, much now depends on whether the hornyness has been taken care of. If it has not, some male versions will now proceed to manifest "full-blown" sexualizing regalia. Perpetual masturbators, however, seldom do.

First off, the usual blue-white rays from the nails and fingertips will now take on the color of blood red and extend themselves up to as much as three feet.

These are quite "strong" rays, and the physical hands increase in gripping strength. In this state, the horny male version will occasionally be seen crunching his genitals through his clothes.

If a male version in this state manages to touch a female version, a sort of hypnosis might ensue and her collections of tiny white chakras denoting the erogenous zones dependably flare up. Strangely, however, they quickly seek escape, and so it would appear that the purpose of the male sexualizing regalia is not particularly to attract females.

If all of this regalia has not resulted in some kind of "success," the small purple chakra in the ass cleft enlarges considerably, and shortly will begin to emit occasional bursts of purple or lavender "lightening."

These streak away outward to who knows where, disappearing into invisibility, but in doing so they streak right through the physical- and energy-bodies of others.

Clairvoyantly seen, they disappear very quickly. But a "seriousness" has now begun to pervade. At this point, most males will accept relief from just about any source, and certainly by now usually do it to themselves.

More stalwart males, however, commence to develop the rest of these already amazing regalia. Long fluctuating "feathers," again red in color, about three feet in length, will now develop at the crown of the head. The "column" mentioned earlier grows more brilliant and its spikes even longer.

Usual clairvoyance might perceive all of this as an extending red field above the head. But with micro-clairvoyance, the "feathers" are seen, and from their tips shower down the equivalent of the white sparklers of the full-blown female versions.

NOW! COILS of pink-red energy, about four inches in diameter, develop from the soles of the feet and twist upward around the calves, knees and thighs, and often involve even the buttocks and the lower lasts of the belly and chest.

Similar coils, but only at about one to two inches in diameter, also emerge from the palms of the hands, twist around and upward involving the forearms, biceps, triceps, and shoulder muscles. The neck muscles seem to enlarge a little, but from within.

The symbolic equivalent of these coils is traditionally placed around the legs and arms of the Mercury archetype, as has already been mentioned.

Since I've never seen these vibrant energy coils regarding female versions, they appear to be unique to the male versions, especially regarding younger ones.

However, knowing clairvoyance to the degree I have experienced it, there is always a first time regarding anything and everything.

The appearance of these coils apparently means business if only in that they apparently impart considerable increases in strength.

I've also seen them appear in angry male versions, or in those preparing for some kind of physical fight combat. They sometimes appear in pumped up prize fighters and long-distance runners, etc. Their appearance also reduces the pain thresholds. Often the strength imparted is "superhuman."

These coils also result in hypnotic increases of ecstasy by anyone finding themselves embraced within them. They often produce a fragrance akin to that of ozone.

These coils mean serious business. Unless females or males are prepared to quickly follow through on the whole thing, I'd advise them not to tease, flirt, or taunt a coil-laden male version. Such males are now rather delicately balanced, and other males should not try to play grab-ass.

If this intensified sexualizing situation has NOT YET been taken care of, the buttocks will become engulfed in red light, and shortly a "flame" or fire will rise up along the spine. This is akin to, but seems

NOT to be, the Kundalini thing.

Male versions so affected will literally feel "hot," if they haven't already. In some cases, "spiky" flowers in a variety of colors will develop around the pectoral nipples.

Naturally, also by now all the collections of white chakras of the erogenous zones will have increased in luminescence, and the male version now appears encased in a rather gorgeous red and white luster. This glows like polished red-silver armor.

Indeed, many artistic illustrations of bygone centuries illustrate the fully empowered male in a suit of shining white and red armor.

Finally, as in the case of the female, the pores of the skin will begin emitting minute liquid-like globules, but these are again reddish in color, and they sparkle. These, too, emit a fragrance detectable to sensitive noses. Its odor it slightly acidic, something like fresh semen.

Strangely through all of this, while the male version suffered frequently from penile erections at the outset of the horny cycle, as the regalia develops into its full-blown magnificence, that organ tends to remain flaccid. The unrequited (as its often said) male version now tends to become somewhat zombie-like in spite of the regalia finery.

Also, or at least within my observing experience, female versions in their full sexualizing regalia don't seem to respond very well to the male versions fully outfitted in their regalia. If this is true, the sexualizing regalias can't be said to refer only to the processes of procreation.

Although I made lengthy attempts over time, and in many different kinds of circumstances, I saw no instance where any energy function of the male versions probe female versions. "Selection," therefore, seems to be left to the female versions, whereas a male version fully outfitted in its beautiful, but somewhat Martial regalia will (as it is often uncharitably said) take on anything that moves or has a hole in it.

Chapter 26
SOME SEXUALIZING ENERGIES OF BIO-PSYCHIC CHANGELINGS

Seen clairvoyantly, the feminine and masculine sexualizing energy forms have enough distinctions to classify them as such. But it must be recalled that the aura energy field IS an entangled manifestation of a complexity that is plastic and changeable and thus always in some kind of fluidic and/or electric-like motion.

To this now must be added the concept that the entangled manifestation apparently plays by its OWN ENTANGLED RULES, and which cannot at all be identified or even approximated strictly in accord with physicality.

This chapter addresses the fact that the sexualizing energies of biological females and males sometimes completely, partially, or temporarily exhibit each other's energetic manifestations, especially with regard to the sexualizing regalia.

This, of course, brings confusions into the nature of the sexes as they are biologically downloaded.

But it is also reflective of the rich world-wide traditions dating from antiquity having to do with the bio-psychic energies peculiar to the androgyne and the so-called hermaphrodite.

The modernist West is abysmally and stubbornly deficient of knowledge in this regard. And so there is no easy point of entrance into the tremendous real issues involved. So I'll just review a few significant contexts, and then get on with the energetic phenomena apparently involved.

THE ANDROGYNE

Information sources on the androgyne are found worldwide,

but the most accessible of them download from ancient China, India, Greece, and Egypt.

In those sources, the androgyne is referred to not as a double-sexed biological entity, but as a state of consciousness where the mind soars above forms of all kinds.

Since the concepts of the sexes refer to forms, whether physical, mental, or energetic, the soaring must eventually range above, bypass, or depart from the sexual divisions.

This, of course, refers to a metaphysical psychic level of existence characterized by "free" formless energy BEFORE it downloads into the "form of existence."

In this sense, the androgyne is the metaphor for the level of non-manifested being, and which, at the same time, is the source of any subsequent manifestations into any kind of form, whether energetic, psychic, mental, or physical.

In ancient Hindu metaphysics, the duality of the male and female polarities of the sexes (represented by Shiva and Sakti) meld into each other in the androgyne state to become the Unity of being-consciousness senior to any manifestation of sexual duality.

But, figuratively speaking, the Unity can morphologically be represented as a double-sexed figure. For example, several such artifacts of Dionysus found in Greece represent both a man and a woman, sometimes referred to as the Erect, the Hybrid, the Man Woman Unity.

Such artistic attempts did not serve to portray a physical double-sexed figure, but the combination of the dual energies toward their unity that lifts the "mind" above the two sexual distinctions (and all their attendant problems).

But one of the implications of the portrayals was that sexualizing energies COULD exist in combination with each other in order to meld and become a unity containing both.

The above is a rather brief review of the essence of the androgyne. But it is sufficient to establish the androgyne as the archetype of sexual-energy combining and ultimate transcendence of the combining into the ecstatic unity of a state of consciousness unfettered by the manifested boundaries of sexual formats and desires relevant to them.

ARCHETYPE

The term ARCHETYPE denotes "the original pattern or model of which all things of the same type are representations or copies."

The concept of the archetypes of the collective unconscious was energetically elaborated at awesome length by the famous psychoanalyst, Carl Gustav Jung (1875-1961).

Jungian psychology is based on psychic totality and psychic energism, i.e., that psychic "stuff" of the unconscious is not merely just existing, but that it has dynamic force and activity.

Jung postulated two dimensions in the unconscious: the personal, based on repressed events and experiences, and the archetypes of a collective unconscious, a dimension shared by every member of our species in a universal group mind kind of way.

There are all sorts of ramifications regarding the nature of the collective unconscious. But Jung's use of the archetypes hinged on the concept that the shared collective unconscious was "inhabited" by specific forms of psychic energy forms each having special dynamic activity. These energetic forms constituted original, or basic, patterns in the collective unconscious of our species, copies of which arose in individuals.

In pursuit of identifying these original patterns, Jung enumerated and described a great number of them.

He and others after him showed that a very large number of the archetypes have similarly arisen as "themes" in almost all cultures, and that a rather large part of human activity is played out, or enacted, in keeping with the archetypal themes.

For example, the archetype of the Wise Man is recognized everywhere, as are the archetypes of the Earth Mother, the Joker or Trickster, and the search for enlightenment, portrayed as a Cup or Chalice brimming full with Precious Liquid or Light.

THE THREE MAJOR SEXUALIZING ARCHETYPES

One of the crucial aspects of the archetypes is not only that they exist in "psychic space," so to speak. They also exist with such universal influence that they require some kind of representational form suitable to their specific kinds of vitalizing energies.

Although the Androgyne archetype can be portrayed as a sexually ambivalent figure, its central meaning denotes a state above or beyond sexuality. But its most representative form is the Zero, denoting the formless before forms manifest. However, it takes a rather super-developed form of consciousness to recognize, achieve, and deal with this.

Meanwhile, back in the realm of psycho-energetic forms, there are three major sexualizing archetypes that are recognized just about everywhere, albeit in somewhat different formats, but all having similar iconography and attributes.

These three sexualizing archetypes have been with us since pre-antiquity, and we in the modern West today still recognize them by their ancient Roman designations of:

- Mars, as the chief Male or Masculine archetype.
- Venus, as the chief Female or Feminine archetype.
- Mercury, as the chief Inter-sexed or Mixed-sex archetype.

As a caution here, it needs to be carried in mind that these archetypes, as with all archetypes, refer to specific kinds of vitalizing energies. Those energies do download into artistic and representational forms, and which are sometimes mistaken for the archetypes themselves.

Many pre-modern societies elevated the sexualizing archetypes to the position of semi-deification:

- Mars, the demi-god of intense masculinity with all His active energies and aggressive trappings.
- Venus, the demi-goddess of intense femininity with all Her passive energies and associated allurements.

The existence of the Mercury sexualizing archetype has always been somewhat eclipsed by the other two. But in its classical sense, it denoted a combination of the Mars-Venus archetypes, a sort of half-and-half affair comprised of both.

But the Mercury archetype had one specific factor the other two did not.

The Mars archetype is obviously associated with the red planet Mars, and the Venus archetype is associated with the glittering and beautiful planet Venus.

But the Mercury archetype appears to be chiefly associated with mercury, the metal, which is liquid, fluid and highly plastic, and can change its shape without being destroyed.

In this sense, the chief attribute of the Mercury archetype is change, and anything that is fluid and shape- or situation-changing is associated with this demi-deity.

In other words, while the attributes associated with the Mars and Venus energy archetypes are expected to remain the same in a kind of static way, the chief attribute of the Mercury archetype has to do with energetic undulations.

Thus, the Mercury archetype is usually represented with undulating coils and small wings on feet and on a helmet denoting psychic power.

Based on clairvoyance of their various kinds of energies, these three archetypes terms now make better sense.

The only apparent mistake is the rather superficial assumption that the Martian and Venusian types are complimentary to each other and somehow fit together.

As far as of my clairvoyant observations have gone, this is decidedly not the case.

SOME CLAIRVOYANT EXAMPLES OF THE THREE SEXUALIZING ENERGIES

However, the Martian and Venusian types of sexualizing regalia I've described cannot be taken as typical or standard, since mixtures of them are far more common.

Regarding the impressive female regalia, I've seen only two examples that fit the ideal feminine bill. One example concerned a sales lady tending a perfume counter in the famous and very elegant Bloomingdale's department store in New York City.

I had gone there with a friend who wanted to purchase some special skin lotions. This was before Carmen de Barazza helped close down my "flaring chakras."

I could see the regalia from across the store, and it turned out that her counter sold the types of lotions my friend was looking for.

I had already seen lesser versions of the female regalia, and had, with difficulty, comprehended what they meant. But this woman was older, although well preserved and quite elegant and stunning. I couldn't resist doing a little research. So I told her I was "developing my clairvoyance."

This interested her, and so I popped the rather brash question: Are you by any chance horny?

Her eyes widened. Oh, My God! You can see that! I'm about to die. So I described what I was seeing, at which point she broke into tears.

It turned out that she was SIXTY-ONE years old, although she looked fifty, and had undergone menopause years earlier at the appropriate time.

My friend and I lingered at the counter for quite some time. We discovered that her studdly live-in boyfriend, who was twenty-four, would be back in town that very night.

And so hypnotic had I become that I ended up buying $125-worth of expensive lotions I didn't need or want.

I've witnessed several versions of the male regalia full blown, each of which were variations on the central theme. Only in a few cases did I venture to pop the horny question and was rewarded with suitable answers.

According to my admittedly clairvoyant lucidity observations, what is more usual is to find either smatterings or full parts of the Martian and Venusian sexualizing energies in the SAME individual energy body.

Such energetic mixtures thus equate to the Mercury energy archetype. The dislocations between the two sexual versions of the sexualizing paraphernalia also have to be considered.

It is also not unusual to find male versions at least temporarily manifesting parts of or the full female regalia (with the exception of the green probing beam) or to find female versions temporarily manifesting the male regalia (with the exception of the coils).

Something here seems to fall within the scope of whatever or whichever energy body the energy sensorium either wants to do or wants to experience.

THE RELATIONSHIP OF HORNYNESS AND
THE DESIRE TO MELD OR BOND

The topic of melding will be more fully elaborated in the next chapter. But setting aside here what might constitute psychological difficulties, blocks, or fixations, the purpose of hornyness seems to indicate a desire to meld with someone or something.

If we add the concept of BONDING to this, arriving at double concept of MELDING-BONDING, we can trace back into antiquity certain rituals designed to inspire and achieve such.

Many modern attitudes can hardly think of such rituals as anything other than sexual, meaning that they can't get much beyond the issues of the physical genitalia having precise, but limited functions.

Even without the asset of clairvoyance, this seems a quite narrow vision. Even though such rituals obviously had their sexualizing concomitants, the ancients could see that there was hardly any logical reason to ritualize sexual activity per se. Something that goes on all of the time hardly needs to be ritualized.

Melding and bonding, however, clearly should be ritualized, since these constitute important issues above and beyond mundane physical intercourse and etc. Even the heterosexual marriage rite today does not ritualize intimate contact; rather it attempts to ritualize melding and bonding.

It's worth mentioning along these lines that perhaps the two potential participants should undergo clairvoyant inspection before the marriage rite. Legalized copulating alone often does not a marriage make.

It is helpful here to remember that the energy body is never static. It is always in flux, or fluctuating. It is also plastic and seems to be enabled to "create" novel energy manifestations.

For example, the pranic chakras (which have been discussed) are not usually seen as activated in most bio-psychic units. On the other hand, some or all of them can magically appear, at least temporarily so, where not one iota of evidence for them has been perceived before.

Thus, something here is obviously owed to the "states of consciousness" the sensorium or vital soul has "decided" to manifest and to meld or bond with.

It's also very worthwhile to mention that the auras of certain people seldom manifest any sexualizing energies, none of the regalia at least.

I noticed that the auras of some people were a gorgeous blue, or a gorgeous light purple. Upon questioning these people, they invariably had higher, aesthetic or spiritual goals, with sex only occasionally being necessary or not at all. It was easy enough to associate such sex-empty energies to the Androgyne archetype.

Earlier this century, many psychologists and philosophers theoretically suggested that the "sex energies" could be "sublimated" into other creative urges and goals.

This is somewhat in keeping with what can clairvoyantly be perceived, although a "shift" in consciousness is also apparently needed.

It is illogical to believe that a sensorium fixated into sex energies can sublimate them without also un-fixating that particular state of consciousness.

THE PROBLEMATICAL NATURE OF MIXES OF THE THREE SEXUALIZING ENERGY FORMS

Before going on, it should be admitted that clairvoyantly I have seen energetic phenomena I have not been able to identify or understand.

Especially prominent among these are the black, right angle bars seen in the auras and inside the bio-body, and the various kinds of shooting in and shooting out radiances seen to leave and enter various energy bodies.

Also mysterious is seeing that an aura field is composed of more than just one personal aura field, or several of them. Some of these, or a mix of then, can be identified as belonging to a female version, others obviously belong to a male version.

The problem with clairvoyant seeing in this regard is that such mixes tend to undulate in and out of each other. They come, they go, they appear, they vanish. But the implication is that it is not an individual or personal aura being seen, but a composite.

From these additional "personal" auras, as it were, can occasionally be seen flare-ups of the male or female regalia. The complications here seem obvious and insurmountable, unless we consider that in some cases the energetic sensorium involved is a composite one, and which will "produce" mixtures of sexualizing energies.

At any rate, there are confusions to be encountered when an individual aura or energy body manifests more than male or female energy manifestations or manifests a mix of them.

Since we can suppose what these mixes or multiplicities probably mean in social terms, there is little point in delving too deeply into them.

As it is, however, some males manifest distinct female regalia and this whether they are seen as physically feminine or butch or built like brick shithouses.

Butch dykes almost always exhibit the protruding pink pseudopodia from their crotch areas, although in those cases that energy organ usually doesn't extend outward very far.

Both female and male versions can emit from their pores the male or female globules, depending, it might be supposed, on circumstances or perceived affinities of external sexualizing attractions.

Sometimes I've seen energy bodies having fully one-half of the male sexualizing regalia and one-half of the female regalia. I've occasionally witnessed married couples, seeming completely happy, but in which the male manifests versions of the female regalia, while the female manifests those of the male.

Thus, the Mercury archetype is perfectly valid, if based upon what can clairvoyantly be seen. In this sense, then the modern terms heterosexual, homosexual, and bisexual seem particularly limiting, narrow, and often just plainly inapplicable. These terms are purely sociological in origin, and don't at all apply to sexualizing phenomena of our species that transcends local sociological idiocies.

It is worth recalling here that the Mercury archetype is "fluid" like the liquid metal mercury. All human energy bodies are also "fluid."

Indeed, fluidity is the hallmark of the human species in all things, including physical motion, mental motion, spiritual and aesthetic motion, About the only thing that can become fixed, thus static, are convictions, and these are exclusively of static psychological origin.

The equivalent of convictions can be perceived in human

auras, usually of the color black, or a darker non-luminous color. These "clouds" or "densities" can usually be seen as sucking in energy, perhaps like a black hole, a vacuum cleaner, or in a vampire kind of way No outpouring can be seen, or only very weak ones.

For more specifics on all this, I'll refer you to Barbara Ann Brennan's competent book, HANDS OF LIGHT (1987), listed in the bibliography.

In her book, among other topics important to clairvoyance, you will find a section headed "The Energy Field of the Schizoid Structure."

This refers to an energy structure characterized mainly by energy-field
discontinuities like imbalances and breaks. These "structures" are not uncommon, but they are outside the scope of this present book.

ENERGETIC COMPLEXITIES TO BE CONSIDERED

So far, although these commentaries might seem strange enough, there are now some energetic complexities to be considered:

1. Some male versions cannot be seen to possess the sexualizing paraphernalia of the purple chakra in the cleft of their buttocks. If it is indeed absent, and not merely reduced to nothing, then this absence seems to leave the male curiously asexual, and often completely uninterested in such matters.
2. Likewise, some females can be seen to have an absence of the complimentary blue-green chakra just inside their vaginas, with much the same result.
3. However, some males and females can be seen to have BOTH—with resulting complications and confusions.
4. A male version can have the female chakra just above his penis or at some point along the penis. The female version can have the male one, although not in her ass cleft, but slightly above it nearer the tail bone.
5. Obviously, these factors begin to make for some complications regarding the bending rays. And since

these complications are so various, its rather senseless to utilize the three stereotypes of heterosexual, homosexual, and bisexual to describe them.
6. One reason is that the mix-up is more frequent than might be expected, and that there is indeed a wide spectrum regarding what can then happen.
7. At times, these mix-ups seem only temporary and impermanent, since in the same individuals they can be seen to change, vanish, and reemerge at various times. Something obviously depends on circumstances here.
8. With equal shiftiness, the tip of the male penis can be seen having the emerald green chakra, while in the female the clitoris can be found having the ruby red one.

These situations usually have unexpected (or expected) results concerning the bending rays, and which results can easily be described as "attractions," or better still as "pulling attractions" which take the intellects involved by surprise.

The presence of the usually red chakra in the crotch is usually the same in both the male and female versions, with the exception that if it is fading, has changed colors, or has darkened or blackened, then almost assuredly the person will shortly be subjected to ill health.

It also appears that if this basic powerful chakra has somehow become jeopardized, then a wide variety of emotional and adverse psychological effects might also manifest.

For example, ANY toxic drugs, and any overuse of alcohol, seems at least to temporarily distort this crotch chakra, not only as in regard to its circularizing shape, but its colors as well.

While this chakra seems to have a great deal to do with sexualizing activities, its impairment is also easily related to increases of faulty judgment. If it is not impaired, it can yield increases in refined judgment.

Chapter 27
THE ENERGETIC MELDING FUNCTION

As has been mentioned, when auras are illustrated on paper, they are seen only in the 2-dimensions the paper represents. Any motional activity of the real aura is frozen on the page, so one can easily come away from the illustrations with the idea that the aura energy fields are static or motionless.

Written descriptions of auras can point up that they are active and motile. But still, in a visualizing sense, the static two-dimensional image has entered into memory, which itself is likely to be predominantly composed of billions of static pictures.

The whole of this leads to the subtle expectation that any clairvoyant perception of the auras will "see" them as they were presented in the static illustrations. The reason is that verbal visual memory storage are two different sectors of the overall memory storage banks.

It would take movie or video film to capture the auras in a three-dimensional way and give the necessary impressions of their active motion.

Motion pictures can capture electromagnetic activity, especially if they illuminate or ionize the atmosphere around them, such as is the case regarding lightening either in nature or in laboratories.

Sometimes, still photographs of people demonstrate glows or other phenomena around them. However, such effects are usually "explained" as trickery or as something amiss with the photo process.

Motion pictures of Kirlian auras have been achieved. These show the energy discharges as scintillating, often as jumping around and changing shape, and exhibiting sudden changes of color.

Conventional analysis dismisses these as mere electrostatic effects, which most assuredly they are in one sense. But the question remains as to why even electrostatic effects should happen.

In the case of the Kirlian effects, it is true that a mild electrical charge is being introduced into the hand, and that it is being discharged out of the hand.

It is these discharges that can be photographed and explained away as such.

But this is indicative of a process whereby any energy encountered by the body or energy field would likewise be absorbed and then discharged. So the Kirlian effects represent a simple model of what would happen to the greater energetic whole.

Similar to the Kirlian effects, which are always dancing and scintillating in motion, the whole of the aura would also be scintillating and dancing in vital motion. Even aura fields that might at first appear to visualizing clairvoyance as motionless mists are composed of micro-energetic particles always exhibiting some kind of energetic motion.

THE DYNAMIC MOTILITY OF AURA ENERGY FIELDS

MOTILE is a term seldom used anymore, but it should be restored to usage regarding aura energy fields.

As an adjective, MOTILE denotes "Capable of motion; characterized by motion."

MOTILITY denotes "Capable of the power of motion (as a quality of organisms")."

The introduction of the term POWER into the above definition is important, at least in its principle and most descriptive definition; "Having ability to act or produce an effect; capacity for being acted upon or undergoing an effect."

The above definitions take on added luminosity if the term DYNAMIC is introduced into them. The standard definitions of that term usually refer only to physical forces or energies.

But the definition of DYNAMICS is more useful and revealing. It denotes "a branch of mechanics that deals with forces and their relation primarily to the motion, but sometimes also to the equilibrium of bodies of matter."

This definition can logically be extended to include the motion and/or equilibrium of "vital life organisms."

Keeping the above in mind, the definition of DYNAMISM

becomes quite interesting and revealing: "The theory that explains the universe in terms of forces and their interplay."

As might be surmised, this "theory" is the modern Western equivalent of the Pranic energies of ancient India, and the Ch'i energies of ancient China.

If these definitions are carefully reflected upon, it is almost impossible to consider any kind of energy as having anything remotely resembling, as it were, effect-less-ness.

Energies, then, rather regularly produce dynamic effects, and they do so whether they are, in any conventional sense, visible or invisible, tangible or intangible.

The distinction between non-visual and visual clairvoyance has been discussed in several different contexts.

Non-visual clairvoyance (a type of telesthesia) has been defined under the connotation of dynamic "sensing" in the absence of any mental imagery that goes along with visualizing clairvoyance.

Although non-visualizing clairvoyance is broadly discounted, it is none the less a quite important form of it, since it most clearly represents the signal feature of energies, its impacting or dynamic effects.

Indeed, the effects are first sensed (because of their impacts), but the initial sensing is almost immediately or simultaneously followed by "knowledge" of from whom or from where the energies emanated.

If one has a form of clairvoyance developed enough to perceive motional qualities of the "knowledge," then the rays, beams or energy tubes conveying the energy can become visible. But this is a kind of clairvoyance that MUST incorporate the "seeing" of the dynamic motility of the energies involved. The meaning here is that if the clairvoyant doesn't expect to sense-see the motility, then it is quite likely to remain in the invisible category.

The thrust of the foregoing discussion has been to bring to light the motile-dynamic nature of aura energy fields, as contrasted to the more usual static, motionless, concepts of them. The reason is that the motionless concept of the energies cannot incorporate something that the motile concept can, that there are enormous qualitative differences among the impacting energies, and this must have something to do with subtle dynamic differences or essences imbedded in their motility.

MOTILE ENERGIES AS CARRIERS OF INFORMATION

Considering the fluidic motility of the auras or fields, their purpose or function cannot be simply to impact and cause random effects.

If that were the case, then all energetic impacts would more or less result in sensing the impact, but without any recognition as to what it represents beyond that.

To get into more refined distinctions of this, it can be said that human bio-psychic organisms are quite good at recognizing the difference, for example, between the emanating emotion impacts of love, hated, grief, happiness, admiration, and especially the impacts of sexualizing energies.

Broadly speaking, the sensing of the emotions (empathy) can sometimes have confusing aspects.

But sensing of the sexualizing energies is usually undergone with high degrees of clarity, the only real obstacle seeming to consist of intellectual damage regarding sexuality as a whole.

Each of the categories mentioned above can, of course, be considered superficially. But each of them can be transliterated into a specific type of "information."

Indeed, most will say that sex, love, and hate, for example, are composed of different vibrations. But the intent of this has to do not with the vibrations per se, but with the different kinds of information they carry.

This implies that the vibrations are sensed as different from each other not simply as different vibrations, but by their different information content.

In support of this, although information theorists are not overly preoccupied with auras, they none the less make a good case for interpreting the whole of existence as Information.

They further stipulate that the Whole Shebang of Information is somehow subdivided into particular information formats, but which must interact in order to discriminate information sets.

This, to be sure, is almost a very grand mystical or metaphysical prospect.

THE EXISTENCE OF ENERGY-INFORMATION

But the fact is that Information Theory can be seen working just about everywhere.

For example, the seeds of apples and the seeds of cacti carry the specific energy-information that invariably produce apple trees and cacti. In principle, it would be possible by genetic engineering to meld these two together to produce an apple cactus.

For the vital life energies and forces to have any meaning at all, it must be presumed that they either ARE or CARRY information. The fact that clairvoyants perceive the information forces as radiances, lights, colors, subtle fluids, fields, etc., is, in this sense, beside the point.

The "point" becomes more clarified in the case of psychic healing where the energetic-information patterns of the healer link into and stimulate a reorganization of the energetic-information patterns of the healee.

Some of the better examples of this have been documented as non-touch healing, where the physical hands of the healer do not touch the physical components of the healee. In cases of non-touch healing, the affect can only be an energetic one.

However, in some sense at least, the information-energies of the healer would have to temporarily meld with the information-energies of the healee in order for a curative energy-information exchange to take place.

But this leads to the prospect (better addressed as psychic force creativity) that vital life information energies and forces are being melded and exchanged all of the time anyway, even across distances, such as in the cases of "absent" healing where the healer and healee are separated by distances sometimes very great indeed.

It's worth noting at this point, that if the fundamental nature of mainstream societal resistance is examined in fundamental detail, all of the vital force phenomena recounted in this book are objected to on the grounds that (under any name) the energies ARE information carriers.

If the energies were just energies that did nothing, affected nothing, remained ovalesque, then there would be no societal problem about them.

From the point of social-control formats, however, one

can't have untamed information running around willy-nilly—either emerging from sensitives or seers or consisting of unsuspected influences that might be problematical to socio-authoritarian monopolies.

THE INFORMATION-EXCHANGE NATURE OF ENERGETIC MELDING

The principle of bio-psychic, energetic melding somewhat flows over into the activities of psychic creativity, in which context its substantive phenomena could be treated in depth.

But the sexualizing phenomena that are the topic of this book are, in themselves, types of vital energy melding, this being more pronounced and exact perhaps in the case of bio-psychic female versions.

In addition, it should be pointed up that the bio-psychic melding principle need not necessarily carry information whose energetic intent is only sexual in nature.

Thus, there are additional energy formats involved. Sometimes these activate during sexual-intent energetics. But sometimes they do not. They are more likely to activate and become clairvoyantly perceivable if the major intent is some kind of communion.

Naturally, one does not want to commune with something that is energy-information unsuitable or non-productive. So, considering the elegance of the vital force energies, it seems logical to assume that such forces have specific energetic formats in this regard.

THE MALE MELDING TORUS

Regarding male versions seen clairvoyantly, when two of them are near one another, a peculiar energy phenomenon might occur.

A torque or torus can be seen horizontally forming around their pectoral areas, running around the biceps and completing the circle at the back.

A torque is something that produces a rotation, a turning, twisting force. A torus is a protuberance or a bulge, which is doughnut-shaped.

The male physical body can be seen standing in the doughnut's hole, while the torquing torus is about two to three feet out around the body. So far as I can tell by micro-clairvoyance, this particular torque is nowhere linked to the bio-body, and so I identify them as free-standing energetic phenomena.

When this torque first forms, it is usually glowing golden in color. The torques of two males can be seen magnetically attracting each other, as if they "want" to meld. If the melding does not shortly take place, then the color shifts to red, and tends to become "disturbed" and "angry." The emotions seem to respond likewise.

Meanwhile, a second, but smaller, torquing might form around the area where the genitals are, and THIS one can be seen to involve the basic red crotch chakra, the genitals, buttocks and upper thighs.

This is not quite free standing, but it forms about a foot outside of the bio-body. The coils, earlier mentioned and always very impressive, might also form.

If by now a melding has not taken place, these torques can be seen releasing curving rays of red and white energy which detach and can whirl independently around, "disturbing" both the male versions and anyone else in the proximity. There is considerable dynamic force regarding the torques and the free-standing rays. The "atmosphere" becomes heavy and tense.

The best example I've seen of these torques was the case of two brothers who had been undergoing psychoanalysis for a long time because they hated each other but couldn't go their own ways.

In analysis, they had gotten so far as to conclude that their "energies were irrevocably incompatible." When they heard of my clairvoyance they asked to visit.

When they walked into my studio, their mutual torques were in such an advanced state of disrepair that they were sending out not only whirling beams, but "sparks" as well. The "atmosphere" of my studio instantly became quite tense, almost baleful.

I decided to get directly to the point by asking if they had hard-ons, which made them red in the face, but got their undivided attention. I then did a rap about torques, and about the angry-heat they could produce, and which had a totally surprising result in that both broke into tears.

I did not ask them to embrace and kiss, but in my explanatory rap it became clear to them what they had to do. After a little mumbling about not being "fags," they physically approached each other.

The magnetic torques around them immediately became one larger torque surrounding both. With the "psychological consent" now available, the torques themselves did the rest largely because the torques are strongly "intelligently magnetic"—which seems to be the best way to put it.

The two brothers embraced tentatively at first, but then "more magnetically." Finally, with no embarrassment, they kissed like Russian men do.

The kissing-embrace did not last very long, but they apparently forgot I was there. Meanwhile, in silence, their combined aura bodies shifted from angry red to a most gorgeous blue outlined in a golden light.

I thought I could see their mutual energy networks duplicating each other, but a good deal of clairvoyant stuff was going on and I couldn't be sure.

Afterward, I made tea (mainly to reorganize myself,) and we then talked for about two hours about clairvoyance and energy bodies. During this time, they nonchalantly held hands, and finally departed with arms around each other's shoulders.

The problem apparently had been that they had interpreted their affinity and attraction to each other as homosexual, and this aroused social fear in them. Their analyst had even diagnosed that this was their "incestuous problem," and had told them so. They had been paying perfectly good money for this "treatment."

THE FEMALE MELDING TORQUES

Female versions produce torques, too, but of an entirely different kind, abundantly more complex, but wondrously so.

Most female versions produce five of them.

The first, and sometimes predominant one is vertical and shaped like a two-pointed oval.

The top point is about two to three feet above the head, the bottom point is beneath the feet and penetrates into the ground and floor.

Conjoined to this one is four more, making five in total. If seen from above, they make the shape of a five-pointed star.

Male versions do not always have their torques, but it seems that female versions always do.

While in the male versions the powerful gold-red melding torques rotate horizontally, the perpendicular torques of the female versions slowly rotate vertically and into and out of each other and can do so rhythmically and in wonderful tempos.

In the female versions, the rotating torques, if in a kind of inactive state, resemble colorless glass tubes about an inch or less in diameter.

When they are energized they become at first golden. If these melding torques are not fulfilled, they then turn sort of an angry electric blue, at which time the "atmosphere" around the female will turn heavy.

I've only occasionally seen these torques throw off free-standing rays, but when they do they are very unsettling to others who experience them.

In color, the flung-out rays are usually a dirty white or gray pink.

When the torques of male and female versions "wish" to meld and duplicate each other's. Information, a kind of template or pattern of the female torques will appear around the male, while the pattern of the male torque will appear around the breast area of the female.

These, however, are quite delicate and transparent, and both sets of torques and templates disappear upon "consent" to meld.

GEOMETRIC ENERGY STRUCTURES

If melding (energy information exchange) has been successful, a temporary illumination will appear in the auras above the head whether the melding is of the two or same sexes.

This is usually glowing white, and often I believe mistaken for the important Pranic crown chakra. Subjected to micro-clairvoyance these illuminations can be seen containing a vast array of different colored lights, usually pastel in color, and also, of all things, a vast array of geometric symbols.

These are rapidly changing and fluctuating into and out of each other. The nearest analogy I can devise is of a computer processing information via symbolized energies, and with exceeding speed so fast that the symbols become indistinct as blobs of light. These illuminations are wonderful and exquisite to behold. When the processing of the melding seems complete, they disappear.

However, when I first saw these symbols I truly thought I was imagining them. But in conducting further research into the literature, I came across papers concerning one Nancy Lansdale (1883-1957).

She had been an artist clairvoyant who saw these symbols as a part of the auras above peoples' heads.

She rendered many beautiful paintings of them, calling them "personal archetypes." Some of these will be reproduced in the companion book to come under the title of PSYCHIC CREATIVITY.

CHAPTER 28
HUMAN ENERGETICS— A SCIENCE DENIED

It is difficult to wrap up this book, because its overall information content obviously extends into other large areas of human energetic activity, especially the areas of creativity and power. Thus, without taking a breath, it would be easy enough simply to segue into both of those topics. Like this book, the central major topic of the two has to do with the existence of invisible energetics, and which, in some sense at least, account for the amazing, but elusive, special phenomena encountered in both areas.

Those special phenomena have been left unaccounted for. There are a number of lesser societal reasons, but the larger one is simply that the science of human energetics has for a very long time been avoided and denied at the behest of powerful mainstream forces.

The exact, bigger-picture reasons that stimulate this denial are quite difficult to fathom. Whatever they are, they certainly go against the overall concept of an unbiased accumulating of enlightened knowledge on behalf of enlarging human understanding and transformative values of it.

OCCULTISM AS THE SCIENCE OF ENERGETICS

Generally speaking, however, interest in universal, cosmic, and organic energetics has never disappeared entirely, and much along such lines has been undertaken by those interested in doing so.

Give or take a little, the entire category of occultism and occult knowledge can be thought of as the science of energetics.

Indeed, the various aspects of whatever has been assigned as occult do deal with invisible factors, and principally with energetics and how various energies are distributed in the cosmos and in organic organisms.

In this sense, "occultism" has fundamental and important roots in antiquity, and much has continuously been derived from them.

But through the centuries they have been added to at various epochs, while in some of the epochs the work was condemned and had to be conducted "underground." Hence, the term OCCULT (meaning "hidden") has a double meaning. The energetics studied were hidden by their essential invisibility and hidden also to avoid mainstream condemnations.

The thread that links most of the occult work into one continuous piece is that the universe is made up of energies, and that these download in different interplaying formats, and the different formats are those subtle vital life energies from which all animated life form can manifest.

Something like this is the essential definition of Prana of ancient India, and of Ch'i of ancient China. There are many other terms for the same idea. The modern West even has one that verges on scientific authenticity. This term, as we saw in the foregoing chapter, is DYNAMISM—a theory that explains the universe in terms of forces and their interplay.

There is a strange aspect to the societal suppression of occult energetic topics.

No matter the suppression, and how trenchantly it is conducted, the topic of energetics simply reemerges again and again, under different auspices, and under different nomenclature.

The most probable reason for the reemergence is that certain individuals perceive the value and meaning of knowing something about energetics, and especially so with regard to human activity.

THE ENERGETIC NATURE OF SECRET SOVIET RESEARCH

As but one rather amusing example, in 1969, the American intelligence community had become unnerved by a surprising discovery—that since the 1930s the Soviet Union had secretly been conducting serious research into psychic phenomena.

Further, the Soviet research was big-time, and involved some nineteen major military research centers.

The whole of this constituted something of a socio-political mystery. Not only was the sheer size of the Soviet effort a shock to American analysts, but the very idea of such research was also in conflict with Communist philosophy.

As informed Westerners understood it, the political sociology of Marxist-Communist thinking ardently held Western psychic phenomena and parapsychology to consist of superstitious beliefs compiled with decadent behavior.

Thus any such phenomena must not only be avoided in the Soviet Union, but actively purged.

But far from being purged, such work was boldly underway in the Soviet Union, and so there were possible scientific and military issues involved, but also political and societal ones.

In the light of this possible ominous Soviet development, a quite large and longer-term effort was made to find out what the Soviets were doing. One of the first larger-picture discoveries was that Russia and other significant portions of the Soviet Empire were Asian in cultural background, and as such possessed deep currents of Asian ethos.

Such guiding principles had historically legitimized such activities as acupuncture, chi gong, shamanism, second-sight, and distant influencing as being energetic functions not only in nature, but as regards the human systems.

In this sense, then, the Soviet scientists did not see such energetic manifestations as arising from psychologically decadent causes, but as bio-energetic (the Soviet term) functions that could be ascertained, explored, and demonstrated in laboratories.

Thus, without too much fuss and bother, the Soviet "bio-energetic" and "bio-communication" research could be incorporated into the socio-political think of the Soviet Union.

Because the distinction here may remain ambiguous at first, it needs to be clearly pointed up.

Contrary to the understanding in the West that parapsychology researched "powers of mind," the Soviets were busily researching biological ENERGIES. Put another way, the Soviets were in the process of developing a science of human energetics.

The developing Soviet science, therefore, had no comparable counterpart in the West, so American analysts were initially unable to grasp what was involved, since they thought in terms of mental phenomena rather than biological energetic phenomena.

The modern West had established no science regarding the field of human energetics, and which field indeed had long been denied acceptance, as we have seen in this book.

THE ASIAN ENERGETIC COUNTERPART

The Soviet energetics did have a comparable counterpart in Asia, and especially in China, and a very ancient and authentic counterpart at that.

It is found elucidated, among other sources, as one of the doctrines of TAO, variously translated as "The Way," or "The Supreme Path of Nature"—which constitutes a philosophy that has permeated the whole structure of Chinese thought and society for over 2,500 years.

As referred to earlier, a rather neat synopsis of the "Supreme Path" is contained in Reay Tannahill's fascinating book, entitled SEX IN HISTORY (revised and updated edition, 1992).

As noted by Tannahill, within the Supreme Path of Nature, Existence appeared as a dynamic, "energetic movement of change, a kind of space-time continuum of fluid energies in which man, beast, trees, mountains, cloud, river and sea were all indissolubly merged."

Weaving and powering an erratic trail through all of these is the force (energy) known as CH'I, the vital essence, the breath of life, and whose path is the Supreme Path of Nature.

In the sense of this vital force (energy) as the fundamental essence of EXISTENCE, the ancient Chinese viewed CH'I as THE primary factor of all that exists. So, the primary factor of whatever exists is first ENERGETIC, and only then do the realms of the phenomenal, including those physical and mental, manifest.

In her book examining sex in history, Reay Tannahill was obliged to make the important connection between Eastern knowledge of CH'I energetics and sexualizing energetics, a connection that has gone missing in the West.

Beyond that connection, however, Eastern knowledge of CH'I resulted in the formulations of acupuncture, ch'i gong (energy healing), cognitive extensions of CH'I force as a basis for many of the martial arts, and for various kinds of shamanism and divination.

Developmental CH'I also led to empowerment of various states of exceptional experiencing easily comparable to certain kinds of energetic PSI phenomena in the West.

In the West, however, such energetic functions were mistaken as psychological powers of mind, not as basic powers of energetics. (Quite a number of the astonishing energetic functions derived from the practice of CH'I gong are described in a recent (1997) book by Paul Dong and Thomas E. Raffill, entitled CHINA'S SUPER PSYCHICS.)

A CHIEF CHARACTERISTIC OF WESTERN PSI RESEARCH

The study of the sociological implications of PSI also revealed a number of things about the West, where the occurrence of energetic phenomena did not enjoy the traditional background as found in Asia and much of Eastern Europe.

To help explain this, Asia had always considered the body-energy-mind as three primary factors of human existence. But the West utilized only the two-part body-mind model. In the West, therefore, all human phenomena had to be attributed to the body or to the mind.

The three-part Asian model, however, was in keeping with most pre-modern societies the world over. Indeed, as established via archaeology and anthropology, most pre-modern societies made allowance for the three-part idea of the human in which the energy part was conceptualized as distinct from, but interrelated with, the other two parts.

In the West, as the modern age condensed and solidified its philosophical and scientific identity, a departure was made from the pre-modern triune of body-energy-mind.

Although energies were still referred to in the philosophies and sciences of the modern West, they were thought of not as things-in-themselves, but only as subsidiary elements of the body or mind.

Another way of putting this is that energy was considered only as amorphous potential until it was manifested either as physical or mental energy.

This resulted in the broad Western understanding that the human entity indeed possessed energies, but that these were internal to and commensurate with the dualism of body-mind, and thus having no separate substance.

In their biological sense, the body energies could simply be thought of as mechanistic in nature. The mental energies were a little more difficult to conceptualize in terms of psychology.

And in that regard a number of fatiguing problems ultimately arose which began serving as background for a number of enigmas, paradoxes, and conundrums. These paradoxes have never really been resolved.

Even so, the philosophies and sciences of the Modern Age moved dynamically forward, deservedly triumphant in very many aspects. But the same philosophies and sciences became increasingly weak regarding such problems, identified as, for example, the body-mind relationship, the body-mind interface, etc. None of these problems could be, and have not yet been, convincingly resolved in the absence of human energetics.

SOME HISTORICAL NOTES REGARDING THE DENIAL OF ENERGETICS IN THE WEST

In terms of its history, the blow-by-blow developments that led to the Western denial of energetics are complicated. But it is quite easy to recognize one of the most important fallouts from the denial.

The fallout is that the phenomena of energies, or energetics, that could not be directly attributed to body or mind gradually collated into the area earlier known as the "occult sciences," but which category was stigmatized as unscientific in its fundamental nature.

In not only the philosophic or scientific sense, but in the broad societal sense, this development demarcating the scientific from the unscientific can clearly be seen as a denial of the major substance of the occult sciences: VITAL ENERGIES.

Since the later psychical and subsequent parapsychological research arose out of the discredited occult sciences, the mainstream sciences needed to be intolerant of them as well.

While it is true that the so-called occult sciences came to consist of many intellectual confusions, their major substance consisted of studies of energetic phenomena as, so to speak, things in themselves, and as having real and natural cosmic existence before they become interactive with subsequent human energy dynamics.

The nexus of all of this had to do with the fact that human energetic organisms can often sense such supernal energies, even if only ambiguously so. Most pre-modern societies made some kind of sociocultural allowance for this type of sensing. The theoretical strictures of the modern body-mind dualism did not.

The reasons for the modern strictures are not easily identified or explained. But it was quite easy to trace the evolution of the strictures.

It can be said, with historical justification, that the sciences of the Renaissance were focused on positive distinctions regarding the "influences" of cosmic, natural and biological "energetics." Within these energies, the triune concept of body-energy-mind had a correct and authentic place.

But at some early point during the post-Renaissance decades, this important trinity almost invisibly passed from mainstream consideration, and this produced two results:

1. that the human was increasingly explained as body-mind only; and
2. that the Renaissance concepts of energetics increasingly were stigmatized as "occult" and hence unscientific.

The chronology established that the Western strictures against energetics had surfaced after the Renaissance, roughly between 1680 and 1730 during which period the negative distinction of the so-called occult sciences was formalized.

This anti-occult trend conditioned societal responses away from occult matters and phenomena and increasing ratios of mainstream social intolerance against them began manifesting.

It was also easy to establish that roughly by 1850 or earlier, the strictures themselves came to constitute the accepted societal, mainstream parameters of knowledge, while practically no consideration was any longer given to actual human experiencing that did not fit into the strictures.

Roughly between 1680 and 1880, the problems regarding the conflicts between occult and scientific knowledge had accumulated to an enormous degree. By 1880, the mainstream sciences had become entirely resistive regarding the issues involved.

Recognizing the existence of this situation, leading thinkers, including many eminent scientists, organized research societies to study the forbidden energetic phenomena independently of the mainstream sciences.

The first and most dynamic of those societies emerged in London 1882 under the rubric of "psychical research."

As we have seen in the text, the early psychical researchers were clearly examining energetic phenomena that were most astonishing. However, many (but not all) early psychical researchers themselves had accepted the assumed authenticity of the body-mind dualism.

And so, between about 1882 and the 1930s, the principle parapsychological concepts advanced ESP, psychokinesis, and telepathy, etc., as being exclusively involved with unknown components of mind.

Throughout the whole of this convoluted saga, the existence of energies per se was not denied.

But the energies were associated in secondary ways with body and/or mind, and no discrete science of primary energetics evolved to consider the energies as factors independent of the body-mind dualism.

It is to be noted that the body-mind dualism IS an ism— ISM always referring to a distinct doctrine or theory, as compared, for example, to distinctly observable phenomena or facts.

During the Progressive Age of Western science and psychology (roughly between 1905-1955), thinkers had expended a great deal of activity and funding in an effort to identify what the "normal" human consisted of.

This effort basically consisted of attempts, in the form of wholesale "testing" of individuals, to ascertain various psychological and intelligence criteria that would identify the "normal" from the "abnormal"—but which criteria more or less had already been decided upon theoretically and philosophically.

By tracing the history of this period, it could be seen that distinctions between normal and abnormal were undertaken in the name of science and psychology theory, not in the name of actual human experiencing. (I.e., anything that tasted of the occult was abnormal.)

But more in fact, the guiding principles of this effort were sociological in conceptualization, in that any results obtained by the effort were ultimately geared toward utilization in sociological management.

THE UNACKNOWLEDGED NECESSITY OF THE ENERGETIC COMPONENT

Whatever else might be said about psychical phenomena, an "energetic" component is necessary to begin any significant understanding of them.

Without this component, such phenomena more or less have to be shunted to the unscientific fringes, since neither the body as such, or the mind as such, can convincingly explain them.

After the disappearance of Renaissance "energetics," and until the Soviet introduction of "bio-energetics," no comparable, official concept really existed in the modern scientific and philosophical West. Although human energies could be talked of in popular, layman terms, no official scientific or philosophical substance existed for them.

It was only by tracing the Western sociological treatment of psychical phenomena that not only the avoidance, but ultimately the denial, of human energetics became identifiable. In fact, however, there are no real scientific grounds for such a wholesale avoiding of energetic phenomena. And so this "avoiding" now stood out like a red flag in a sea of white ones.

ENERGETICS—THE BRIDGE TO UNDERSTANDING SEXUAL AND CREATIVE ENERGIES

It is, of course, a great leap from Soviet and Chinese energetics to the topics of human sexuality and creativity. But those two topics are among the most commonly and frequently experienced and sensed as being energetic in nature, with the advantage that they are always sensed as energies much before anything else.

In any event, it can be said that nothing happens unless some kind of energetics is involved. It would seem, then, that establishing and enlarging studies of human energetics would contribute to empowerment in many areas.

SUGGESTED READING

NOTE: The topic of psychic sexual energies is seldom found directly addressed in published materials, or in relationship to the field of human energetics now growing. There are two principal reasons for this.

First, information during the modern period was increasingly compartmentalized into mainstream fields, disciplines, and specialties. One of the ultimate results was that various categories of information were insulated from each other, and so greater integration of all knowledge seldom took place.

Second, various kinds of information were treated as taboo during the same modern period, and as such none was permitted to intrude into any of the compartmentalized categories as established. The topics of human energetics, PSI, and sexualizing energies were excluded from entry into any established field, or any field seeking mainstream acceptance.

The advent of the Sex Liberation Age (c. 1965) served to establish a new compartmentalized field for sexual behavioral studies and the bio-mental aspects of sexuality. But as the new field opened up and developed, it remained insulated from most other established fields, with its interests avoiding the taboos of PSI, human energetics, and the topic of sexual energies.

Even if oblique, all of the sources listed below have some kind of reference to sexual and human energetics, the latter a new field still seeking authenticity. But as is the case with most of the sources, one has to read between the lines in order to grok the hidden implications regarding meaning and implications via a vis the topic of sexualizing energies. It is also to be understood that the lines between sexualizing energies and other kinds of human energies can be very miniscule.

*

Allen, Paula Gunn, *Grandmothers of the Light: A Medicine Woman's Sourcebook.* (Beacon Press, Boston, 1991.)

Bagnall, O., *The Origins and Properties of the Human Aura.* (University Books, New York, 1970.)

Bailey, Alice, *The Light of the Soul, Its Science and Effect: A Paraphrase of the Yoga Sutras of Patanjali.* (Lucis Publishing, New York, 1950.)

Baraduc, H., *La Force Vitale: Notre corps fluidique sa biometrique formulation (The Vital Force: Our fluid bodies and their biometric patterns).* (Georges Carre, Paris, 1893.)

Beck, Peggy and Walters, Anna Lee, *The Sacred: Ways of Knowledge, Sources of Life.* (Tsaile, Navajo Nation: Navajo Community College Press, 1971.)

Becker, Robert O. and Gary Selden, *The Body Electric: Electromagnetism and the Foundation of Life.* (William Morrow, New York, 1985.)

Beesely, R. P, *The Robe of Many Colors.* (The College of Psychotherapeutics, Kent, England, 1957.)

Bennett, Hal Zina, *The Lens of Perception: A Field Guide to Inner Resources.* (Celestial Arts, Berkeley, California, 1987.)

Bergler, Edmund, *The Superego.* (Grune & Stratton, New York, 1952.)

Besant, Annie and C. W. Leadbeater, *Thought-Forms.* (The Theosophical Publishing House, Adyar, India, 1901. Quest Book edition, 1969.)

Best, Simon and Cyril W. Smith. *Electromagnetic Man.* (St. Martin's Press, New York, 1989.)

Bloch, George J., *Mesmerism: A Translation of the Original*

Medical and Scientific Writings, of F. A. Mesmer, M.D. (William Kaufmann, Los Altos, California, 1980.)

Brennan, Barbara Ann, *Hands of Light: A Guide to Healing Through the Human Energy Field.* (Pleiades Books, New York, 1987.)

Buranelli, Vincent, *The Wizard From Vienna, Franz Anton Mesmer, A Biography of the 18th Century Doctor Who Laid the Foundation for Modern Psychiatry.* (Coward, McCann & Geoghegan, New York, 1975.)

Burr, Harold Saxton, *Blueprint For Immortality: The Electric Patterns of Life.* (Neville Spearman Publishers, London, 1972.)

— *The Fields of Life: Our Links with the Universe.* (Ballantine Books, New York, 1972.)

Cantarella, Eva. *Bisexuality in the Ancient World.* (Yale University Press, New Haven, Rhode Island, 1992.)

Carpenter, Edward, *The Art of Creation: Essays on the Self and Its Powers.* (George Allen, London, 1904.)

Carr, Donald E., *The Forgotten Senses.* (Doubleday & Co., Garden City, New York, 1972.)

Carrington, Hereward, *Modern Psychical Phenomena: Recent Researches and Speculations.* (Dodd, Mead & Co., New York, 1919.)

Chuvin, Pierre, *A Chronicle of the Last Pagans.* (Harvard University Press, Cambridge, Massachusetts, 1990.)

Cohen, Kenneth S., *Qigong: The Art and Science of Chinese Energy Healing.* (Ballantine, New York, 1997).

Cole, K. C., *Sympathetic Vibrations: Reflections on Physics as a Way of Life.* (William Morrow, New York, 1985.)

Conway, David, *Secret Wisdom: The Occult Universe Explored.* (Jonathan Cape, London, 1985.)

Cox, Edward W., *Spiritualism Answered by Science.* (Longman and Co., London, 1871.)

Crookes, William, *Spiritualism Viewed by the Light of Modern Science.* ("Quarterly Journal of Science (London)," July, 1970.)

Dong, Paul, and Thomas E. Raffill, *China's Super Psychics.* (Marlowe & Company, New York, 1997.)

Dubrov, A. P., *The Geomagnetic Field and Life.* (Plenum Press, New York, 1978.)

Edwardes, Allen, *The Jewel In The Lotus: A Historical Survey of the Sexual Culture of the East.* (Julian Press, New York, 1959.)

Fiske, John, *Outlines of Cosmic Philosophy* (in two volumes). (Houghton, Mifflin & Co., Boston, 1874.)

Fodor, Nandor, *Freud, Jung, and Occultism.* (University Books, New Hyde Park, N.Y., 1971).

Geley, Gustave, *From the Unconscious to the Conscious.* (Harper & Brothers, London, 1921.)

George, Leonard, *Alternative Realities: The Paranormal, the Mystic and the Transcendent in Human Experience.* (Facts On File, New York, 1995.)

Gray, William E., *Know Your Magnetic Field.* (Christopher Publishing House, Boston, 1947.)

Green, Elmer and Alyce Green, *Beyond Biofeedback: Pioneering Research that Explores the Mind's Power to Control the Body and Its Unconscious Functions, the Emotions, and States of Consciousness.* (Delacorte Press, New York, 1977.)

Grim, John A., *The Shaman: Patterns of Siberian and Ojibway Healing.* (University of Oklahoma Press, Norman, Oklahoma, 1983.)

Gunther, Bernard, *Energy Ecstasy: And Your Seven Vital*

Chakras. (The Guild of Tutors Press, Los Angeles, 1978.)

Harding, M. Esther, *Psychic Energy: Rs Source and Goal*. (The Bollingen Series published by Pantheon Books, New York, 1948.)

Heline, Corinne, *Occult Anatomy and the Bible*. (Rosicrucian Fellowship Press, Oceanside, Calif., 1937.)

Hunt, Valerie V., *Infinite Mind: The Science of Human Vibrations*. (Malibu Pub. Co. (P.O. Box 4234, Malibu, California 90265) 1995.)

Inglis, Brian, *The Hidden Power*. (Jonathan Cape, London, 1986.)

Johari, Harish, *Tools For Tantra*. (Inner Traditions International, Rochester, Vermont, 1986.)

Johnson, Basil. *The Manitous: The Spiritual World of the Ojibway*. (New York: Harper Collins, 1995.)

Karagulla, Shafica, *Breakthrough to Creativity: Your Higher Sense Perception*. (DeVorss & Co., Los Angeles, 1967.)

Karagulla, Shafica and Dora van Gelder Kunz, *The Chakras and the Human Energy Fields*. (The Theosophical Publishing House, Wheaton, Illinois, 1989.)

Kiefer, Otto, *Sexual Life in Ancient Rome*. (Dorset Press, New York, 1993.)

Keiffer, Gene (Ed.), *Kundalini For The New Age: Selected Writings of Gopi Krishna*. (Bantam Books, New York, 1988.)

Kilner, Walter J., *The Human Aura*. (Originally, *The Human Atmosphere* (London, 1921). (University Books, New Hyde Park, New York, 1965.)

Krippner, Stanley and Daniel Rubin (Eds.) *Galaxies of Life: The Human aura in Acupuncture and Kirlian Photography*. (Gordon and Breach, New York, 1973.)

— *The Kirlian Aura: Photographing the Galaxies of Life.* (Anchor Press/Doubleday, Garden City, N.Y., 1974.)

Krishna, Gopi., *Kundalini: The Evolutionary Energy in Man.* (Ramadhar & Hopman, New Delhi and Zurich, 1967.)

Kunz, Dora van Gelder, *The Personary Aura.* (Quest Books, The Theosophical Publishing House, Wheaton, Illinois, 1991.)

Laucks, Irving F., *A Speculation in Reality.* (Philosophical Library, New York, 1953.)

Leadbeater, C.W., *The Chakras: A Monograph.* (Sixth edition, The Theosophical Publishing House, Adyar, India, 1961.)

— *The Inner Life* (in two volumes, first published in 1910. Fourth edition, The Theosophical Publishing House, Wheaton, Illinois, 1967.)

— *Man Visible and Invisible: Examples of Different Types of Men as Seen by Means of Pained Clairvoyance.* (The Theosophical Publishing House, Adyar, 1902. Quest Book edition, 1952.)

Lee, Sang Myung, *Super Magnetic Field: Prana Science.* (Printed in Korea, 1991.)

Licht, Hans, *Sexual Life in Ancient Greece.* (The Abbey Library, London, 1932.)

Lovgren, George K., *The Art of Inner Seeing.* (Karl Bern Publishers, Sun City, Arizona, 1977.)

Mann, W. Edward, *Orgone, Reich and Eros.* (Simon and Schuster, New York, 1973.)

Mavor, James and Dix, Byron E., *Manitou: The Sacred Landscape of New England's Native Civilization.* (Rochester, Vermont: Inner Traditions international, 1998.)

May, G., *Social Control of Sexual Expression.* (Allen & Unwin,

London, 1930.)

Merleau-Ponti, M., *The Phenomenology of Perception.* (The Humanities Press, New York, 1972.)

Merrel-Wolff, Franklin, *The Philosophy of Consciousness Without an Object: Reflections on the Nature of Transcendental Consciousness.* (Julian Press, New York, 1973.)

Mosse, George L., *Nationalism and Sexuality: a Respectability and Abnormal Sexuality in Modern Europe.* (Howard Fertig, New York, 1985.)

Motoyama, Hiroshi, *The Functional Relationship Between Yoga Asanas and Acupuncture Meridians.* (I.A.R.P., Tokyo, 1979.)

— *The Correlation between PSI Energy and Ki.* (Human Science Press, Tokyo, 1991.)

Payne, Buryi, *The Body Magnetic.* (Self-published? Printed in Santa Cruz, California, 1990 (no other information given.)

Pierrakos, John C., *The Energy Field in Man and Nature.* (Institute for the New Age, New York, 1971 (Monograph).)

Popp, Fritz-Albert (Ed.). *Electromagnetic Bio-Information.* (Urban & Schwarzenberg, Munic-Vienna-Baltimore, 1979).

Powell, Arthur E, *The Etheric Double.* (The Theosophical Publishing House, London, 1925. Fifth edition, 1969.)

— *The Causal Body and the Ego.* (Theosophical Publishing House, London, 1928.)
— *The Astral Body.* (The Theosophical Publishing House, London, 1972.)

Presman, A. S., *Electromagnetic Fields and Life.* (Plenum Press, New York, 1970.)

Purucker, G. de, *Occult Glossary: A Compendium of Oriental and Theosophical Terms.* (Theosophical University Press, Pasadena, 1972.)

Reichenbach, Charles von, *Psysico-Physiological Researches on the Dynamics of Magnetism, Electricity, Heat, Light, Crystallization, and Chemism in their Relation to Vital Force.* (First published in 1851, republished by Health Research, Mokelumne Hill, California, 1995.)

— *Vital Force.* (J. S. Redfield, Clinton Hall, New York, 1851.)

— *The Od Force: A Newly Discovered Power in Nature.* (First published in 1854, republished by Health Research, Mokelumne Hill, California (no date).)

Rubik, Beverly, *Life at the Edge of Science.* (The Institute for Frontier Science, Philadelphia, 1996.)

Schiffman, H. R., *Sensation And Perception: An Integrated Approach.* (John Wiley & Sons, New York, 1976.)

Scott, George Ryley, *Phallic Worship: A History of Sex & Sexual Rites.* (Luxor Press, London, 1966.)

Sharaf, Myron, *Fury on Earth: A Biography of Wilhelm Reich.* (St. Martin's Press, New York, 1983.)

Shattuck, Roger, *Forbidden Knowledge: From Prometheus to Pornography.* (St. Martin's Press, New York, 1996.)

Taimni, I. K., *The Science of Yoga: The Yoga-Sutras of Patanjali.* (The Theosophical Publishing House, Wheaton, Illinois, 1961.)

Talamonti, Leo, *Forbidden Universe: Mysteries of the Psychic World.* (Stein and Day, New York, 1975.)

Talbot, Michael, *The Holographic Universe.* (HarperCollins, New York, 1991.)

Tannahill, Reay, *Sex in History.* (Scarborough House, Lanham, Maryland, 1992.)

Tansley, David V., *Subtle Body: Essence and Shadow.* (Thames and Hudson, London, 1977.)

Taylor, G. Rattray, *Sex in History: The Story of Society's Changing Attitudes to Sex Throughout the Ages.* (Vanguard Press, New York, 1970.)

Thurston, Herbert S. J., *The Physical Phenomena of Mysticism.* (Henry Regnery, Chicago, 1952.)

Tiller, William A., *Science and Human Transformation: Subtle Energies, Intentionality and Consciousness.* (Pavior Publishing, Walnut Creek, California, 1997.)

Tillett, Gregory, *The Elder Brother: A Biography of Charles Webster Leadbeater.* (Routledge & Kegan Paul, London, 1982.)

Vasiliev, L. L., *Experiments in Distant Influence.* (Dutton & Co., New York, 1963.)

Walker, Benjamin, *Encyclopaedia of Esoteric Man.* (Routledge & Kegan Paul, London, 1977.)

White, John, *Kundalini, Evolution and Enlightenment.* (Anchor Books, New York, 1979.)

Wilson, Colin, *The Misfits: A Study of Sexual Outsiders.* (Carroll & Graf, New York, 1988.)

— *Beyond The Occult: A Twenty-Year Investigation into the Paranormal.* (Carroll & Graf, New York, 1989.)

Wyckoff, James, *Franz Anton Mesmer: Between God and Devil.* (Prentice-Hall, Englewood Cliffs, New Jersey, 1975.)

Zolla, Elemire, *The Androgyne: Reconciliation of Male and Female.* (Crossroad, New York, 1981.)

Zukav, Gary, *The Dancing Wu Li Masters: An Overview of the New Physics.* (William Morrow, New York, 1979.)

A BIOMIND SUPERPOWERS BOOK FROM
SWANN-RYDER PRODUCTIONS, LLC

www.ingoswann.com

OTHER BOOKS BY INGO SWANN

Everybody's Guide to Natural ESP
Master of Harmlessness
Penetration
Penetration: Special Edition Updated
Preserving the Psychic Child
Psychic Literacy
Purple Fables
Reality Boxes
Resurrecting the Mysterious
Secrets of Power, Volume 1
Secrets of Power, Volume 2
Star Fire
The Great Apparitions of Mary
The Windy Song
The Wisdom Category
Your Nostradamus Factor

www.ingramcontent.com/pod-product-compliance
Lightning Source LLC
Chambersburg PA
CBHW030050100526
44591CB00008B/91